THE CHILD ABUSE INDUSTRY

THE CHILD ABUSE INDUSTRY

Outrageous Facts & Everyday Rebellions
Against a System that Threatens
Every North American Family

Mary Pride

CROSSWAY BOOKS • WESTCHESTER, ILLINOIS
A DIVISION OF GOOD NEWS PUBLISHERS

OTHER CROSSWAY BOOKS
BY MARY PRIDE

The New Big Book of Home Learning
The Next Book of Home Learning
Schoolproof
Unholy Sacrifices of the New Age
The Way Home
All the Way Home

Sixth printing, 1990

Printed in the United States of America

Library of Congress Catalog Card Number 86-70290

ISBN 0-89107-401-5

TABLE OF CONTENTS

INTRODUCTION

One Saturday in March of 1985, I was at home minding my own business. This business included writing a resource book on home education (*The Big Book of Home Learning*, also published by Crossway Books), mothering my three children, and being *very* pregnant. A good friend called, and I was happily talking to her, when she dropped this bombshell:

"Mary, you won't believe what I just heard on KSIV! They had a man on who had been waiting in a Division of Family Services office and overheard—really, you're not going to believe it. He heard a social worker telling her manager that she had been out to see a family who wouldn't let her into their house. She had seen the children and they looked OK, but she didn't know what to do next. The manager told her to *phone the child abuse hotline several times and accuse the family of child abuse*—just make up a story and phone it in. That would give her enough evidence to get a pick-up order and take the children!"

I couldn't believe what I was hearing. On second thought, I *could* believe it. Aren't anonymous hotlines an open invitation to this kind of malicious slander? Was there anything in the current anti-family climate that would stop a social worker from lying in order to yank a child away from his natural parents—all "in the best interests of the child"?

On that wild and crazy Saturday I made phone call after phone call. The sequence of calls, which I had not planned in any way, led me to Laura Rogers, the founder of Missouri Parents and Children (Mo-PaC). Laura had wide experience with the laws governing children and families. I talked to her for an hour, and trembled when I put down the phone.

Now, I'm not the twitchy type. I don't run to the basement every time the Tornado Watch siren goes off, nor did I cower under my bed at night after the next-door neighbor's house was broken into. But the last thing a happily pregnant woman wants to hear is that bureaucrats have actually maneuvered themselves into the position of having the power to take all her children, *without* any evidence and *without* any appeal.

My husband Bill and I had already had some inklings of how the system operated, having worked at one time in a foster home and having followed the tribulations of home schoolers in our state and elsewhere. But, all the same, we hadn't believed the system was really *that* bad. We weren't prepared to discover that today's family has *no* civil rights, as far as child abuse legislation and enforcement is concerned.

We immediately got to work checking this out. Bill went to a local law library and photocopied the Missouri statutes. He also went to the local school of social work and scrutinized the texts being used in the courses, buying one and bringing it home for me to agonize over. Bill went to visit Laura and talked with her for three hours, taping the talk for me to listen to at home. Laura gave him boxes of material, which we painstakingly picked our way through—copies of government reports and recommendations, books on child abuse, letters, legislative bills. I got the number of a lawyer who had worked with Laura and interviewed him, thus gaining some insight into how our legal process treated suspected child abusers. We also began clipping everything we could find on the subject from the papers, and spent hundreds of dollars on an electronic information service to get back issue clippings from magazines. Bill attended hearings and talked to legislators, eventually becoming the new president of MoPaC. I talked for hours to all sorts of people involved in the child abuse issue— parents who had been hotlined, adults who had been abused as children, bureaucrats, former social workers, political activists. Between us we read dozens of reports about child abuse.

The more we investigated the child abuse laws and the way they were being enforced, the more shocked we became. Often parents who raped or severely beat their children were allowed to retain custody. Yet, parents who had no evidence against them of any crime, and were not charged with any crime, were being threatened with losing their children and in some cases had actually lost them! The two facts, spelled out over and over again by personal testimonies and professional reports, and documented in this book, didn't seem to make sense.

Neither did a lot of other things that were starting to bother us. Take, for example, the question of qualifications.

"Who *are* these modern saviors of children?" we began to ask.

- Do they have the simplest qualification of all—wonderful children of their own?

- Do they have a good working knowledge of normal family life? (Or does all their training center around children in institutional settings?)

- Do they have a clear definition of what is and what is not child abuse? (And does their public definition match their private definition?)

- Do they hold out realistic promises of a brighter future?

- Do they understand and respect the different life styles of the American people?

- Are they responsible with their power, using force only when absolutely necessary?

- And the most fundamental question of all—*Have their solutions worked?*

This book will show that the answer to *all* the above questions is no. The amount of child abuse and neglect has markedly *increased* since the child abuse industry was established. When it comes to solving child abuse, today it is the blind leading the blind.

When it comes to building bureaucratic empires, however, we find a different story. Under the new child abuse laws, empire-building has been a booming success. Trading on the public's goodwill and the halo which floats over those who dedicate their lives to "helping children," the child abuse industry has enjoyed years of exponential growth virtually untroubled by any need to justify its methods.

Here, as this book shows, is the explanation for the seeming contradictions of the child abuse system.

The truth, simply stated, is that those acting "in the best interests of the child" frequently, repeatedly, consistently act in *their own* perceived best interests, regardless of the needs of the child or his family.

No one could have predicted the rapid rise of the child abuse industry; it is useless to blame ourselves. Nevertheless, it remains true that little has been done to prevent the child abuse industry from expanding its unchecked power over our families. The result has been a nightmare for millions of North Americans falsely accused of child abuse—and for the tens of thousands of seriously harmed children whose most basic needs are being shockingly ignored.

As Douglas J. Besharov, former head of the National Center on Child Abuse and Neglect, puts it, the present child protection system is "like a 911 emergency phone call system that cannot distinguish between a murder in progress and littering."[1]

The child abuse industry roared into action with dazzling ad campaigns and universal public acclaim. It has, however, not produced. As this book will show, its methods combine the self-serving and the inept, and its very reason for existence is highly suspect, being founded on inflated statistics and misleading definitions of "abuse."

This book will suggest some *proven* ways to significantly reduce genuine crimes against children *without* disrupting innocent families. The methods suggested have a proven track record both historically and trans-culturally, unlike the child abuse industry's experimental solutions whose only apparent common factor seems to be a desire to smash all American families into a white, upper-class, post-Christian mold.

There *is* a solution to the problem of crimes against children that does not involve infallible state decisions on who is or is not fit to raise their own offspring. Our problem is not that there is no solution (the solution as you will see is absurdly simple), but finding the moral courage to implement it.

For several generations now many North Americans have been ducking the responsibility of raising their own children. Now the state changes the rules of the game so that all parents are either actually or potentially guilty of child abuse by definition, meaning we get to keep our children only as a temporary favor that can be denied at any time. Is this what we have subconsciously wanted? Do we actually *want* to lose our children? Or are we going to wake up, realize at last what's going on, and throw the rascals out? Because we *can* throw the rascals out, as you will also see.

This book, then, began with fear but ends with hope. The truth of what is going on is horrible, but the story does not end there. We can make a difference. We *must* make a difference. For our children's sake.

Outrageous Facts I

CHILD ABUSE HYSTERIA VERSUS THE FACTS

YOU ARE 1
THE TARGET

Last year, over one million North American families were falsely accused of child abuse.

These families, people just like you and me, suffered in varying degrees.

Some merely went through the humiliation of an investigation for child abuse and were "cleared." Although their names remain in government files as suspected child abusers for a period ranging from five years to forever, these are the lucky ones.

Others, not so fortunate, found themselves in compulsory counseling programs. Still others lost their houses and emptied their bank accounts fighting these unjust charges. Many lost their jobs. Others, the saddest of all, lost their children.[1]

I hate alarmist books, and I rather suspect that you do, too. After the twentieth time the shepherd boy calls "Wolf!" the villagers feel uninclined to charge to his rescue. For years people have been warning that the family is under attack, and yet here we still are. So what's the big deal?

The big deal is that the worst fears of all those alarmists are actually coming true. Sooner or later those who were quietly negotiating to gain total authority over our families had to start using the power that we sleeping citizens had let them grab.

I don't totally blame my fellow parents: we're not greedy for power ourselves and find it hard to understand those who are. All we want is to be let alone, and getting involved in politics is not only tedious but takes time from worthwhile activities. But we made a mistake in going along so meekly with bureaucratic solutions for our family needs.

While mothers followed fathers in migrating out of the home, leaving their young children in day care and dropping off the older ones at a variety of clubs; while adult society became more rigid in excluding children; while television replaced family togetherness; while pulpiteers vied with each other inventing excuses for divorce "for any and every reason"; in short, while those of us who still had families were creating a job market for our replacements, those who claimed to speak for our children managed to ram through child abuse laws in every state that

- defined "abuse" so vaguely that *all* families are guilty;[2]

- installed government-operated hotlines and solicited anonymous reports of child abuse;[3]

- required all professionals who had any contact with children, and even workers like mailmen, to hotline families if they *suspected*, without any evidence, that abuse (which was vaguely defined to mean anything) was occurring or *might* occur at some time in the future;[4]

- allowed bureaucrats to invade homes without search warrants, and to remove children without showing any evidence (other than an anonymous hotline call) for why the children should be removed;[5]

- denied those accused of child abuse the right to a fair trial and due process;[6]

- made hotline callers, even malicious callers, immune to lawsuits or prosecution;[7]

- made the bureaucrats immune to lawsuits.[8]

Seeing is believing. I could feed you statistics on the huge number of false child abuse reports called in each year on state child abuse hotlines (65% by a recent, conservative figure).[9] I could list, category by category, the actual "crimes" that are considered "substantiated" cases, categories that include "inappropriate punishment," "lack of supervision," "threatened harm" (don't dare *scold* your child!), "emotional neglect" (whatever that is), and even "home schooling."[10] I could point out that, once hotlined for any reason, you are guilty until proven innocent and it's up to you to prove that you have never done any of the things social workers object to.[11] I could mention that the list of things for which social workers have threatened to remove children from their parents includes

- scolding and spanking (or permissiveness);

- withholding TV-watching privileges (or neglecting chidren by using the TV as a babysitter);

- raising your voice in anger (or failing to show proper emotion);

- failing to exercise 24-hour supervision (or repressing children by exercising 24-hour supervision) . . .[12]

The list goes on. I could show how children have actually been taken from their homes for these, or even more trivial causes, and that once they are taken the average time till they are returned is almost two years for whites and over four years for blacks—*even in cases where it is conceded that they were taken wrongly in the first place.*[13]

But let's not talk statistics and theory at this point. Let's see how the system works.

CASE 1—THE SMALL CHILD

Most people aren't aware of this, but it can be dangerous today to have a small child. You see, our child abuse and neglect statutes and regulations cover a strange condition known as "failure to thrive." It seems that some psychologists have determined that *all* children should be a certain height and weight. If your son or daughter doesn't meet this standard, he or she is "failing to thrive."

"But," you may say, "I feed him plenty." That doesn't count. "Failure to thrive" is considered a sign of *psychological* abuse. According to this logic, Junior's smallness cannot be the result of having small ancestors and inheriting their genes. All smallness is supposedly caused by some horrible trauma he suffered in your home.

Now you can understand what happened to poor little Christina Whitt. Social workers formed the theory that Christina was "not growing or developing properly because of neglect."

> The first investigation, conducted in 1980 when Christina was 2, resulted in her placement in a foster home for nine months. The second time, social workers visited the Whitts' home repeatedly and ordered numerous medical tests to determine if Christina was a victim of abuse and neglect.

Let's put this all into perspective. The "evidence" that Christina was failing to thrive was her height. Now, at age 6

> Christina is 42 inches tall and weighs 38 pounds. According to medical growth charts, five percent of children her age nationally are about the same size.

So if your children fall into that five percent, you're in trouble.

Christina's parents tried many times to explain to the Department of Social Services that both Christina's mother and her maternal grandparents were small. "Nevertheless, their action was to proceed with the case (dismissed December 15, 1985)."

And just how small are Christina's relatives? Debra Whitt is 33, weighs 92 pounds, and is 4 feet 10. Her grandfather is 4 feet 7 and her grandmother is 4 feet 9.[14]

CASE 2: DON'T PROTECT YOUR CHILDREN FROM SEXUAL ABUSE

You play the judge. The facts are this. A son in British Columbia, Canada, accused his non-custodial father of sexual abuse. The father was investigated, but no charges were filed. A judge said he "was satisfied that the son had been abused, but was not convinced that the son was correct in naming the father." The daughter also disclosed abuse, but that too did not lead to charges.

At this point the social workers step in to "help" the family. This "help" took the form of arranging access visits by the father, in spite of the children's hostility towards him and unwillingness to see him. The mother (let's call her Sarah) for obvious reasons did not want these access visits. She also put pressure on the social workers to obtain therapy for the children.

Next the social workers, disdaining the idea of therapy, indulged in some pop psychology.

> Two human resources social workers . . . thought Sarah was not coping well with court-ordered access visits by the father. They alleged that she was encouraging the children—a son, 7, and a daughter, 5, to show extremely distressed behavior whenever the visits occurred.
>
> Sarah said the two workers told her that her son's behavior was because she was giving him too many negative messages and not making him feel secure enough.

Apparently insecure children automatically accuse their fathers of sexual abuse—right? Well, the state knows how to cure that!

> In July they [the sensitive social workers who were handling this case] raised the possibility of taking the children away from Sarah.
>
> The reason for the apprehension in the court document was that Sarah was unable to provide a stable, secure environment and that she was unable to distinguish her own needs from those of her children. . . .

Now comes the really gruesome part . . .

> Sarah's accounts and the workers' court reports indicate the apprehension was a scene of chaos. The workers were trying to get the two children in their car when a neighbor, Jim Mattinson, drove down the road.

The social workers flagged him down and asked him to help get the children into the car, Mattinson said. He described the scene as he first came upon it:

"There were two kids and a woman running after them. (He later realized the woman was one of the social workers.) The kids, they were screaming. My first impression was there had been an accident.

"The kids were screaming for their mother. They were trying to grab their mother." . . .

The two social workers managed to get the children inside the car, Mattinson said, and then began to drive away, with Sarah hanging on to the car.

At this point, he said, he grabbed Sarah and pulled her off the car because he was afraid she would hurt herself.

Mattinson said the social workers never appeared to be in control of the situation.[15]

Now let me ask you. Would *you* tear children who wanted to stay with their mother away from her *because* the children were complaining their father sexually abused them?

These social workers, who "never appeared to be in control of the situation," had the power to snatch Sarah's children on the basis of an accusation that *she* was not in control of the situation! Sarah was not charged with abuse or physical neglect. The only charge against her was psychological. She didn't behave like the social workers wanted her to. She wanted to protect her children from sexual abuse.

Children are not supposed to be forcibly removed, according to the B.C. regulations, unless there is evidence of neglect, emotional abuse, or physical abuse. Carol Beauchamp, the co-ordinator of the Nelson's Women's Centre, a social worker who has done apprehensions for Ontario and Alberta provinces, said in Sarah's case, "I can't see any evidence that the children were in need of protection." That must be the understatement of the year. However, Wayne Nickel, the Ministry of Human Resources regional manager, was quite pleased with the way his social workers acted. As he said, "Our primary concern is for the safety of the child,"[16] and that obviously makes tearing a screaming child away from the mother he loves all O.K.

Another interesting thing about Sarah's case: the visits. The father, who was accused of sexual abuse by both children,

has had lengthy visits with the children, where he has been able to take them out on the ferry and to the hot springs, while she and the children have been visiting for little more than an hour in a small human resources office. Sarah said this is because the supervising worker wants to monitor what she says to her children.

Beauchamp wonders,

if the abuse actually took place, what kind of impression this creates on the children.

The children "visit with the dad for a big chunk of time and do fun things and then visit with the mother in a small MHR room that is not really fun," she said. "What parallels do they draw?"

Is Sarah's case unique? Unhappily, no.

Beauchamp often gets calls from women having difficulty dealing with the human resources ministry, and has seen a rise in the number of calls regarding apprehensions. . . .

Normally there might be one or two calls to the Women's Centre for help dealing with an apprehension in a year, she said. This spring, she started working on four cases and has recently received "eight to ten" calls for information.

Beauchamp said it feels like the emphasis has changed from keeping families together to taking the child out of the home.[17]

CASE 3: THE SHIRT BUTTONS

I'm starting to think that Scrooge is alive and well, because so many completely illegitimate removals occur at Christmas time. Here is one of the Christmas stories in my bulging file folder, as reported by a local journalist.

In the U.S.S.R., a vindictive neighbor can anonymously accuse you of nebulous offenses. The state bureaucracy then does its best to build a case against you, starting by carting you off to the local police station and conducting a coercive interrogation. This is exactly what happened to a couple we can only call Steve and Peggy Doe, because their names are withheld from the press while their lawsuit against the bureaucracy is being decided.

Just before Christmas, 1982, two police officers arrived at the door one morning after Steve had gone to work. They said someone had phoned the child abuse hotline and accused Steve of sexually molesting his own two-year-old daughter. They discovered later that it was a neighbor who phoned after the two-year-old, sitting on his lap, tried to undo his shirt buttons. That, according to the neighbor's odd thinking, indicated child abuse.

Just when you think you've heard them all, here comes a new one. Didn't this neighbor know that all children love to button and unbutton? Maria Montessori especially invented a buttoning apparatus for use with children of this age in her early childhood development program. If Dr. Montessori had heard this accusation, she'd turn over in her grave.

Unhappily, those investigating serious charges like child sexual abuse don't always act rationally.

No, the police officers didn't want to talk to Steve, only to ask Peggy if the child was being abused. After hearing her answers and seeing the children [who categorically denied any abuse], the police seemed satisfied. But child protection workers got an order to seize the children.

That evening, as Peggy gave the children supper, four police officers arrived at the door. She shuts her eyes as she describes the horror of that scene—the four-year-old running and hiding under the bed, the two-year-old totally confused as the men carried her off.

It was several weeks before the couple got back their two children from a foster home, and the experience has left them with emotional scars they will always carry. The legal costs ruined them, and they lost their home.[18]

CASE 4: FOR THE LOVE OF BASEBALL

Just to round things out nicely, I thought I'd include a story told by the victim herself. Most appropriately I found an excellent one in the Victims of Child Abuse Laws newsletter of September/October 1985. (Documentation is available for this, as for the other stories, if any journalist out there is interested.)[19]

"There is a nine year old little boy who, for the last six years of his life, has been in love with a game called Baseball. (I know. I am his mother.) At age eight, he tried out for the 'Lambert Little League' and proudly became a single A Angel.

"In 1984, he won a trophy for being the Good Sportmanship Player of the whole league. Chris won a Certificate of Award from the Laurel Elementary School PTA for the Reflections Contest, when he drew a picture of a baseball diamond with himself at bat titled, 'I Have a Dream of Being a Baseball Star.' This was in the second grade.

"This year, 1985, Christopher tried out again and now he plays for the double A Angels. Only now I am afraid for him to play baseball at all!

"On May 6, 1985, Monday afternoon, Christopher was practicing pitching and catching in the front yard of our house with two neighborhood boys. They were using a tennis ball and a pitchback. This is an aluminum frame with a net designed to pitch the ball back to you. (It was a Christmas gift from his aunt.) During the game he missed the ball with the mitt and was struck in the nose, in fact, right between the eyes. It left a red mark on his nose and the side of one eye. It didn't hurt much and there was no bleeding; so instead of being a sissy in front of his friends, he did not come in to the house crying that he was hurt. I was not aware of any injury.

"The next day Christopher was forty minutes late coming home from school. I sent my sister, his aunt, to look for him and thinking the baby (Jenny, age 16 months) might enjoy the ride, she took her along. They went up to the school looking for Chris. There she was met by police officers and Christopher, who was scared to death and crying. In front of Chris, the policemen removed my baby from her aunt's arms and told her that they were taking my children for child abuse and we could not see them.

"The children's aunt came back home in a state of total hysteria. She stood in the middle of the living room crying and screaming. It took several minutes to find out what was wrong. She kept saying, 'They took our kids! Oh God, Oh God! Why did they take our kids?'

"The police took my children to La Mirada Community Hospital to be examined for possible child abuse. (The hospital has since sent me a bill for $373.00.) The hospital report on Chris said, 'a small bruise on bridge of nose, redness around one eye and a couple of small scratches on face' (due to baby Jennifer). They recommended no treatment. They x-rayed all of both children's bodies and neither had ever broken a bone in their lives (thank God). They found no signs of abuse of any kind on Jennifer.

"The DPSS then had Chris placed in a foster home which already had two children sleeping on the floor and whose playground was the local high school where the children played unsupervised after school hours.

"Jennifer was placed in Mac Laren Hall where she sustained numerous bruises on her face, ear, arms, and legs. Only Jenny can't talk to tell me how it happened.

"Christopher told the teacher, school nurse, and school principal about the baseball accident; he told the police and the DPSS workers; he told anyone and everyone, and they still took my babies away. They wouldn't believe him or even telephone me.

"After three days of being unable to eat or sleep, we had a dependency hearing, where the judge ordered my children detained until the trial on July 22, 1985.

"On Friday I was finally allowed to visit Jenny in Mac Laren Hall.

I found her sick, dirty, and covered with bruises. The only answer they could give me was that 'maybe another child got to her.' By Monday I was hospitalized for stress and severe dehydration.

"The following Wednesday we finally went before a judge who released the children to me until trial.

"I have pawned my jewelry and am in the process of selling my car and furniture. I have called every attorney I can find. My job put me on a personal leave of absence so that they would not have to pay my salary until I have solved my personal problems. I'm broke! Now I have two very frightened kids at home besides myself. Am I guilty? I did buy him his first baseball!"

You'll be glad to hear that this case has since been thrown out of court, where, as the newsletter also says, it should never have been. Justice, however, did not prevail until both children were abused and neglected *in state custody*, the mother was hospitalized, and the family was ruined financially. She had to pay (literally) for the blind fixations of school, police, and social work personnel who simply were determined to believe that abuse had occurred no matter *what* the little boy said.

Are these cases unique? Unfortunately, no. I have hundreds of them on file. Families accused of child abuse because they were providing an excellent home education for their children;[20] teachers hotlining every family in their classes out of spite;[21] a little girl torn screaming from her home because she lied to make an impression on the school nurse;[22] a teacher who coveted another woman's daughter and hotlined her;[23] foster parents accused of sexual abuse by the alleycat teenagers they had innocently taken in (in one case, because they didn't allow the teen to go on overnight dates);[24] an adopted daughter removed because her new three-year-old foster sister, who had been previously sexually abused, told the therapist "Daddy" did it, and although she called *all* men "Daddy" nobody investigated her story or her previous record;[25] babies born dead because their mothers were hotlined and miscarried out of stress;[26] and perhaps most ominous of all, the Christian couple who were accused of "delusional religious beliefs" for believing in the Rapture and who not only lost their daughter but were placed in a mental institution.[27]

"People don't realize what can happen," said Steve Pell, a Ventura [California] lawyer who has represented local families in these "dependency" cases.

"Parents in general don't know about this unless they are touched by it," Pell said. "Ninety-nine percent tell you no one can take the kids. One hundred percent of my clients are shocked when they find out someone can come and take their child."[28]

As Don Feder, writing in the Boston *Herald*, states,

> Children are being taken from their parents on the basis of rumors and suppositions—a telephone tip or unexplained bruise. They are placed in uncaring foster homes and institutions where they're often victimized by other children or adults. . . .
>
> Basic civil liberties are regularly violated in the course of investigations. Intervention often is based on an anonymous report phoned to a hotline. Warrantless searches are conducted . . . Children are removed from the home on the slightest pretext, including the parents' refusal to cooperate with investigators. . . .
>
> A suspected murderer has more rights in this country than a parent charged with child abuse.[29]

The North American public has given unprecedented support to government child abuse programs because we honestly believed these programs would help children. Everyone from the Daughters of the American Revolution to the NEA endorsed the new child abuse reporting and investigating system in 1974. In the schools, prevention programs were introduced with the help of the Parent-Teacher Associations. Little did we know that these programs would be directed *against* parents, teachers, and anyone who associates with children.

Government abuse of families has been swept under the rug for ten years. But there is simply too much of it to ignore it any longer. From the mayor of Spartanburg, South Carolina whose career was ruined by his ex-wife's accusation[30] to the unwed mother losing custody of the baby she has not even yet delivered,[31] the net spreads ever wider.

We thought we were installing a system that would protect children from those *other* people—those wicked abusers over there somewhere. We didn't realize the system would be aimed at *us*.

Nothing in the law protects you from a malicious accusation of child abuse. Nothing in the law guarantees that an ummarried social worker fresh from college won't find your particular family's life style objectionable. Every weapon aimed at *them*—the genuine child abuser—is pointing straight at *you*.

You are the target.

THE PLAGUE THAT ISN'T 2

One day Chicken Little was scratching in the barnyard. As a carriage drawn by a weary old horse rattled by on the nearby road, a dirt clod flew off the horse's hoof and hit Chicken Little on the head. "The sky is falling!" shrieked Chicken Little. "A piece just hit me on the head! I must go and tell the King!"

You know what happened next. Chicken Little convinced some of his barnyard friends that the sky was indeed falling; they rushed off in a body to tell the King; and the whole pack was decoyed into a fox's den and eaten.

We are apt to laugh at Chicken Little and to imagine we would have been much wiser in his place. Journalists, especially, who like to think of themselves as a hard-boiled bunch, are often sure *they* would never be taken in by foolish theories masquerading as fact.

Yet just as Chicken Little screamed "The sky is falling!" on evidence one can only charitably describe as flimsy, so the media have been inundating us with horrifying reports of a "plague" of child abuse, based (as this chapter will show) on evidence that is at best contradictory and at worst downright false.

Let me make it clear, right at the start, that I am not saying there are no such thing as crimes against children. I know, and you know, that there are some bad people out there, and some of those bad people have children. But we are not being alerted to an outbreak of violence among skid-row degenerates. Instead, we are being asked to believe that

- huge numbers of North American children are being severely harmed every year;

- parents are the group inflicting the greatest harm;

- we ought to be suspicious of *all* parents, not just drug users, alcoholics, those with dubious sexual arrangements, and the like.

A whole ideology of "child advocacy" has developed, based not on facts, but assumptions, whose main point seems to be that children are always better off when their parents are replaced, either physically or legally, by government bureaucrats and their dependents. *Every* family is suspect. And the only cure for this "crisis" is to monitor, threaten, survey, harass, and coerce *all* parents into surrendering their parental authority to the State.

Is North America overrun with child abusers? Is it really true that child abuse, unlike every other child-rearing behavior, is homogenized throughout "all economic, racial, ethnic, and religious groups"[1] as the dogma has it? Is it true that, in order to root out child abuse and neglect, we have to practically abolish all civil rights for families, as our state and federal legislators and judges have been led to believe?

You've seen and heard the hysteria—on TV, in the papers, in magazines, on the backs of milk cartons.

Now let's look at the facts.

MARSHMALLOW STATISTICS

I subscribe to a newspaper clipping service, and every week I see literally piles of statistics on child abuse. Although each new statistic is trumpeted by the media as proof that child abuse is rampant, these statistics blatantly *contradict* each other.

In my files, I have quotes from various reputable people and organizations that place child abuse at anywhere from one out of every two hundred children per year[2] to one out of every forty children per year.[3]

From one out of every two hundred to one out of every forty children abused per year is quite a jump—one that the media seem not to have noticed. But things get even stranger when people talk about sexual abuse. I have a clipping that proclaims (citing no source) that five million children are sexually assaulted each year[4], and dozens that declare (also citing no source) that one out of every four girls and one of every eight boys will be sexually molested by age 21[5]. Or, if you prefer, take the clipping which said (once again, citing no source) "Annually, some 300,000 female minors are known victims of sexual assault."[6] Contrast these wild figures, apparently pulled out of thin air, yet spread from paper to paper without investigation, with facts. The known number of rapes in 1980, including those *not* reported to the police, for *all* age groups, was less than 200,000.[7] But my favorite clipping of all is the one which solemnly states

Statistics show that one out of every four children will be sexually abused by the time they are 18. . . . Only one out of every ten cases is reported.[8]

This is marshmallow land, friends. If "statistics show" that one-quarter of the female population will be unwillingly defiled by age 18, and only one-tenth of the cases are reported, that means over 200 percent of the female population are victims of sex abuse. Twice as many girls will be raped as exist. Come on, now. Isn't that carrying things a mite too far?

Why do we believe this rubbish? Are one out of four adult women (or one out of three, or two—the statistics keep getting wilder) really the victims of savage lust perpetrated in their youth? Isn't it possible to organize a bridge party without staring at an abused woman across the table? Where do these wild statistics come from?

What we have here is a major problem. The major problem is that the public has been convinced that child abuse is a major problem. "Child abuse" is identified in the public mind with rape and severe brutality, but in the bureaucratic mind with something entirely different. When the public gets figures on "child abuse," *nobody points out where these figures come from*, or that they reflect *a different definition of "child abuse."*

I can't complain too loudly about those taken in by child abuse hysteria because I was duped by it myself. In a previous book, I quoted the estimate of a California psychiatrist who said that one out of every six girls is the victim of incest. But sober facts do not bear this, or any of the other alarming statistics, out.

What the public needs to know is that

(1) The only accurate statistics on child abuse in the U.S.A. are compiled by the American Humane Association. The AHA is under contract with the National Center on Child Abuse and Neglect to compile the statistics prepared by the individual states into a comprehensive report each year. Canada has no national statistics: some provinces have some statistics, others not. Nobody in North America, anywhere, besides the AHA has access to this information on a national scale.

(2) The statistics so widely reported in the media are not, in fact, statistics (except those from the AHA, which rarely get quoted). Instead, they are *estimates*, which means they are somebody's *guess*. Now, you may be as suspicious as you like; you may estimate that one out of two of your neighbors is a Mafia hit man; but in most cases we do not build national policy on these kinds of guesses. Only in the

never-never land of child abuse do guesses outweigh the sober facts.

(3) Even when quoting actual government statistics, child advocates have a deplorable tendency to cite the number of *reports* of child abuse (which include at least 65 percent totally false reports)[9] as if they were the number of *proven cases* of child abuse. Even those advocates who, more carefully, talk about "substantiated" cases fail to inform the public that "substantiation" only means the social worker suspected you could have been abusing your child, or might abuse them at some time in the future. Substantiation does not mean any evidence at all was found. Cutting down the number even finer, we find that the vast majority of "substantiated" cases involve trivial categories such as "Threatened Harm," "Emotional Neglect," or "Educational Neglect," the latter of which, otherwise known as truancy, has nothing at all to do with child abuse, coming as it does under the jurisdiction of the compulsory attendance laws.

When the wheat is sorted from the chaff, what is left? Only 2 to 5 percent of all reported cases involve actual crimes against children. In Missouri, for example, in 1984 less than 1,600 incidents of serious crimes against children occurred, and since in Missouri we list up to five types of abuse per child, there could have been as few as 320 actual victims. Let's say for the sake of argument that double this number of children were actually involved. That amounts to less than 1 percent of the children reported on that year.[10]

Missouri, under the aggressive child advocacy leadership of Representative Kaye Steinmetz (D-Florissant), has the highest reporting rate in the country: 55.13 children per 1,000, just double the national average of 27.3 per 1,000.[11] This could either be because we are zealously catching more abusers or because we in Missouri have been more intensely propagandized into turning our neighbors in for nothing at all. (My research inclines me to the latter opinion.) However that may be, the U.S. figures include a higher percentage of serious crimes. In 1984, the latest year for which national figures are now available as of this writing, major physical injury accounted for 3.3 percent of substantiated cases (about 1.36 percent of reported cases), and sexual maltreatment for another 13.3 percent. The latter category, however, includes such non-provable categories as "fondling." Again, duplication of incidents occurrs. When all this is taken into account, you wind up with, in the entire U.S.A., out of a child population of over seventy-two million, less than ten thousand cases of major physical injury, a few thousand of actual incestuous rape, and a few thousand more of serious starvation and other genuine serious neglect.[12]

It's not great that several thousand North American children are severely harmed each year by their caretakers (*not* necessarily by their parents),[14] but that's a far cry from the supposed millions of child abuse cases.

How, then, has the public been so shoddily misled?

Here's a quick lesson on how to mislead people with statistics.

HOW TO MISINFORM ABOUT CHILD ABUSE

(1) Skip the statistics and use guesses. Dress this up by announcing the guesses as the "estimates of experts." For fun, vary this with the fudge factor approach: "Only one out of every X cases is ever reported." Make X as large as you like.

(2) Introduce your article or newscast with a gut-gripping horror story. Then proceed to introduce your child abuse statistics. Your readers or hearers will come away with the impression that all those statistics refer to crimes like the one you described. Fail to disillusion them by pointing out that gruesome crimes against children are exceedingly rare:[14] instead, let them "draw their own conclusions."

(3) With horror in your voice, read the latest government numbers on child abuse. "More than a million cases a year! How awful!" Never explain that most of these reports were proved to be unfounded, and that, of the remainder, most involve trivial charges. Also forget to mention that these statistics include the possibility of multiple reports per child, so that the most severe categories may refer to relatively few children.

(4) If you really want to impress people, take a poll. Ask the right people the right questions and you can, if you wish, "prove" that 100 percent of the population were abused as children. Be careful to ask undefined questions like, "Were you abused as a child?" or "Were you emotionally neglected?" Ignore the fact that "abuse" means "anything I didn't like done to me" and that almost everybody has at least one period of self-pity in his or her life. Or, if you prefer, you can "discover" huge amounts of family violence by asking questions in such a way that every parent who ever used corporal punishment is labeled violent. One good way to do this is to substitute the word "hitting" for "spanking."

Credulously accept all positive responses without requiring corroborating evidence (such as medical or police reports). To further pad the figures, you might try giving the poll in Southern California, the strangest spot in the country, with a divorce rate double the national average. Again, fail to distinguish between abuse perpetrated by *parents* and abuse from outsiders. In this way, you can lump the bad behavior of all teenage girls' dates into the sexual abuse category and wow the world by revealing that One Out Of Every Four Women Was Sexually Abused As A Child.

(5) You can even skip the polls and the experts with their estimates, and boldly invent your own statistics. For example, speaking
before a civic group a Missouri juvenile officer said,

> Nearly 60,000 children across the state are abused in a given
> year. Of these cases about ninety percent are sexual molesta-
> tion.[16]

This is hogwash. The official Missouri statistics for 1984 (the
latest available at the time of the juvenile officer's speech) showed
about 30,000 children involved for all forms of abuse and neglect, of
which most fell in trivial categories. The statistics showed less than
2,663 incidents of all forms of sexual abuse. The vast majority of these
sexual abuse reports, being either trivial, unfounded, or false, never
made it into court. Even counting each of them as true, an extremely
naive assumption, sexual abuse amounted to less than eight percent of
the total.[16]

Headlines can also be used to invent untruths. Consider this one:
"Incest is the most common form of child sexual abuse,"[17] when
alleged incidents of incest account for less than ten percent of sexual
abuse reported in that state.[18]

(6) Propound the idea that the best way of learning about child
abuse is to ask convicted abusers. Criminals never lie, you know; they
never play for sympathy. If a child molester sobs "I was abused myself
as a child!" believe him. Now you can prove not only that abuse
always causes abuse (thus killing all hope in the hearts of abuse
victims who would like to be parents someday) but that child molesters are innocent victims.

Can it really be true that every child with abusive parents grows
up to abuse his or her own kids? Let's say that, back in 1700, there
were only one thousand mean, nasty abusers in the American colonies. Let's say that each of them married, and each family had only
two children (considerably less than the birthrate back then). Let's say
their children grew up to be abusers, married, and so on. By 1980
you'd have over 330 million abusers—more than double the adult
population of the U.S.A. and Canada combined.

Statistically this idea is nonsense; ethically it is wicked. Children
are not little machines that spit out whatever is put into them. If
children always aped their parents, where in the world did the Dr.
Spock generation come from? Spanking doesn't even always lead to
spanking, let alone abuse to abuse.

I took so much time with the "abuse causes abuse" dogma because
I wanted to make a point. The point is that the child abuse industry's
slogans are just that: slogans. They are uttered unthinkingly, taught

unthinkingly, learned unquestioningly, and repeated unquestioningly. Let's start questioning them.

EXPERT HUNCHES AND THE MISSING MISSING CHILDREN

Gut hunches are all very well when little is at stake. Nobody cares if John Doe takes the "A" exit off Highway XYZ because he has a hunch the "B" exit might be clogged today. But what we're staring at today is a totalitarian social policy based on gut hunches, not facts. Experts "just know" that there's a lot more abuse going on than the facts show. So they add a fudge factor of ten, or twenty, or fifty to the facts and proceed to clamor for police state powers to deal with the "crisis" they have just fabricated out of thin air.

A recent example of how this works is the "Missing Children" scam. For a while there we were hearing that millions of American children were being abducted each year by strangers. The public swung into action. Pictures of missing kids started appearing on TV broadcasts, on mail advertising pieces, on milk cartons, and (this is bizarre) on schoolroom walls.

The "missing millions" campaign even took in our legislators. Missing children legislation popped up everywhere. Fingerprinting programs blossomed, and parents willingly subjected their children to this invasion of privacy formerly reserved for criminals. We now have a whole bureaucracy devoted to the missing children problem.

This campaign is still going on today, although it has somewhat abated since the disclosure that most of the "missing" children were runaways or had been taken by their own non-custodial parents. Reliable estimates of the number of stranger kidnappings per year now run between sixty-seven and several thousand—a far cry from the millions claimed at first.[19]

As I heard it from a man at the FBI, the parents of children that had been taken by divorced spouses got together and deliberately exploited the concern over stranger kidnappings to get their own kids' pictures plastered all over America. Their motives were entirely understandable, although the means were far from laudable. But the fact remains that these people took in the entire American media—including some journalists who still are writing about the "missing millions" years after the whole mess was exposed.

Have any victims of stranger kidnappings been found through this vast campaign? So far, it seems not. But the campaign kicked off by marshmallow statistics continues unabated, in defiance of its shaky base and outstanding lack of success. It seems you can build a whole empire on marshmallows.

A PLAGUE OF LEECHES

It's bad enough that child abuse hysteria is turning us into a nation of busybodies. But it goes further: we're a nation of paranoid busybodies. Not only are we suspecting that an occasional friend or neighbor might be abusing his children, but we're suspecting *all* our neighbors. If those ridiculous statistics of one in four girls sexually abused, and millions of children in general being abused each year, were right, then you could literally look to the house on the right, the left, and across the street and be sure that at least one of your neighbors was an abuser (because abusers are supposedly evenly mixed in the population).

It came as a great relief to me personally to find out that there is much, much less abuse in America than we have been told. The reason? A great, glaring gap between what you and I mean when we talk about abuse and what the "experts" mean. You and I think of bloodied children, battered children, raped children. The "experts" think of parents who scold and withhold TV-watching privileges. Abuse, you see, is undefined by law. That means it can mean anything an expert wants it to. And, increasingly, "experts" are redefining abuse to include such things as "failing to provide sympathy and support." (That quote was from the National Committee for Prevention of Child Abuse.)[20]

A more dangerous example: authors Richard Gelles, Murray Strauss, and Suzanne K. Steinmetz in their study of family violence (one based on interviews with just over two thousand people) deliberately redefined "violence" in such a way as to include physical punishment, which by their own admission "is used by 84 to 97 percent of all parents at some time in their child's life."[21] As Gelles, Strauss, and Steinmetz reveal,

> Although the current thinking about slaps and spankings of children is that they are legitimate parenting tools, our view is that slaps and spankings are simply one end of a continuum of violent acts. . . . We chose to use the word "violence" and to employ a broad definition that includes acts which are not normally thought to be violent because we wanted to draw attention to the issue. . . . We call this hitting "violence" because we would like to have people begin to question the acts which traditionally they have taken for granted as necessary, useful, inevitable, and instinctive.[22]

Then, after using this misleading definition of "violence" throughout their book, the authors end with some proposals for reducing what they naturally discovered to be an epidemic of "violence" (as they defined it) in the home. Proposal Number One is to eliminate spanking, and to implement a propaganda campaign against it.[23]

This is a classic case of begging the question. In the same way, we could define failure to dispense wheat germ at every meal as "nutritional deprivation" (while acknowledging the fact that up to 99 percent of American families engage in this behavior), go on for hundreds of pages about the horrors of nutritional deprivation (using the scariest stories we could find and claiming they are "typical" of what goes on in American homes), and then end with a proposal that parents be forced to include wheat germ in every meal. We could even prove that force is necessary to implement the Wheat Germ Proposal, because after all practically everyone is incapable (read, unwilling) to do it on their own.

What makes Gelles et. al. dangerous is that their studies and conclusions are taken more seriously than actual government statistics. The American Humane Association, in its last report on child abuse, gave more credence to Gelles et. al.'s estimates of child abuse than to their own report.[24] Yet, as we have seen, the whole approach of Gelles and friends is tainted by ideology. They are not open-minded scientists trying to discover truth. They know in advance what they want to force the rest of us to do, and are willing to bend the English language and label 97 percent of families "abusive" in order to achieve their end.

Neither do Gelles, Strauss, and Steinmetz stand alone. They are just the point men for a whole corps of "child advocates" who have found a way to impose their elitist, white, upper-class, post-Christian parenting philosophies on the rest of us under the guise of "fighting child abuse." When this group talks about vast numbers of "abused" children, what they mean is "children who are raised in ways we disapprove." That number can, of course, be as large as they like.

Marshmallow statistics, then, serve a purpose.

(1) Money. It's a lot easier to get millions of dollars for your program when you are supposedly fighting an epidemic of child abuse. If people knew how few cases of genuine child abuse there are, it would be hard to keep the money rolling in.

(2) Power. Those who dislike the traditional family (and they are a significant minority) find it convenient to preach about abuse. By inflating the statistics they "prove" that the family does not work and needs to be replaced by state-run institutions, or at least controlled by them and their friends.

We are suffering a plague, all right. But it's not a plague of child abuse. It's a plague of leeches.

3 HOME, HORRIBLE HOME

Many children fear the dark. More fear falling. And every child fears getting lost or otherwise separated from his parents. Even our folk tales reflect this fear—Hansel and Gretel lost in the forest, Thumbelina carried off by a frog.

Yet, in spite of every child's deep need to be with his own parents, no dogma is more common in the child abuse camp than this: home is horrible. This is variously expressed as home being the most dangerous environment for children, all homes being abusive homes, all parents being abusive parents.

Richard Gelles and Murray Strauss, who as you have seen are influential authors in the child abuse field, put it this way:

> With the exception of the police and the military, the family is perhaps the most violent social group, and the home the most violent social setting, in our society. A person is more likely to be hit or killed in his or her own home by another family member than anywhere else or by anyone else.[1]

Declarations like that above increasingly find a home in the media and in the proposals of our elected officials. Instead of the lavender-scented memories of "home, sweet home" purveyed in former days, "home" and "family" are becoming dirty words.

I don't know how it is with you, but in my everyday life I don't encounter hordes of bruised, battered, bewildered children. The few children I've seen who appeared neglected or otherwise potentially abused also were not from "all socio-economic strata," but from the poverty-stricken, single-parent, somewhat immoral group—just where we have historically expected to find them.

With this in mind, I decided to investigate. *Is* home a den of depravity, or is it still the safe haven we had always thought? Do most children need protection from their parents—or does the family need protection from usurping bureaucrats who are drumming up an anti-family hate campaign not based on facts?

DEATH

The death of a child is a terrible thing. However, since America seems to be developing a taste for terrible things (witness the latest TV offerings), we are treated every so often to a splashy story on how some poor child was done to death by his or her parent(s). Cumulatively, the effect of these stories is to make it seem that parental murder is common.

It struck me that, if the murder of one's own children were so commonplace, it wouldn't be headline news. And, in fact, this heinous crime is extremely rare. An average of 1,000 children die each year at the hands of their parents or guardians.[2] This number may seem large, but out of a total child population of 72,444,127 in 1980[3] it comes to less than 1 out of 72,000, or .00138 percent. Out of the total of about 80,000 deaths for youths aged less than 19,[4] the deaths from child abuse amount to just over 1 percent of the total.

When you look into it further, it becomes clear that most deaths attributed to "child abuse" actually occur at the hands of persons other than the parents. Live-in boyfriends are the most common offenders, as both the raw statistics and newspaper reports bear out.[5] Nor are the "families" where these deaths occur necessarily normal American households in other respects. Drugs, alcohol, promiscuity, and a previous criminal record are factors in most child abuse deaths.[6]

Now let's compare child abuse deaths with deaths about which child advocates are remarkably silent.

- Although 1,500,000 abortions occur each year, most after the baby has developed her nervous system and consequently can feel great pain, this is not considered child abuse by child advocates. Abortion, which by definition causes the baby to be torn apart while alive, cut to pieces, or burned to death in a saline solution, is torture of a kind which one would expect to arouse those guardians of the rights of children. But it doesn't. Although annually 1,500 abortions occur for every death by child abuse, and the death by abortion is far more violent than most child abuse deaths, child advocates either are totally silent on this topic or endorse abortion. They are not even pressing for laws to limit abortion to before the fetus can feel pain, although this kind of law, which would not even make abortion illegal, but would only accord unborn humans the rights now granted to live dogs, has at least a chance of being found constitutional. (It's one thing to endorse a woman's "right to privacy," and another to endorse her right to torture her own child. The first does not at all imply the second.) Nor do child advocates oppose the abortion mentality, although it directly and inevitably leads to real child abuse, as a Canadian study has shown.[7] A mother who may legally torture her 8-month-old unborn baby will find it difficult to understand why she can't slam her 8-year-old against the wall.

Even if I still resided in the far-left wing of the feminist camp, as I did for years, I would find it difficult to justify *torturing* a baby. None of this gutless copping out about the unborn being a "blob of tissue," either. Any book on fetal development can tell you better. And in a day when premature babies have been known to survive as early as five months gestation age, to allow abortion literally until the moment of birth is, as Germaine Greer says, ghoulish.[8] A woman who has been indecisively wondering "Should I have an abortion or shouldn't I?" for nine months is certainly not prepared for the nurturing mindset of motherhood. This is why West Germany has consistently refused to legalize abortion—because of the disrespect for all life to which it leads, and which they so graphically experienced under Hitler.

The connivance of child advocates and legislators at upholding the torture of unborn children renders their child protective rhetoric suspect.

- Automotive deaths claimed the lives of 10,000 children annually.[9] Again, we know why most of these occur—drunkenness. But do child advocates speak out against booze and drugs? No. Blame is again placed on the family, for failure to strap the youngsters into seat belts, and legislators pass mandatory car seat laws. No car seat in the world will save you from being killed when a drunk driver going the other way on the highway hits your car with a cumulative impact of 120 miles per hour. But forcing families to buy larger cars and invest in expensive car seats does distract public attention from the drunken, irresponsible drivers who kill twenty times as many children annually as die of child abuse.

- Many writers have pointed out that the hospital newborn nursery is a fruitful source of disease. Add to this the practice of oversedating mothers before birth and all the other hazardous interventions to which the newborn is exposed, and you can make quite a convincing case that the hospital nursery ranks third as one of the most dangerous environments for babies. Nobody knows how many infant deaths, or deaths of hospitalized children, can be attributed directly to modern medicine's passion for intervention, but with one of the highest child mortality rates in the developed world, the U.S. hospital system must take at least some of the blame for the 40,627 deaths of children under the age of 1, at least 870 of which were directly attributed to "infections specific to the perinatal period," i.e., infections the hospital either caused or failed to prevent. If you include all of the "certain conditions originating in the perinatal period" we find a death rate in children under one of 522.1 for each 100,000—almost five hundred times the rate of deaths from child abuse.[10]

● Murder by those other than parents and deaths from legal intervention together claim more than three times as many lives as child abuse.[11]

● Suicide accounted for 4,000 child deaths in 1980, four times as many as died from child abuse. But suicide is government-endorsed, with compulsory "death education" classes in the public school where children learn how to do it and are desensitized to the horrors of dying by their own hands.[12]

Actually, almost every cause of death claims more victims than child abuse. More children die every year from heart disease or pneumonia than die of child abuse.[13]

So the most dangerous place for a child is not the home into which she is born. It is

(1) Her mother's womb—and the child abuse industry supports the parent's right to torture the unborn.

(2) Anywhere around a moving vehicle—and the government and child advocates continue to allow drunken driving with minimal, not to say trivial, penalties.

(3) The hospital—and as you will see, the child abuse industry desires to require more and more hospitalization of children as part of their "networking" strategy.

(4) Anywhere around non-family members or police officers.

(5) Public school classrooms and the negative influence of peer cliques.

Is the traditional family really the cradle of violence? No. Highway fatalities and even heart disease significantly outstrip child abuse as causes of death for children.

Yet the child abuse industry continually strives to make the traditional family (mother, father, and their original children) appear as a pathological institution that cannot care for its members. The rare cases of abuse involving the natural parents are seized upon with glee and publicized nationwide as typical. But in the cases where a child dies in his home, very, very rarely is he the member of a stable two-parent family. Only if a writer is willing to get sloppy and consider adulterous, extramarital, homosexual, and other alliances as "families," and to include foster homes and other "primary caretaking institutions" as well, will he ever find that the family poses any statistically observable danger to a child.[14]

SEXUAL ABUSE

Nowhere is the child abuse hysteria more evident than in discussions of sexual abuse. The statistics get wilder every day: one out of ten girls sexually abused, then one out of five, one out of four, one out of three, and even, ridiculously, two out of one. What goes on in porn magazines is supposedly a model of cleanliness when compared to what's happening at home, and virtually all your neighbors, if not you yourself, are statistically indicted as child rapists.

What the child abuse industry fails to tell us is that *the vast majority of sexual abuse occurs in non-families or broken families.* Even the social work text that first opened my eyes to the child abuse industry's crusade to make incest a mere "taboo" reveals that incest occurs, not in traditional settings, but elsewhere.[15] We even have a profile of the typical perpetrator: promiscuous, often remarried and even more often not married (i.e., a live-in boyfriend), alcoholic, often with a criminal record.[16] They could have added that this type of man (because, in spite of foolish feminist desires to see women equally numbered among these villains, men do 90 percent of it) is a heavy porn user.[17] And there you have it. Hardly the picture of the traditional family.

A friend of mine who has spent years working with spouse and child abuse victims told me that, in her experience, "It's extremely rare to find incest in an intact, original marriage. When previous generations also had intact marriages, the rate of incest is virtually zero." But the child abuse industry says just the opposite!

What do we *know* about the crime of incest, a crime so heinous the Bible says we shouldn't even desensitize ourselves to it by discussing it (Eph 5:3-12)? Let's look at some statistics.

The U.S.A. national statistics blur sexual abuse by lumping together incest with attacks by outsiders. The AHA report points out that

> the tremendous increase in 1984 in the proportion of sexual maltreatment . . . is not due only to growing public awareness, but is also associated with the expansion of definitions to include extra-familial abuse. . . .[18]

In other words, every kid who gets molested by a step-uncle, a boyfriend, or a stranger on the street gets added into the "sexual abuse" category, which then is used as "evidence" that the home has become an unsafe environment.

A newspaper report on sexual abuse explains that the sexual abuse figures also include "anything from fondling to actual sexual intercourse."[19] Since, in most cases, there is no way to prove either that fondling did or did not occur, and all a social worker needs to substantiate a sexual abuse charge is her suspicion that the abuse might have occurred, including fondling in the sexual abuse figures greatly increases those figures. In New Jersey, for example, almost half of sexual abuse reports involve "mild fondling."[20]

Some states, however, do make it possible to get a handle on how much in-family, as opposed to out-of-family, sexual abuse is going on. The Missouri statistics split off incest (all forms of sexual crimes involving family members) from sexual abuse (sex crimes perpetrated by outsiders). After all the hype about the degeneracy of the family, you'd expect incest to outnumber sexual abuse 10 to 1, but actually the ratio is reversed. There were ten times as many substantiated reports of sexual abuse in 1984 as there were of incest.[21]

Again, sexual abuse is loosely defined. One mother called me to complain that she was substantiated as a sexual abuser because she washed her seven-year-old's foreskin for him when he was sloppy about the job. My husband has been told by a major day-care chain operator that her workers are fearful about touching the children when changing their diapers because they might be accused of sexual abuse. The day-care workers' fears are justified, because the law includes fondling as part of sexual abuse. Generations of mothers who greased their baby's bottoms with Desitin would have been shocked to be called sexual abusers, but that's where we are today. No wonder sexual abuse has the highest substantiation rate of all kinds of child abuse. As an article in *American Spectator* magazine aptly observed, "Hug Your Kid, Go To Jail."

But leaving the sloppy definition of sexual abuse aside, and even assuming that 237 cases of fondling and what-not did occur in Missouri in 1984, this is not where the action is. It is certainly true that a large number of girls are sexually used by the time they reach eighteen or twenty-one, but not at the hands of their parents. Fornication, widely encouraged by the schools and the media, is the reason so many girls and boys approach eighteen in a non-virginal state. Public school courses indoctrinate children in the rightness of nonmarital sex, tell them how to do it, and practically order them to go out and practice sex as a homework assignment. In these circumstances, date rape outweighs parental sexual abuse by enormous margins.

Consider the case of a typical fourteen-year-old girl on a date. The young man sitting in the driver's seat, if he is like his fellows, expects sex by the third date, at the very latest. Eighty percent of single males in a recent survey indicated they expected sex by the third date, and 50 percent expected it on the first.[22] Add to this the "philosophy" popularized by *Playboy* magazine, that every woman really wants sex at all times from anything in pants, and where does that put the fourteen-year-old? Flat on her back. And then child advocates have the nerve to complain about the problem of unwed teen mothers!

Pregnancy is caused by sex, not by social conditions. As long as our leaders endorse non-marital sex, we're going to have non-marital pregnancy, and lots and lots of girls are going to end up with no husband at all.

Home is not the most dangerous sexual environment for a child. Dating is.

ENCOURAGING CHILD ABUSE THROUGH "PREVENTION" PROGRAMS

However, home can *become* a dangerous sexual environment, if the next generation can only be desensitized to incest. This is what the so-called "child abuse prevention" programs do so well. Young children, as their very first exposure to sex, are told to suspect Mom and Dad of evil intentions on their bodies. Their older siblings are taught that incest is only a "taboo" and that almost everyone is doing it. In a groupthink society such as ours, saying that incest is common amounts to an endorsement—"Hey, Johnny, join in, everyone's doing it!" Thus pubescent males are being taught to eye their defenseless little sisters' bodies as possible release valves for their sexuality. If these curricula (which nobody has ever proved do the slightest good)[23] are allowed to proliferate, we will produce for the first time an entire generation of males who have been trained to consider raping their sons and daughters as passably normal behavior.

LITTLE PIG, LITTLE PIG, LET ME COME IN

Sexual abuse *is* increasing. The questions are, How much? and Who is to blame?

The answer to the How much? is that incest is up significantly, but is nowhere near an epidemic. If, as one article suggested, incest occurred at about the rate of one in a million families in 1940,[24] it is certain that it is not, as the same article claimed, occuring in one out of four households today. On the most rudimentary level, if that were true, we would have enough people voting *for* incest to prevent any laws against it from ever passing. Wild claims like these—"one out of four families incestuous"—have no basis in reality.

On the other hand, it would be surprising if incest were not on the rise, now that the media is actively promoting it. What has been euphemistically called the "sex industry" (e.g., *Hustler* magazine) has been increasingly featuring children and child figures in its cartoons. In May 1984, *Hustler* published a cartoon of a father sticking his hand into his daughter's pants and leering in her face while she tells her boyfriend on the phone, "Gee . . . I'd love to go to the drive-in, Tommy, but my dad has some, ah, extra household chores for me tonight." *Penthouse* and *Playboy*, while not quite so blatant, regularly depict child-adult sexual interaction, in the words of researcher Judith Reisman,

> as something that the child *desires* and *seeks out*, something that is *harmless* to the child and something that the reader can interpret as *viable interaction.*[25]

We even have a female psychiatrist and pediatrician who goes about touting the thesis that children *should* have sex with adults, and that incest is *good* for children.[26] Physically, of course, that is horsefeathers—prepubescent children are not physically designed to have sex. It can even kill them. (The doctor in question encourages sex as early as age four, and masturbation from birth.)[27] Morally, the suggestion is outrageous. But the reporter who conducted the interview with this woman thought she "has an argument that should be heard." *Why* should her argument be heard? Because "she wants to save the children too."[28] And that, friends, is about as low as child-saving can go.

Now I hope you are closing in on the answer to the question, "Who is to blame for sexual abuse increasing?" It is those who *knock the traditional family*, who *oppose traditional religion*, and who hope to cover up their own depraved actions by *forcing depraved standards on the rest of us under the guise of "mental health" or "saving the children."* The root of the problem is social attitudes which disconnect sex from marital responsibility; an increase in unmarried living arrangements and remarriage, with a consequent increase in men living with girls who are not their natural daughters; pornographic propaganda; and the media's desire to cash in on the shock value of child sex. The traditional family stands squarely *against* all these things. Yet the increase in sexual abuse is being used as an excuse to kick traditional families in the teeth!

The home, that is, the *traditional* home of mother, father, and their natural children, is not the cradle of violence. It is the best protection children ever have had, or ever will have. And all the furor over "fighting sexual abuse" looks more like a bid for state control of every family than a sincere attempt to address the problem. The wolf is knocking at the door of the Little Pig's house and crying, "Little Pig, Little Pig, let me come in! I have just finished a study that proves your home is a mess, Little Pig! I have solutions to your problems!" The Little Pig in the story was too smart to believe that a wolf in the house would do him any good.

Are we that smart?

THE IMMACULATE CONFESSION & OTHER CHILD ABUSE DOCTRINES 4

Where there's smoke there's fire. Or so the saying goes. But sometimes lots of smoke comes from a small fire; sometimes a fire can be under control and people still call the Fire Department. Sometimes there's no real fire at all, just a heavy cloud of cigar smoke oozing out a bedroom window or the dark exhaust from an untuned car gushing from a garage.

By now you're probably wondering: why is there so much noise about child abuse when there so little actual abuse? Why do people garble the facts about child abuse so badly? Why are the statistics inflated, the terms redefined, and the whole problem blown so out of proportion?

Statistically we see that child abuse does not even begin to approach an epidemic. Only one child out of 72,000 dies from child abuse;[1] less than one out of three thousand is seriously harmed each year.[2] Sexual abuse affects only about one in a thousand children,[3] and most of these cases do not involve the natural parents. Reports of abuse and neglect are increasing, but so is the malicious use of child abuse hotlines by ex-spouses.[4] Actual severe physical abuse is even reported on the decline.[5]

Why is there so much smoke with so little fire? Because social workers and other child abuse industry employees are trained to ignore the facts. Instead, they are taught *doctrines*: ideological slogans that fly in the face of reality. When a contradiction appears between facts and ideology, they are trained to dismiss the facts and go with the doctrine.

This is not the first time in human history that people have become so gripped with an idea that they were willing to ignore reality. The history of fanaticism is almost as old as history itself. And child advocacy is stated in just those terms: a "crusade," a "war." Schools of social work guard and disseminate the faith; the media propagate it.

This new jihad, or holy war, against the family is different from other such movements, however, in that it claims to be rational and scientific. No archangel appeared from heaven to initiate Doctors

Gelles and Strauss into the mysteries of why families are schools of violence. The movement doesn't even have a Fuhrer or little red book. All it has is its "scientific" revelations, all of which combine to form a body of excuses for a system that anyone can see is vastly overblown and isn't working.

The beauty of scientific pronouncements is that you can rationally test them, and even disprove them. Since child abuse theory claims to be scientific, we can check it out against facts and logic.

Let's do it.

THE DOCTRINE OF UNDERREPORTING

Just like any cult, the child abuse industry has its own set of defensive doctrines designed to explain away the inconsistencies of its actions. First among these is *the doctrine of underreporting*. This doctrine asserts that, although it's true that no evidence exists to prove we have a plague of child abuse, it's only because people are failing to report.

The American Humane Association, for example, ignores their own carefully-compiled statistics based on actual reports. Instead, they accept a study done by Richard Gelles and Murray Strauss, extrapolate from that study to posit one and a half million children aged zero to seventeen from intact families subjected to very severe violence in 1985, and then conclude that "only one child in seven who is physically injured is reported."[6] So a study which the authors themselves admit was created in order to kick off a propaganda campaign,[7] one which furthermore uses an extremely dubious definition of "violence"[8] (paddling, for example, falls into this category), is allowed to override the actual statistics. In spite of the fact that the proportion of false reports is rising, which would indicate we are at least approaching the point of diminishing returns, the AHA took the position that "the C[hild] P[rotective] S[ystem] still has a long way to go if the goal of providing protection to even the seriously abused is to be achieved."[9]

THE DOCTRINE OF UNDERINVESTIGATION

The one-sidedness of child abuse logic also shines through in *the doctrine of underinvestigation*, which parallels the doctrine of underreporting. This doctrine claims that the only reason so many reports are unsubstantiated is because "we don't have time to investigate them thoroughly."

Again, the AHA, while claiming every single "substantiated" report is a genuine case of child abuse (although "substantiated" means only that social workers suspect abuse, not that abuse has been proven), is unwilling to admit that any unsubstantiated reports are false. As the 1984 report says, "Unfortunately, cases which are unsubstantiated may actually involve an incident of child maltreatment."[10] The evidence? "Sixteen percent of unsubstantiated cases were opened."[11] This is a classic case of begging the question: because social workers were willing to open a case without any proof their intervention was needed, that proves intervention was needed. By this reasoning, if Joe the bully down the street decided to kick your son in the teeth for no reason, that proves your son needed a kick in the teeth. Quid pro quo and a happy New Year to us all.

If the AHA had been willing to recognize the possibility that some "substantiated" cases were inappropriately substantiated, we could perhaps forgive their overeagerness to claim some unsubstantiated cases are genuine. But since no such disclaimer exists anywhere in their report, the obvious conclusion is that the AHA is in the grip of doctrine, and using its considerable influence simply to defend the bureaucratic system.

BLAME THE PARENTS FOR EVERYTHING

We also have the *blame-the-parents doctrine*. This declares that parents are always to blame for everything that happens to their children, even if it occurs without their consent or knowledge.

St. Joseph's Health Center of St. Charles, Missouri, even asked to have this doctrine enshrined in law. Seems that the folks at the hospital ran into cases of rape perpetrated by those who *weren't* the parents. They could have reported this to the police, but then they would have had to run the risk of being liable for their actions. Preferring to claim the protection of absolute immunity afforded reporters on the child abuse hotline, St. Joseph's suggested a novel idea. Perhaps they could *report the parents for neglect* (for having allowed this to take place, although against their wishes and without their knowledge)! As St. Joseph's so thoughtfully put it:

> Some instances in which the suspected abuse is by a person other than one who has care, custody and control of the child may involve neglect by those who do. Where a child is secreted from her bedroom during the night and sexually abused by a neighbor, the parents may be neglectful for failing to notice the disappearance. Similarly, where the perpetrator is a temporary member of the household, the parents may be neglectful for leaving the child unattended. . . . Thus, in certain circumstances, the Child Abuse Hotline should accept reports of abuse by persons other than those who have care, custody and control on the basis of neglect by those who do.[12]

How much more sensible to subject a family to the threat of removal for their alleged "neglect" than to face "the possibility that an alleged perpetrator will charge the health care employee, physician or institution with slander."[13]

We could call this the Doctrine of Limited Liability—do whatever benefits the institution, not the family.

THE DOCTRINE OF TOTAL DEPRAVITY

And families are easier pickings these days, thanks to the *doctrine of total depravity*. *Every* family, it states, is depraved. *All* families are abusive. Therefore, any and all state interventions are justifiable. As a prominent social work text states,

> Child maltreatment exists on a continuum; at some time everyone has been abusive and has been abused. . . . No one has a corner on committing violence against children. Most parents at some time have abused or neglected their child or a child who was entrusted in their care.[14]

With logic like this, it's hard to see why child advocates even bother to use child abuse hotlines to gather their reports. Wouldn't it be simpler just to remove *every* child from his family at birth? (You think I'm kidding, but a plan very like this has already been suggested, endorsed by a governor, and sent around to every state, as you will see in a future chapter.)

THE DOCTRINE OF THE IMMACULATE CONFESSION

Now you have enough background information to understand the strangest doctrine of all: *the doctrine of the immaculate confession.* This is the Catch-22 of child abuse.

Social workers are taught that anytime a child accuses his parents (even if his confession occurs under pressure from the worker), this confession must be taken as gospel. However, if he denies everything from the start, or later denies his accusations, his denials means nothing.

Here's the Catch-22: *you're only supposed to believe the child if he accuses the parents.*

People are actually pushing for laws to embody this doctrine. They would make all recantations inadmissable in court (on the theory that the parents forced the child to retract). A step toward this, allowing the earlier confession to be introduced in court in spite of later denials, was signed into law by Missouri Governor John Ashcroft in 1985.[15]

The child abuse industry at present has full powers to pressure children for hours, days, or even weeks in order to squeeze out an accusation. Investigators can ask leading questions, or even make up stories and coach children in them. In this way, virtually any family unfortunate enough to be accused of child abuse can be found guilty sooner or later.

Consider this bit of actual courtroom testimony, given by a five-year-old girl.

Direct examination

Q. *Did anybody ever hurt you when you were living in your real home?*
A. Yes.
Q. *... What was that?*
A. Spanking
Q. *... Was there anything else?*
A. Yes.
Q. *What was the other thing?*
A. Touched on the private parts.
Q. *... What are your private parts?*
A. Crotch.
Q. *... Did anybody ever touch you, other than your crotch, in your private parts? Do you remember?*
A. My butt.
Q. *... You said somebody touched you in your crotch with their finger; is that right or wrong?*
A. Right.
Q. *... Did anybody tell you you should make these things up, that they weren't true?*
A. No.
Q. *... You didn't make them up?*
A. No.
Q. *Did they really happen then if you didn't make them up?*
A. Yes.

Cross examination

Q. *Do you remember when Tom [a social worker] said, 'Now it's time to practice for court . . .'?*
A. Yes.
Q. *... And you practiced saying, 'I'm telling the truth,' with Tom, didn't you?*
A. Yes.
Q. *And you practiced with Tom saying that your mom and dad touched you in the private parts, didn't you?*
A. Yeah.
Q. *... And during practice, if you gave a wrong answer, Tom would correct you, wouldn't he?*
A. Yeah.

Q. . . . *And they kept telling you, 'You have bad secrets,' didn't they?*
A. Yes.
Q. *And before you were taken away from your real parents, you didn't have any bad secrets, did you?*
A. No.
Q. . . . *You told a lot of people it was just pretend, didn't you?*
A. Yeah.
Q. *And you kept telling them that nothing happened last year, didn't you?*
A. Yes.
Q. *But they wanted you to tell them that something happened, didn't they?*
A. Yes.[16]

As if this kind of manipulation of children by child abuse industry agents weren't enough, we now have something called the Child Sexual Abuse Accomodation Syndrome to explain away any inconsistencies in courtroom testimony against the parents. Briefly stated, the CSAAS says

- sexually abused children tend to contradict themselves;

- sexually abused children cover up the incident;

- sexually abused children often show no emotion after the event;

- sexually abused children often wait a long time before making their accusations

In other words, all the evidence typically used to show *no* sexual abuse occurred (contradictory or nonexistent stories, child not upset, child only coming up with story much later) has now been captured to "prove" the very opposite![17] According to this logic, if it looks like a cheeseburger, smells like a cheeseburger, and tastes like a cheesburger that proves it is *not* a cheeseburger.

Lack of physical evidence of abuse poses no problem to True Believers, because "touching" has been added to the category of sexual abuse. If accused, it will be up to you to prove that you never touched your child "sexually." The state does not have to prove touch is sexual: touch is *presumed* to be sexual. Fathers who diaper their daughters are in deep trouble because of this definition (another blow for women's rights).

Given the pressure put on children, once removed, to confess something, *anything*, that will justify their removal, the next dogma seems almost laughable. Yet a big part of child abuse theory centers around the belief that *the child cannot lie*. As one victim of the system pointed out,

> "There is a general feeling among attorneys and child protection authorities who say a child cannot lie . . . The reason given is that children don't know enough about sex to lie about it . . . but [I know] of at least four books on sale in local bookstores specifically aimed at teaching children about sex so they can avoid sexual abuse."[18]

The man has a point. What good is it claiming children "cannot lie" about sex because they know nothing about it, when the child abuse industry is diligently introducing this very information into every schoolroom it can reach? Parents buy books on sexual assault and read them to their children. Networks air prime-time shows on the subject. Yet we are supposed to believe that it's the days of the Hardy Boys and Nancy Drew, when children didn't even know they *had* "private parts," let alone that these could be misused.

Another, more serious, point, is that children can and do tell stories, and can and do lie. Little Sally might knock over Baby Ricky's block tower and then angelically claim that Brother Sidney did it. Brother Sidney, in turn, might tell his friends some outrageous story about his father's (wholly fictitious) secret life as an F.B.I. undercover agent. Baby Ricky, too little to talk, will quickly crawl away from a mess he knows he shouldn't have made and try to look like somebody else did it. Part of human nature is to try to excuse oneself and to try to please others by saying what they want to hear.

But the child abuse industry ignores the obvious fact that if adults lie, they must have learned to as children. Instead, they draw children on to tell stories. Children are shown films, and then asked "Did this ever happen to you?" (a clear invitation to be the center of attention—the material for their fantasies has already been supplied). Children are given dolls to play with, and then their most innocent behavior is seen as "acting out sexual abuse."

More about those dolls. Lee Coleman, a Berkeley psychologist, is one of a mounting number of doctors condemning the use of "anatomically correct" dolls. These dolls are, as one newspaper article says, a "major tool" for those involved in investigating and prosecuting juvenile sexual abuse cases.[19]

Why does Coleman condemn these dolls? Not because they're not cute. They're soft and huggable and squeezable and thoroughly non-threatening. And that's just the problem. As Coleman says, "You don't give a kid a doll and then tell them to tell the truth . . . A doll is for fantasy, not for truth."[20]

As Diane Schetky and Harold Boverman, both M.D.'s, pointed out in a paper entitled "Faulty Assessment of Child Sexual Abuse" presented at the 1985 Annual Meeting of the American Academy of Psychiatry and the Law, "Nor has anyone yet to demonstrate how normal children play with these dolls." The fact is that normal children know a doll is a plaything, not a person, and their behavior when playing with a doll has nothing to do with their own real-life experiences. Little Sally might throw her doll on the floor and step on it, although she never acts like this with her baby sister. Little Sidney might twist the doll's head around to see if it comes off, although nobody has ever twisted *his* head in his life. Yet untrained state personnel hand a preverbal or barely verbal child one of these dolls, with its huge, bulging genitals ("anatomically correct" dolls are anatomically complete, but *not* anatomically correct), and believe that if the child even *notices* the genitals that he or she is "acting out sexual abuse"!

Can't you just see what would happen if Baby Ricky got his hands on an "anatomically correct," lovable, soft rag doll? He'd pull its hair and squeeze it and chew on its nose . . . and on any other part that happened to protrude. Oh, oh! Baby Ricky has just "acted out sexual abuse"! He didn't know Rule #1 for playing with dolls—never touch them in the private parts! (He probably doesn't even know that bit of soft rag is supposed to symbolize "private parts.") And off goes Ricky to a foster home, and here come the officers to take Mommy and Daddy away.

I know this all sounds silly, but it's no laughing matter. You can end up in jail because of how your child plays with one of these dolls, even if there is no actual evidence against you. As a *Newsweek* article of February 18, 1985 said, "every state but Nebraska permits the conviction of a molestor on the uncorroborated testimony of a child,"[21] and this "testimony" can and does include a child's behavior in a session with dolls. This means the state needs *no* evidence, *no* witnesses, *no* adult testimony, and not even verbal testimony by the child to convict a parent of sexual abuse. And in juvenile court, where laws of due process don't apply, the only testimony the state needs is the caseworker's.

"We're just not supposed to believe that children do or can lie," says Tim Stanton, a social worker at California's Naval Hospital Clinic . . . "I was trained in school to believe that the child wouldn't bring up such an awful topic if it were a lie." Stanton's faith has been shaken because in the last two years he has treated a half dozen children who either fabricated or knowingly embellished stories of sexual abuse.[22]

As an article in the *American Spectator* explained,

Some children do lie. In a not atypical case, a Southern California junior high school girl accused her teacher, William Gillett, of molesting her. Gillett was carried off, handcuffed, by the local police. Three weeks later, after Gillett had quit his job, the girl admitted that she had made up the story to "get" him for giving her a low grade.[23]

And even if a child is not consciously lying, as that same *American Spectator* article pointed out,

adults' expectation can shape children's perceptions . . . for children, the line between lying and truth-telling, between experience and fantasy, is far from clear.[24]

Cullen Cline, a Missouri lawyer, says part of the problem is that

"children are so suggestible. If you ask a child the right questions, possibly you can get the child to say the right thing." . . . Sometimes the child can be over-rehearsed before a trial so that the child repeats what has been said.

The system leans absolutely towards the child in these cases, Cline said.[25]

Are we seeing, not an epidemic of child sex rings and parental sexual abuse, but of Salem witch hysteria? Dr. Ralph Underwager, a clinical psychologist who "has testified as an expert witness in child abuse cases from Florida to Alaska and who himself treats abused children," told a *Toronto Star* reporter

there is a remarkable similarity in the images children produce under interrogation—whether or not they have been abused. "You see the same progression," he said. "First they speak of fondling, then penetration, then monsters, leading on to the killing of small animals and finally the ritualistic murder of babies and adults."

Society, he said, believes children can't lie. But when they're pressured by adults, they lose their ability to distinguish between fact and fantasy. Many of the children now involved in the U.S. cases "will be destroyed," he predicted. "Some of them will become criminally psychotic." That, he said, amounts to child abuse.[26]

In real life, sexual abuse and physical abuse leave evidence. As psychologist Holly Wakefield comments, "Anal and vaginal intercourse is excruciatingly painful for the child and causes tissue damage." [27] Physical abuse leaves broken bones and other tell-tale signs. Male sexual activity leaves liquid traces. Screaming can be heard by witnesses. And so on.

Nobody is saying children can never tell the truth in court, or that sexual abuse and other crimes never occur. But these child abuse doctrines appear in a swarm of cases where *no evidence exists* except for the word of a child in state custody. Child abuse workers can easily *create* these cases, using these doctrines as "evidence."

The way the prosecutor behaved in the much-publicized Jordan, Minnesota case shows child abuse doctrines can be used in just that way. She, an ardent feminist, and one must consequently suppose an enemy of the traditional patriarchal family, interrogated children for hours until they confessed something. Even the children who refused to accuse their parents were not returned. Then the earlier accusations started breaking down; the children started admitting that they only accused their parents to get out from under the pressure; and medical evidence revealed the little girls' hymens were all intact. The prosecutor was unmoved. Although no parent in Jordan has ever been found guilty, she vowed that none of them would ever get their children back.[28]

Child abuse doctrines are both unreal and dangerous. They tell us more about the prejudices and frustrations of those who invent and propagate them than they do about reality. They can be used to "prove" child abuse occurred in *any* family, even the most innocent. They are the creed of hysteria.

A society that accepts these doctrines will be a society without civil rights . . . and of families without children.

NEGATIVE IMPACT OF THE CHILD ABUSE HYSTERIA 5

For the first time in 24 years, a San Diego high school counselor now asks another adult to be present any time he meets with a female student.

"I've been helping young people for more than two decades, and now I find myself wondering whether some adolescent girl will go home and say, 'This man's trying to get friendly with me,'" he said, asking not to be identified.

A young mother has quit her job to care for her 3-year-old son rather than entrust him to strangers at a day care center.

"It may sound silly since I've been relying on the center for nearly a year, but now I get panicky when my son's not with me," said Cindy Gasher of Greenbrae, California.

A grandfather of two no longer smiles at toddlers.

"I really had a shock recently in the supermarket when I grinned at a little girl who was winking at me, and the mother grabbed the child and fled," said silver-haired Zygmunt Pawlak of San Bruno, California.

Although its exact extent is uncertain, public attention focused on child abuse has had a chilling effect on family relations and counseling. . . .

As a consequence, child development experts said in interviews, some adults have become so fearful of having a simple gesture of friendship or affection be misinterpreted as a dastardly deed, they are withholding "nurturing" touches that are crucial to a child's development. . . .

Dr. Alvin Rosenfeld, director of psychiatric services at Jewish Child Care Association of New York, says the massive publicity about missing and molested children may be doing more harm than good.

"We are terrifying parents and children into unhealthy lifestyles. Some parents are afraid to let their kids go out of the house. And we may be instilling undue fear of the world in children, who are confronted with a constant assault of what may be a one-in-10,000 case of abuse."[1]

Hysteria: spell that D-A-N-G-E-R. A hysteric harms both himself and others as he lashes out at imaginary foes. A hysterical nation may, in the very process of trying to solve its problems, add more problems to them.

Think what we are coming to. Do we want to be afraid to hug our children, to talk to one another or show affection, to smile in the supermarket?

The number of crimes against children has been exaggerated, as we already have seen. But this exaggeration is no ho-hum mistake we can yawn about and ignore. It is setting children against parents, neighbor against neighbor, friend against friend. Whole communities are being rent by the largely unfounded hysteria.

Consider, for example, what is happening to blacks.

> "Black parents are faced with the dilemma of raising their children by both white and old traditional black standards of discipline," the study says. "Many traditional methods of discipline in the black family are considered child abuse today.
> "This leaves black parents in a real dilemma on how to raise their children."[2]

It is surely ironic that the very people who have always considered themselves sympathetic to blacks, namely, liberal whites, are now terrorizing the black community, threatening to remove its children. Who decided to, overnight, define black standards of discipline as "child abuse"? The very same people who supposedly are champions of pluralism and black culture. Hear this cry from the blacks you claimed to respect:

> "Parents, and I mean very good parents who are used to administering heavy spankings out of love, are becoming afraid to discipline their children at all.
> "Someone has changed the rules very fast and a lot of good black people are confused.
> "In very close black families, it is understood that if parents love their kids, they spank them a little harder. It's a system where parents not only deliver a message to your ears, they deliver a message to your behind.
> "Black parents simply don't know what to do to replace spanking, switching, and whipping. All that's left is a mystery. They are afraid that if they don't do it at home, the police will do it, and their kids will go to jail."

So said Otis Woodard, coordinator of outreach ministry for Lutheran Family and Children's Services of Missouri. Woodard began a campaign, supported by other black leaders, including the vice-president of the Association of Black Social Workers St. Louis chapter. He saw what was going on, how his community was being threatened—all in the name of "love" and "compassion."

Woodard contends that permissive child-rearing theories, spawned by "liberal people who call themselves experts," have been adopted by the white middle-class and are being institutionalized in laws.

His comments, reported in a *Post-Dispatch* article of May 16, 1985,[3] were supported by other black leaders. Lottie Wade, the director of the St. Louis City Office for the Division of Family Services, said Woodard and the other black leaders "have a good issue."

"I understand the concern," she said. "It's one I have expressed and we here at the Division of Family Services have had expressed to us by parents."
Ms. Wade said the law allows parents to spank their children. But it also defines any injury as abuse, she said.
"There's a tendency after a parent has been reported to the hotline (for inflicting bruises or welts) to back off and not discipline their child at all. Also, a child who is used to being disciplined by corporal punishment doesn't necessarily respond to other forms of discipline."[4]

So, whereas formerly a social worker would have left strong black families alone, approving parents who exercised strict discipline, now black parents who try to fulfill their responsibilities are targets of the law.
Another unanticipated side effect of the child abuse hysteria is a leap in the number of false accusations of sexual abuse.

There is some evidence that false accusations [of sexual abuse] are a growing phenomenon. At the beginning of this year, Brian Taugher, a special assistant to California Attorney General John Van de Kamp, was found innocent of molesting a 9-year-old girl. A California paper reported that Taugher said since his arrest dozens of people have told him "horror stories about being falsely accused of child abuse."
Wayne Anderson, a university professor who counsels people with sex-related problems, said a certain hysteria surrounds child abuse. Many people don't appreciate the distinction between crimes, he said.
Compare the difference between someone running a hand up a child's leg and someone who abuses the child for many years.

In addition, some families spank their children and those who don't use corporal punishment might see spanking as child abuse, Anderson said. . . .

Columbia lawyer Cullen Cline said part of the problem is that children are "so suggestible."

"If you ask a child the right questions, possibly you can get the child to say the right thing," Cline said. Sometimes the child can be over-rehearsed before a trial so that the child repeats what has been said.

The system leans absolutely towards the child in these cases, Cline said. Safeguards for the defendant in these cases have been reduced. . . .

In child sexual abuse cases, it's the child's word against the adult's word.[5]

About the only way a divorced man or woman can get sole custody without visitation rights for the ex-spouse is to accuse the ex-spouse of sexual abuse. Does this happen? Yes, more and more. Such an accusation adds more fuel to the hysteria, by pumping up the statistics. At the same time it can permanently damage the reputation of the innocent spouse, and may even result in the deserving spouse losing custody. With all the accuser stands to gain (revenge, custody of the child), an anonymous hotline looks almost too good to pass up. Especially when the state *invites* callers to accuse parents on mere "suspicion."

Right now, anyone can accuse you of sexual abuse without evidence. A social worker and policeman will come to your door. The social worker will take your children off individually and ask them leading questions, like "When does Daddy put his finger on your crotch?" If the social worker is able to get the children to say anything that remotely sounds suspicious, away go your children. No hard evidence is needed—no physical signs of rape or sodomy, no witnesses. You are another "substantiated" case of sexual abuse, and you might never get your children back.

Parents are not the only ones who can be victimized by malicious hotline callers. In today's climate, to be accused is to be guilty. Anyone who works with children can have his career ruined at the twirl of a telephone dial.

Paul Wallin, an attorney who represented 40 teachers accused of sexually abusing students across the country in the last year, reports that not one was convicted. Describing the cases of four of his clients in particular, Mr. Wallen says, "All four were excellent, caring, considerate, model teachers. If a kid was crying and needed a hug, they would do it. All four were accused. All four were exonerated. All four of their lives were ruined. And not one of them is teaching any more."

Teachers have become just as wary as the kids are supposed to be. One elementary school principal in Chicago said that he used to invite a few of his students to join his family at Christmas time. He would not consider it today. "You've got to be careful even putting a hand on a child's shoulder or arm as you're moving kids out of the room in a line."

A Kansas City school administrator remembers when a teacher's best technique for quieting a fidgety pupil was to sit close and put a hand on the child's knee. But no more. She advises teachers to keep their hands off. "Back then," she says, "you could touch them and they knew to cut it out. Now they get a different message."[6]

Is all this helping the children? Some people would say that damaged reputations and separated families are just the price we have to pay for catching abusers. To carry this view to its logical conclusion, *every* family should have to be periodically investigated. (A Tennessee School Boards Association representative has actually proposed such a law.)[7] But this kind of blanket suspicion is actually *harming* children.

Some child protection workers defend the reporting system, saying it is necessary to identify any child who may be in danger. But [Douglas J.] Besharov, [the first director of the National Center on Child Abuse and Neglect], said it has gone "far beyond anything reasonable."

"This flood of inappropriate cases is not just unfair to the parents who are investigated. It also created real danger for children who are in true jeopardy. These children who need to be protected are getting lost in the avalanche of new cases," he said.[8]

The very children who need the investigations most *are not getting reached in time and with adequate resources* because the child abuse hysteria is dispersed so evenly. If *all* parents are guilty, or could be guilty, then resources end up spread thinly. There is no way to separate the criminals from the average Joes. Jane Doe could face the same penalties for spanking or scolding as Jack the Ripper for raping or mutilating. A system that fails to distinguish crimes from unfashionable child-rearing practices cannot protect children.

Most ironically of all, the hysteria prevents parents from seeking help. Consider this plaintive plea, found in the "Open Mind" column of the St. Louis *Globe-Democrat* of September 3, 1985:

I am not enclosing a return envelope, and I cannot give you my name and address. Please answer in your column: What should a mother do when she finds she cannot tolerate one of her children? I am afraid to go for counseling because I could be reported for child abuse.

So the very laws instituted to protect children, and the very publicity which is supposed to "prevent abuse," are having the opposite effect. Instead of seeking help, parents with problems are being driven into hiding. Instead of concentrating on criminal cases, hotlines are crammed with trivial and malicious reports. Children are being made fearful of their own loved ones, for no good reason, and being trained to think sexually about family members. This training in incest could bear hideous fruit in the next generation. Civil liberties won with blood and tears are cast away overnight in a hysterical attempt to "protect the children" from what isn't happening anyway, in most cases. The public is being systematically, if not willfully, misled into believing that these drastic measures are necessary, measures that open the door to totalitarian enslavement.

The fruit of the child abuse hysteria is isolation, suspicion, and fear—the very opposite of the bonding, togetherness, and trust children need. Thus, life outside the system, for those who have not yet been caught in the net, is becoming more difficult daily. This, however, does not equal the pain of those caught in the system, as the next chapters will show.

Outrageous Facts II

THE MYTH OF CHILD PROTECTIVE SERVICES

"WE JUST WANT TO HELP" 6

Warm fuzzies. In the television, in the newspapers, in the legislative chambers, in the hearts of the people. Americans get the warm fuzzies when they think about the pathetic little tykes who are victims of child abuse. I do myself.

But, just as the warm fuzzy little Tribbles grew and multiplied and took over the good starship Enterprise, our warm fuzzies about abused children are threatening to wipe out the North American family. Somehow, our warm feelings about the *children* have become transferred to warm, uncritical feelings about *anyone who claims to help the children.* "Give them money! Give them power! Don't question anything they do!" rings the current cry.

Now, human nature has not changed since Lord Acton penned his immortal phrase, "Power tends to corrupt, and absolute power corrupts absolutely." Give any group of people a blank check on the American family; make it work in their own interest to discover or invent more and more family problems; reward them for aggressively imposing their personal prejudices on families; and what do you have? A social work industry growing out of control. We should have expected it.

We have already seen that the "epidemic" of child abuse has been grossly inflated, and that all statistics on the subject come from those who have most to gain by magnifying the problem. Yet inflated statistics alone do not explain the phenomenal growth in the child abuse industry. The alleged epidemic of child abuse could have just as easily, and more logically, brought about stricter laws for prosecuting abuse offenders. Instead it has concentrated power over *all* families, not just over family criminals, in the hands of the social work bureaucracy. The police have actually *less* to do with family violence than before.

How is it that, in the face of a supposed outbreak of violent crime against children, society's response has been to increase the social work bureaucracy rather than expedite these matters via the police and the district courts?

The answer is one word.

59

"Help."

Sensing that very few people support the idea of bureaucrats breaking up families, social work bureaucracies have taken care to project a cozy image of *helping* families. As it says in the Missouri Division of Family Services pamphlet, *What Everyone Should Know About Child Abuse*, "Helpers seeks to protect the child and help families learn to live together and cope with crisis. . . ."[1]

This pamphlet, a typical example of those put out by social work bureaucracies, attempts to convince average citizens that civic duty impels them to report even unfounded suspicions of child abuse to a social workers' hotline. Wide-scale informing supposedly helps parents who are trying to raise their children: the pamphlet goes so far as to claim that families *want* to be reported.[2]

We can see why some malicious busybody, say old Aunt Kate who spends her days peering with binoculars at the neighbors' windows, might like to think that her tale-spreading is a vital social service. But the claim that families want to be reported, or benefit from being reported, ought to sound odd to the rest of us.

Please keep in mind that we are not talking about reporting crimes to the police. Everyone, a small minority of criminals excepted, agrees that individuals who smash up or rape their children ought to be reported. The problem is that, with the introduction of the new child abuse legislation, the rules of the game have changed. The public is not being asked to report suspicious evidence like multiple broken bones. Nor are we told to report to criminal justice authorities, who at least are properly trained to investigate and who usually can tell the difference between a murder in progress and littering. Instead, the criteria for opening up a family to social worker intrusion include

- Neglected appearance
- Overneatness
- Disruptive behavior (of the child)
- Passive, withdrawn behavior
- Critical parents
- Isolated families who "don't share in school or community activities"[3]

In other words, if your child is shy or aggressive, neat or dirty, allowed to run around the neighborhood or kept close to home, your neighbors are being encouraged to report you for child abuse. And if you become afraid to let these potential informers into your home, you can be nailed for being "isolated."

The pamphlet urges readers to "use caution and good sense in identifying child abuse." But how are we supposed to exercise this good judgment? Not by personally investigating the situation before rushing to hotline our friends, nor by waiting for actual evidence of physical or sexual abuse. Instead, if the reader sees it is becoming "plain that this [i.e., any of the behaviors above] is a PATTERN or becoming one, then IT'S TIME FOR HELP . . . "[4]

So, one incidence of shyness does not conclusively prove child abuse, but if a child seems consistently shy, IT'S TIME FOR HELP. If your children are scrupulously clean one day, that's O.K. But if you insist on dressing them nicely for all public appearance, IT'S TIME FOR HELP. Notice the assumption that these "patterns" are infallible proof of child abuse: the Division should have said IT'S TIME TO INVESTIGATE, since at the time of the report, nothing would have been proved.

People are much less likely to phone in their friends and relatives if they think a hotline call will cause a family trouble. But "help" is a different story. Everyone could use "help." You don't even have to prove a parent is guilty to offer him "help."

What kind of help do social workers offer to families?

REPLACING THE COMMUNITY, CHURCH, AND EXTENDED FAMILY

First, the child abuse industry is in the process of replacing or co-opting all traditional family and community support structures. Those who detect or suspect abuse are never encouraged to confront the suspected perpetrator directly, hear his or her side of the story, or offer him or her advice or help. (Remember, we're still talking about cases of "overneatness" and other non-crimes.) This role is reserved exclusively for government employees and contractors, under penalty of law. All who might feel competent to counsel or rebuke the parents, or to provide help, are required by law to report even suspicions of child abuse to the "proper authorities." Doctors, ministers, and other professionals who have traditionally helped troubled families are forbidden to trust their own judgment as to what is or is not abuse, or how it should be handled. And, although in most states average citizens are not mandated by law to inform on their neighbors, child advocates are working to change this.[5]

Penalties for failing to inform the authorities of the factors they consider suspicious brings with it a fine and up to a year in jail.

Remember, we're not talking necessarily about rape and murder. The normal little problems of child-rearing—and even non-problems such as a child's temperament—have suddenly become matters for state intervention. Grandparents, pediatricians, ministers, rabbis, and even mail carriers—anyone who in decades past might have possibly been in a position to help families is now, or soon might be, forbidden by law to offer help. This massive usurpation of power is a direct blow to the entire social fabric. Those who know you, and those you trust, have overnight been replaced by strangers. All our child-rearing problems are supposed to be handled by these strangers.

Having rammed through this power play, toppling even doctors and other experts from their previous post of family confidant and advisor, you would expect child advocates to have something better to offer.

What *do* social workers do to help?

MEDICAL AND PSYCHIATRIC TREATMENT

The Missouri pamphlet goes on to say,

IMMEDIATE TREATMENT must be given for urgent problems, such as physical injury, malnutrition, serious neglect.

CHILDREN may also need developmental testing or psychiatric therapy.

PARENTS may need a doctor's help, too, for physical problems, mental distress, depression, alcohol abuse, etc.[6]

Social workers cannot provide this treatment. Only doctors can. But doctors are forbidden to get involved with a family suspected of abuse until they have informed on the parents to social workers, thus upsetting a centuries-old tradition of confidentiality between a family and its medical advisors.

One of the real tragedies of the child abuse hysteria is that, because medical confidentiality has been destroyed, parents have less and less incentive to have their children medically helped. Abusive parents know they can lose their child at the emergency room door. Because doctors are required by law to report all "suspicious" injuries, abusive parents are adding to their abuse an unwillingness to help the children medically. Little Tammy Nelson of Kansas City *died* after being sold to a man for sex because her prostitute mother was afraid of being turned in for child abuse if she brought her vaginally hemorrhaging daughter in to the hospital for treatment. And don't think that Tammy would have been helped by the medical personnel informing on her mother—social workers already knew about what was going on with Tammy. All that the law enforcing mandatory reporting accomplished was to cost an eight-year-old her life.[7]

As the criminal classes discover the drawbacks of having their children medically treated, we will see *more* deliberate medical neglect, not less.

Even totally innocent parents are learning to avoid doctors and hospitals. As Dr. Robert Mendelsohn, a highly respected medical authority and best-selling author, reveals,

> Lately, I've been involved in more and more cases in which my function as a physician has been to spring children from hospitals. The usual story is this: The child has a temperature of 103 or 104 and may have a throat or ear infection. He's taken to the hospital where the doctor sees that he's got a couple of bruises on his body. The social worker is called in, and after a few questions the finger is aimed at the parents. The child is hospitalized, presumably for his own protection. Then the parents have to find somebody who will testify that there is no possibility of child abuse and that the bruises are from some other cause.
>
> At one time, child abuse was obvious to doctors. It consisted of children who came in with multiple broken bones. Today, that definition has been extended so that if you take a child into the emergency room and he or she has a few bruises, you're immediately questioned by a social worker. With the thousands of empty beds in hospital pediatric units, it's to everybody's advantage—except the family's—to try to establish a charge of possible child abuse. . . .
>
> I now warn parents to be extremely careful when they bring their children to a hospital emergency room because you never know what can happen once a doctor starts to examine a child.[8]

Isn't it ironic? The very laws supposedly designed to help children are preventing families from seeking help.

SUPPORT SERVICES

The next area where the child abuse industry claims it will help the family is in support services. As the Missouri pamphlet continues,

> SUPPORT SERVICES from visiting nurse, homemaker, social worker, concerned friend or relative are often family-and-life-savers. . . .
> In some cases, all that's needed is a HELPING HAND—and the knowledge that someone cares.[9]

How true. However, the concerned friend or relative is being urged to turn in the family, not to help them directly.

Social workers who want to help families today have been saddled with a crippling handicap. The problem is that their role has been redefined as *coercive,* forcing families to comply under threat of removal, instead of *supportive,* offering voluntary services. As an exam-

63

ple of how this works: Six years ago I was chatting with my father (who lives near Boston) on the telephone. He mentioned that the liberal activist organization with which he worked in his spare time had become involved in helping a poor mother with two children. For lack of funds, her heat had been turned off. Social workers found out about the situation.

Now let us ask, What would you and I do? Give her a personal gift of money to get the heat turned back on? Sign up the mother for a fuel assistance program? Get her some government financial aid? The social workers found her guilty of "neglect" for failing to provide a heated apartment, and took her children! My father and his friends ended up trying to contact state agencies to help this poor mother out so she could recover her children, a job that should have been done by the social worker in the first place.

Believe it or not, many states have laws that define "neglect" as "failure to provide" rather than "*willful* failure to provide." The difference between the two definitions is that poor people are constantly guilty of "failure to provide" what middle-class people think their children should have. These laws are being used to remove children from homes where they are wanted and loved. Just like it happened to that poor woman whose children my father's organization ended up trying to rescue from the social workers.

Some help.

That's why social work "help" isn't helping, and why it never will until we get better laws. Today, social worker "help" is just another word for coercion. You accept their services, or you lose your child. And these "services" too often are *not* needed financial aid and other help, but compulsory counseling and other meddling. Those who need aid the most are unlikely to get it through our present social work industry. The reason? Once a family's pressing needs have been met they are no longer a "client." Paying the fuel bill so the heat can be turned back on solved the "neglect" and one more case has been lost to the bureaucracy.

This brings us to the one and only "service" you can consistently count on from social workers.

EXTENDED COUNSELING

As the Missouri pamphlet explains,

EXTENDED COUNSELING for children and parents is a must. Because abuse develops over a long time, it requires long-term professional treatment.[10]

64

No one has ever proved that counseling forced on unwilling clients is successful in changing criminal behavior. Nor has anyone demonstrated that it is ethical to force behavior modification on families who are *not* guilty of crimes—the majority of so-called child abusers under our present laws. Even willing clients have found a conspicuous lack of positive results with modern psychiatric therapy, as William Kirk Kilpatrick documents in *Psychological Seduction* and Garth Wood, an English practitioner, demonstrates in *The Myth of Neurosis*. In spite of the religious fervor with which pop culture clings to a belief in the legitimacy and efficacy of psychotherapy as a healing art, it has failed to produce.

But the lack of results with the extended counseling into which families accused of child abuse are typically plunged is only one side of the issue. A darker side is stated by those who have gone through this regimen:

> Many people in VOCAL (Victims of Child Abuse Laws) have found themselves involved with such therapists, but with no opportunity for choice. We are not "consumers" of therapy but court ordered into such therapy that is, in actuality, not therapy, but a phase of the investigative process. What makes matters even more difficult is that too often the courts place our fate, and that of our children, into the manipulative hands of such therapists. They alone are given the ultimate say in whether or not they believe a problem exists. Needless to say it is to their benefit to either "find" abuse where none may exist, or to request of the courts additional time and ongoing sessions to determine whether or not the situation warrants continued treatment. Their training, methods of treatment, and testing often go unchecked and unquestioned. Many of these therapists go into a case with the preconceived notion that the individual is in fact guilty and seem only interested in substantiating the claims.[11]

Surprisingly, a social worker confirms VOCAL's accusations. In the May/June 1985 issue of the National Association of Social Workers newsletter, an article by Eileen Anderson appeared, entitled "Therapists and Power: The Unexamined Addiction." The article said, in part,

> After more than nine years as a professional therapist and counselor, I have concluded that many therapists are addicted to power. . . .
> As alcoholics manipulate their world to hide their drinking addicted therapists disguise their own drives for power. They do

so by proclaiming a desire for service, responsibility, and the right to use their expertise. . . .

Most professionals, including doctors and lawyers, function according to defined and established rules and procedures which they apply to specific cases. Therapists, however, may define their own rules and procedures. This is absolute power.

Significantly, individuals who choose therapy as their vocation score high in personal power motive on the Thematic Aperception Test (TAT), a psychological test that measures adult drives and attitudes. The TAT defines power motive as an individual's desire to arrange the world to suit themselves by gaining power over others. . .

Too often a therapist experiences a conflict of interest between the pocketbook and the cure.

The counseling, the support, and the medical services social workers offer as their panacea for child abuse have always been available on a voluntary basis. What is new is the funneling of families accused of child abuse through a compulsory network of state employees and state contractors. These state agents have built-in-conflicts of interest with those of the family, as the longer the family is in their hands the more these agents get paid and the more money social work bureaucrats can demand from the state. The increased load of phony cases also feeds the coffers of all those federal agencies and private sector firms whose livelihood depends on fighting an "epidemic" of child abuse.

Let's stop calling force and harrassment "help." The more proper term is "harm." True help does not grow, as Mao Tse-tung said political power grows, out of the barrel of a gun. Those who wish to apply force to families that have been charged with no crime are criminals themselves.

I'm not condemning individual social workers (with the exception of the few that enjoy power games), but the system. Who enjoys going into a family knowing that they are going to fight him every step of the way? Who wouldn't rather serve people who actually respect her and want her help, instead of jamming unwanted "services" down the throats of reluctant clients? What good is a system that prevents those who need aid from requesting it, for fear they will be automatically labeled child abusers and possibly lose their children?

Coercive help is tyranny, and tyranny can expect to meet resistance.

What is this tyranny of our current system based on? Legal kidnapping. The threat of removing children from their families if the parents don't cooperate. And the threat has force. Read about it in the next chapter.

"WE DON'T WANT TO SEPARATE FAMILIES" 7

> Foster care has become a tool to force change in families. In the words of one social worker, "It's easier to work with the family after removal because that gives us a bargaining tool." (From a government-sponsored study of foster care)[1]

A rose is a rose is a rose. Or, to put it another way, removal of a child from his family is removal is removal. Threats to remove a child are threats are threats. What they are *not* is "helping the family stay together."

Despite all the rhetoric about "helping families," child protective agencies do not offer help. Once you are investigated, any "services" offered are *compulsory*. Your private behavior is now controlled by bureaucrats. You *must* attend bureaucrat-prescribed counseling sessions. You *must* pay whatever fees they demand. If they subject your children to medical examinations, you *must* pay for the examinations. If they take your children, you *must* (unbelievably) pay for the privilege by making regular contributions towards their foster care.

Why do parents put up with this meddling? Fear. Or, more precisely, terror. You talk to hotlined parents, you look them in the eye, and all you see is terror. Terror of what? Terror of losing what they most love: their children.

ABDUCTION WITH OR WITHOUT LEGISLATION

Under the current laws, social workers can remove your children any time they choose. All they must do is find you guilty of some trivial, undefined offense like "emotional neglect." Then your children are torn screaming from your arms and put into "protective custody." They will be placed in an institution, in a foster home, or even in jail, to "protect" them from you. Within a day or so some bored juvenile court judge will hold a hearing to determine whether the children should continue in foster care. If he decides they should, your next shot at getting them released could be as much as six months away.[2]

Our social bureaucrats would like us to think that families hardly ever get separated. As the Missouri pamphlet *What Everyone Should Know About Child Abuse* puts it:

> Temporary separation is sometimes necessary to protect the child and give the parent(s) a chance to 'cool off.' *Permanent* separation is a LAST RESORT.[3]

Permanent separation, however, is not a last resort but the almost inevitable result once a child is taken into protective custody. Unless you get your child back almost immediately, you will probably never get him back at all. "Temporary" separation, which most people imagine to mean a day or two, actually means an average of three to six years. In Missouri, this translates to a median length of stay in foster care of 21 months for white children and 51 months for blacks.[4]

Missouri, a state that considers itself a "leader in the fight against child abuse"[5] (and with some reason, because Missourians report proportionately more child abuse than any other state in the nation), is a shining example of what the child abuse industry would like to do in your state. Naturally, this means much more foster care. Missouri's experience with foster care, then, might be instructive as a peek at what lies in wait for the families child advocates claim they don't want to separate.

In 1981 a study was done in Missouri's foster care system. The study found, among other things:

- "In 45 percent of the cases a dispositional court hearing had not been held for more than twelve months prior to the date of the case reading. This means that nearly one-half of the children in our sample had no 'day in court' for over one year."

- "At least 5 percent of the Division of Family Services children now placed have no court order authorizing their placement."[6]

The tremendous illegality of taking children from their families without even a court hearing, and afterwards not even reviewing their case for another year, did not result in any widespread firing of judges and social workers. Instead, the *Post-Dispatch* ran a prize-winning series on Missouri's foster care system which made a strong plea for terminating parental rights earlier and putting removed children up for adoption.[7]

ABDUCTION WITHOUT JUSTIFICATION

Some of the reasons for which parents lost their children, as stated by the study, were

- "Inadequate parenting skills"—144 cases

- "Educational neglect"—41 cases

- "Unspecified neglect" (i.e., "neglect" that was *not* shelter neglect, nutritional neglect, medical neglect, or educational neglect)—71 cases

- "Lack of supervision"—115 cases

- "Emotional abuse or neglect"—70 cases[8]

More than one reason could apply to each child. However, it is alarming that the above reasons could be considered sufficient excuse for removal at all. As the report itself notes, "Unemployment, lack of adequate income, or substandard housing may indeed be the 'real' reasons for removal."[9] The report also noted a "strong anti-family bias on the part of agencies."[10]

The anti-family bias is a fairly recent development in the history of social work, emerging openly nationwide around 1982 with the doctrine of "erring on the side of the child," meaning erring on the side of removal. It extends also to how children are treated in the system. They are not only separated from their parents, but from their brothers and sisters[11] and, repeatedly, from their friends.[12] If the purpose of foster care was to create confused, rootless children, it couldn't serve it better.

According to Douglas Besharov, "In 1963, about 75,000 children were placed in foster care because of abuse or neglect. In 1980, more than 300,000 children were in foster care for those reasons."[13] Not only that: while the total of hotline reports continues to rise, the proportion of opened cases resulting in foster care is also increasing. Now it stands at just under one in five.[14]

For people who don't want to separate families, the child abuse industry seems to do a lot of it.

Do social workers break up families unjustly? The evidence is mounting that they often do. A lady from Texas named Jean Coyle, who fought a long battle with the Texas Department of Human Resources over her grandson whom the DHR tried to remove on the basis of an allergic skin reaction (they called it "abuse"), has written a book called *Bye, Bye Baby: The Stealing of America's Children*. Look at the end of this book for information on how to order a copy. *Bye, Bye Baby* documents numerous case histories where social workers lied, falsified evidence, and outright stole children from their parents. Jean is traveling around the country forming "Parents and Children Together" groups to spotlight social worker abuses.

Even establishment folk find reason to criticize the huge increase in foster care placements. According to data collected by the Federal Government, "it appears that up to half of these children were in no immediate danger at home and could have been safely left there."

In the words of Michael Wald, Professor of Law at Stanford University, "many children are removed from home unnecessarily, sometimes because the state does not offer services that would enable their families to provide adequately without removal [the classic case of this is removing a child because the mother lost her job and couldn't pay the heating bill] and sometimes where the state was wrong to believe the child was endangered in the first place."[15]

Some of these foster care placements are downright illegal, like the five percent of Missouri placements performed without the benefit of a court order. The only practical difference between these "placements" and kidnapping is that the people performing them are salaried by the taxpayer. Besharov recounts a couple of horror stories (a few leaves among a forest):

One court of appeals, for example, recognized a damage claim by a mother who was told that the temporary care of her three children could be arranged only if she signed a six month, voluntary placement agreement. She signed, based on "assurances," apparently later ignored by the agency, "that her children would be returned whenever she found suitable housing." The mother had to bring a lawsuit to regain custody of her children.

In *Duchesne v. Sugarman*, the mother never consented to her children's removal and yet, in violation of state law, the agency refused either to return her children or to seek a court order to legalize its continued custody of them. The day after the mother was unexpectedly hospitalized for emotional problems, the agency had taken custody of her two children, one seven years old and the other six months old. The mother refused to sign a consent form authorizing the agency to continue caring for the children. The caseworker reported the mother's refusal to his supervisor, who advised that no consent was necessary at that point. Five days later, the mother was released from the hospital, and she "immediately . . . demanded that her children be returned. However, the children were not relinquished." For the next 27 months, the mother unsuccessfully sought to have the agency return her children. But the agency continued to rebuff her and never sought a court order legalizing the situation. Finally, she filed a petition in the New York Supreme Court seeking a writ of *habeas corpus*.[16]

In the same spirit, Bob Horner, a Florida Department of Health and Rehabilitative Services subdistrict administrator, has gone on record as saying his department is not bound by the law.

> Horner says assessment can last for an "indeterminate" period, usually longer than 30 days.
>
> But the state's child abuse law requires that HRS complete its investigation within 30 days of receiving a complaint, determine whether abuse is indicated or the complaint unfounded, and report its findings to HRS' abuse registry in Tallahassee.
>
> Horner says HRS "is not bound by that. We can go as long as it takes to make a case for the protection of the child."
>
> When asked what rights parents have during the assessment period, Horner replied, "None." . . .
>
> Terry Ackert, executive director of the Orange County Legal Aid Society, which provides low-cost legal services to indigent county residents, says HRS is breaking the law in several areas.
>
> "They are violating the 30-day rule and they can't weasel out of that and they are structuring a voluntary agreement that's not in writing," he says.
>
> Ackert, whose organization represents parents whose child dependency cases go to juvenile court, labeled HRS' actions "outrageous."
>
> "If HRS isn't following the written rules, they are abusing their authority beyond reason," he says.[17]

The amazing thing is that so far the public hasn't reacted against this illegal gangsterism. It's one thing for agencies to remove children unnecessarily in accordance with the law—a deplorable situation, but one for which they can hardly be blamed. It's another when crusading anti-family zeal causes agencies to *break* the law. And yet nobody complains! Can we be so passive, so mesmerized by television politics that we will let any person with a state I.D. card do anything he or she wants, even if their actions are illegal?

My personal feeling is that the low level of public concern reflects the very successful agency campaigns to persuade voters that the agencies hardly ever use their power. Thus, each horror story of children removed unnecessarily, or in violation of law, is treated as a "one in a million" accident. In this way, the agencies have a free hand to do as they wish with the poor single women who are their most frequent "clients," knowing that these individuals lack the resources to fight them and that the public is willing to ignore them.

> "They would have you believe that the system works so well that they only separate children when it's absolutely necessary," says Marvin Guggenheim, former director of the family law clinic at New York University Law School. "That's bull——.

71

They separate children for petty reasons and for no reason all the time."

Guggenheim believes more than half the children now in foster care could have been safely left at home.[18]

ABDUCTION AND DISCRIMINATION

Of course, some kinds of people get hit harder by social workers than others. After Jean Coyle was on a television show in Kansas, Kansas Parents and Children Together received forty-nine calls from people complaining that social workers had threatened them unfairly or actually removed their children.

Forty-eight of them were Christians.[19]

A group called the Coalition of Concerned Citizens has filed a $1.5 billion lawsuit against State of Washington officials. This group, composed of parents and friends of parents who claim their children were unjustly separated from them and placed in foster homes, is basing their suit not on specific cases but on departmental procedures which they say consistently violate the Constitution.

"The state is guilty of misusing its authority, in the name of child protection, in the most blatant and illegal manner by not following mandates of state law," said Sandy Schneider, a spokeswoman for the Coalition of Concerned Citizens, a Seattle-based group which claims about 7,000 members in seven local chapters.

"We have gone to the Senate, the courts, the governor and every single available governmental source for relief from the injudicious actions of the state," Schneider said. "We've gotten no relief, so now we're going to the people through the courts."

The suit, filed as a class action, seeks $750 million in damages for physical and emotional injury and $750 million in punitive damages. It also asks that various procedures allegedly used by state agencies be declared violations of constitutional rights and prohibited.

The suit is on behalf of "all parents and children who have been separated and forced to reside apart by the defendants where the children were not in danger of harm at home, or where such danger could have been adequately addressed by the use of in-home services, and where the defendants knew or should have known that there was not necessity for the separation."

Schneider says this group might include more than 1,500 families.

Some of the practices listed in the suit involved removing "children from their homes without notice, hearing, or adequate investigation of complaints of abuse or neglect" and "without regard to the emotional and physical traumas which result." . . .

Schneider said the coalition is a group of parents and friends of parents whose children have been unjustly placed in foster homes.

The 27-page civil complaint does not detail any specific cases, but lists 20 state policies, procedures or practices it says violate portions of the U.S. Constitution.[20]

What I find particularly interesting about this group's suit (besides the outrages it asserts) is the part where it names the groups the government's arbitrary policies have most harmed:

> The state's policies are applied most heavily against the poor, handicapped, minorities, foreign nationals, single parents and Christians, the coalition alleges in its lawsuit.[21]

These lawsuits are becoming more common, and will continue until either the Supreme Court decides to enshrine child-stealing as a constitutional "right" (they could do it, you know), or until a number of these suits are won. The Massachusetts Civil Liberties Union has filed a class action lawsuit,[22] and it is to be hoped other state civil liberties unions will follow suit.

Child-stealing by social agencies is so prevalent that an organization has been formed expressly composed of parents who have become victims of the system. VOCAL, or Victims of Child Abuse Laws, now has 7,000 members and chapters in thirty states. Their membership would be far larger if so many parents weren't clinging to the hopes their children would be returned, and afraid of offending the social workers.

The situation is, if anything, worse in Canada.

In 1975 John R. Caswell, whose wife is a politico in Saskatchewan, received a reply from John Diefenbaker concerning children who had been taken from a foster home in Prince Albert and put in a home in the United States. It stated in part:

> "It appears there are many cases of youngsters who have been removed to foster homes in the United States. To me this is a grave injustice to them, and I will endeavor to secure some action by the federal government to prevent what I might describe as a 'traffic in Canadian blood.' "[23]

As John Caswell has written,

> It is now 1985, ten years later, and the public has no way of knowing if the abuses Diefenbaker described have been corrected. The Department of Social Services continues to have absolute power over the children of Saskatchewan with no means of accountability. The present legislation has such a vague description of a child in need of protection that virtually any parent could be in danger of losing his or her child to the state. . . .
>
> If there is a probability that your child had a problem, has a problem or will have a problem, even though you are not responsible and cannot control it or are working on controlling it, your child and family are in danger of state intervention. . . .
>
> There are two ways the state can get your children. One is by supervision. It can intervene in the home, emasculate the role of the parents, destroy the child's confidence in the parent's judgment and right to discipline, destroy the cohesion and privacy of the home. . . . The state can build a case and take your children. The other is, it can pick them up, leave a note and make a brief oral statement in passing. Then you go to court and have to prove that your scenario for the child's future is better than one a social worker can think up and implement by services paid by you and other taxpayers.[24]

Scary, isn't it? But still it is easy to find defenders for the system. As Richard Wexler says in his article in *The Progressive,*

> The Child Savers see the current laws as a trade off. "I'd rather see a family disrupted than a bunch of dead children," says Jean Schafer. Unfortunately, the laws tend to give us both. Of all the children believed to have died of child abuse or neglect, an estimated 25 percent were known to child protective agencies at the time of their death.[25]

We haven't quite scraped to the bottom of this barrel yet. Yes, state agencies are stealing children. Yes, they admit they would rather steal children unnecessarily than let one abused child slip through the cracks. This is defended as a "trade-off" between the rights of parents (who are big and tough and can take the pain of losing their children) and children (who are small and helpless and need state protection). But in real life this trade-off doesn't exist. The state cannot provide effective protection for children. Find out why in the next chapter.

"WE MUST ERR 8
ON THE SIDE
OF THE CHILD"

It happens, of course, that some children are improperly and unnecessarily removed from their homes . . . but I firmly believe an error must be on the side of the child.—Missouri Representative Kaye Steinmetz (D-Florissant)[1]

Now that fewer and fewer North Americans can read, slogans have become an important feature of national life. Of course, some slogans are more effective than others. Try this slogan on for size:

"It's Better for a Thousand Innocent Children to Be Messed Up by the State Than for One Abused Child to Be Overlooked."

Or how about this one:

"We Must Be Prejudiced Against Parents."

Don't sound too good? Couldn't work up much of a P.R. campaign with those slogans? Yet these are the child abuse industry's own mottos—just rephrased in honest terms. You read them in the paper every day: comments on how it's better for innocent families to be needlessly disrupted than for one abused child to be overlooked, noble-sounding statements about "erring on the side of the child."

Even those who sense something is wrong with the child advocates' ideology have fallen into the trap of accepting their slogans. We hear now of "parents' rights," which need to be "balanced" with children's rights. You can talk this way if you want to, but you should be aware that you're accepting the child abuse industry's basic doctrine: that parents' rights are *different* from children's rights. There is, in this view, no such thing as *family* rights: the right to be left alone, the right to stay with the ones you love. Family life has been replaced with the Marxist ideology of "class warfare": not parents *helping* children (and vice versa) but parents *versus* children. And, of course, if this were true anyone with half a heart would tip the scale in favor of poor, defenseless children.

When challenged about their callous destruction of families, child advocates invariably retort, "If we must err, we should err on the side of the child." Now they have redefined the terms: they're not breaking up families, but liberating children! And their needless interventions now sound *good*: they're "on the side of the child"! Thus they win the battle without even having to fight.

The rhetoric sounds good, but the assumptions underlying it are bad. Let me list them for you:

(1) Parents' desire to keep their children conflicts with the children's "best interests" in even non-criminal cases. Children have no need for their parents, and do not bond with them. As one state agent put it, "To them, it's just another bed."[2]

(2) Child advocates are infallible and, unlike parents, always know what is best for a child.

(3) Child advocates are selfless beings who have no interests of their own. They act entirely out of altruistic love for children.

(4) If a child advocate thinks a child should be taken from his family against the child's own protests, that is all right. Children's wishes never matter when they conflict with a child advocate's.

(5) If a parent thinks a child should remain in his family against the child's expressed rebellious wishes, that is all wrong. Children's wishes always matter when they conflict with a parent's.

We need not spend time discussing these five assumptions, upon which much of child advocacy is based. To name them is to expose them. Besides, we plan to search out the noble, selfless child abuse industry in a future chapter and find out what makes it tick.

For now, let's concentrate on the biggest presupposition of all: the one that sways judges and legislators, the one responsible for our current batch of anti-family laws. This is it:

(6) The state can guarantee absolute safety for children it removes from their homes.

Our legislators need their eyes opened to the enormous, glaring assumption that strangers serving for money are less risky prospects as care-takers than a child's natural parents. In all the rhetoric about "erring on the side of the child," the underlying thought is always that the state can provide something *better* for a child than his own family can. Legislators do not weigh the risks of placing children with strangers, nor do judges consider them. The only question these authorities (until recently) have asked is, "Are the parents perfect?" If the parents are not perfect (and who is?) then in the child's "best interests" he can be removed.

Thus we have a strange double standard. Everyone who knows anything about foster care deplores the system. But, although nobody dares claim that foster care is a perfect emotional environment for a child, or even that it is adequate to meet a child's emotional needs, the number one reason for removing children from their homes is "emotional maltreatment." More cases are opened, and more children are removed, because of "emotional maltreatment" than because of sexual maltreatment or major physical injury.[3] Yet the state has never proved it can help children emotionally! Government is rushing in to break up families when *it can't provide anything better than what it's destroying*!

This is not to say that all foster parents and institutional staff members are bad. Many are sincere, and do their very best. But it's ridiculous to believe that foster and institutional care is by nature *superior*, which seems to be the assumption on which so much child welfare policy is currently based.

An "error on the side of the child" is still an error, and not necessarily on the side of the child. In child advocacy lingo, to err on the side of the child means to err on the side of removal.

If legislators or judges, instead of being objective as they are supposed to, feel they must pick a side on which to err, the wise decision would be to err, not on the side of foster care, but of parents.

Why?

Because parents go through the pain of pregnancy and childbirth for *free*, then actually *pay* for the privilege of keeping their children; foster parents do not suffer the pain or serve for free, let alone pay for their foster children. Parents are bonded by blood to their children; foster parents are not. Parenthood is a lifetime commitment, symbolized by sharing the family name and actualized in law; foster care is temporary, and even when foster parents want to provide a stable home for their foster child a social worker can at any time step in and remove him to another foster home for no apparent reason. In spite of the often-quoted marshmallow statistics, natural parents have a very low rate of child abuse; in foster care, the rate of child abuse rises dramatically.

The bacon thinks twice before jumping from the frying pan into the fire. Sanctions against "emotional neglect" and all the other ill-defined categories of "abuse" are only possible when one assumes that these things never happen in state care.

Which they do.

Let me tell you about it.

CASE 1: ILLINOIS

In Chicago, one case made headlines a few years ago because a three-year-old child, who had already been removed from her parents, was beaten to death while in a state-approved foster home. The natural parents previously had complained to the responsible agency, the Department of Children and Family Services, that this child and other children placed in foster homes were being abused.

After the death of the three-year-old, Judge Mary Hooten of the Cook County Juvenile Court took the family's other children from the guardianship of DCFS and awarded custody to the grandparents. The judge said she had no confidence in the Department's ability to protect these children. . . .

But what did Judge Hooten gain from her pro-family action? The governor of Illinois said the judge had probably overstated the case against DCFS, and he recommended placing more children in state institutions. DCFS then went to court to attempt to prohibit the judge from hearing cases involving child abuse and neglect.[4]

CASE 2: FLORIDA

During the days following the death of a baby boy at the most severely overcrowded home in Pinellas County, state officials have been forced to admit the shocking truth about the way they sometimes care for children abused or neglected by their own parents. In some cases, the state removes youngsters from their own homes and places them in situations that are not much better or safer.

Another way to put it is that children are removed because of *alleged* abuse or neglect only to suffer *actual* abuse from state-provided care. Read on . . .

When little Corey Greer stopped breathing on a Sunday afternoon . . . there were too many children in the home for the foster mother to look after them safely. That was the fault of the Department of Health and Rehabilitative Services (HRS). Judith Lundy's state license permitted three state-dependent children in addition to her own daughter; HRS gave her twelve. . . .

Corey's death also forced HRS officials to acknowledge that:

- They cannot guarantee that children with special medical needs get proper attention and are placed with foster parents who know how to care for them. Corey required a breathing monitor while sleeping but was not attached to the device when he was found dead in his crib. The monitor was in a closet.

- A child in the state's care can disappear, end up in a morgue and not be identified for eleven months.

- Children . . . have been put in homes where they were abused physically and sexually.

- HRS workers who are supposed to check regularly on children in the state's care sometimes do not and are oblivious to problems in the homes.

- The mortality rate for children in state foster care is *more than double* the death rate in children in the general population. [Emphasis mine.]

HRS Secretary David Pingree says that Corey's death surprised him. But he was forewarned—a year and a half ago. In January 1984, HRS's own inspector generals' office issued a blistering report on the emergency shelter program. . . .

Corey's death is damning evidence that the report was not acted upon and that reforms were not made. . . .

And what do you think the official Chief Child Advocate, the one who administers the program to take children away from their parents for "the best interests of the child," had to say? "Asked about the report, Pingree talked about the need for more money to make the system work better."[5]

Only in the never-never land of bureaucracy can a man whose agency's negligence contributed to the death of a child think this gives him authority to demand more money.

CASES 3, 4, 5, AND 6—FOR OUR FRIENDS IN CANADA

Jan 18, 1985: British Columbia (Canada) Supreme Court Justice Ross Lander made public the case of Infant X, a physically-handicapped girl who had been sexually abused at age 12 by a foster father with a criminal record for sexual offenses. The government paid a $42,000 out-of-court settlement to Infant X and her guardian, who had sued MHR for negligence and breach of contract.

April 22, 1985: Shawn Thomas, 2½, was found suffocated and his juvenile foster brother was charged with second-degree murder. Welfare mom Gloria Thomas had lost custody of Shawn to the boy's father in December, but the boy had eventually been placed in a foster home without the mother's knowledge.

May 1, 1985: Williams Lake foster dad William Cook, 50, was sentenced to two years for molesting his own stepdaughter.

Judge Cunliffe Barnett said MHR had failed to conduct a proper check on Cook, who had cared for a dozen foster children over a eight-year period despite having a conviction for assault.

May 14, 1985: Foster parent Terrence Turrell was convicted on two counts of gross indecency involving one of his foster daughters and sentenced to seven years in prison. . . . MHR had approved the Chilcotinarea home for placement of foster children.[6]

CASE 7: ERRING ON THE SIDE OF THE SOCIAL WORKER

One big reason that child protective agencies can't protect children is that they are so busy protecting themselves. Needless intervention and out-of-home placement is encouraged by one-sided liability laws that hold social workers responsible for any injury that happens to a child left in a home but gloss over abuses that occur in foster care.

As the first head of the National Center on Child Abuse and Neglect says,

They are under great pressure to take no chances, and to intervene whenever they might be criticized for not doing so. The dynamic is simple enough. If the child is subsequently injured, the worker can face negative media publicity, an administrative reprimand, a lawsuit, even a criminal prosecution, but there will be no critical publicity if it turns out that intervention was unneeded. . . .

As in the case of defensive medicine, no one knows exactly how much defensive social work exists. However, most observers would agree with Peter Schuck, Professor Law at Yale University, that [s]ocial workers may more quickly—but prematurely—remove children from troubled families rather than risk being sued on behalf of an abused child. Leroy Schultz, a social work professor at the University of West Virginia, found at least one worker in his survey of child protective workers who "tries to get state custody of all abused children just to protect himself from liability." In another state, a program director describes what happened after he was indicted for "allowing" a child to be killed:

"Upon learning of the indictments, caseworkers and their supervisors became aware of their own vulnerability. As a result, paperwork increased to account for everyone's actions and for a while more children were removed from their homes. Supervisors told me that these removals seemed unnecessary but that caseworkers were afraid."[7]

One Missouri mother found out the hard way how needless intervention can harm children. She was maliciously hotlined for obviously trivial reasons. In the course of the interview she failed to cooperate with the social worker, not taking the accusation seriously.

That was a big mistake.

As Laura Rogers, past president of Missouri Parents and Children, told the story to a committee of state legislators:

> The mother was overcome with shock and grief when she called me. But she had only begun to suffer.
>
> A few days later she called again. This time she said, "They killed my son. They killed my baby."
>
> The state had taken two boys from their natural mother who had protected them for twelve years. In all those years of youthful playing, she had kept them from serious injury. And now, less than a week after the state had orphaned them, taking them from their mother and placing them in "protective custody," one was dead. The other one was in shock after helping fish his brother's lifeless body from a swimming pool. The foster parents had a swimming pool, but they had neglected to find out that the dead boy couldn't swim.[8]

There's even more to this atrocity. After the boy's death, the caseworker told his brother that *the death was his fault.* Undoubtedly, that will help the surviving brother cope with his emotional trauma much better.

The mother, of course, is suing, but her chances look dim. Social workers are given immunity in the law: it's almost impossible to win a lawsuit when a child is removed in error. However, you *can* sue a social worker for *not* removing a child who is afterwards harmed in his home.[9] This one-sided liability makes it impossible for social workers to "err on the side of the child." They are under pressure to err on the side of themselves.

I could go on and on, but why be cruel? The facts speak for themselves. Foster care has been called a "national disgrace" by Marion Wright Edelman, President of the Children's Trust Fund.[10] This verdict is echoed and re-echoed. The U.S. Supreme Court calls the foster care system a "limbo."[11] As Douglas J. Besharov says,

> Long-term foster care can leave lasting psychological scars. It is an emotionally jarring experience which confuses young children and unsettles older ones. Over a long period, it can do irreparable damage to the bond of affection and commitment between parent and child. The period of separation may so completely tear the fragile family fabric that the parents have no chance of being able to cope with the child when he is returned. . . .
>
> Increasingly, the graduates of the foster care system evidence

such severe emotional and behavioral problems that some thoughtful observers believe that foster care is often more harmful than the original home situation. Yet, according to data collected for the Federal Government, it appears that up to half of these children were in no immediate danger at home and could have been safely left there.[12]

What makes this most ironic is that, as Besharov also points out,

The reason for intervention in most cumulatively harmful situations [i.e., non-dangerous but non-approved situations] is emotional harm to the child. . . . Ironically, placing the child to safeguard his health often leads to greater emotional harm, as the child is taken out of the family environment.[13]

So "erring on the side of the child" to protect him from supposed emotional harm results in *causing* severe emotional harm. In fact, the graduates of foster care are the group at highest risk of becoming genuinely abusive parents—not so much because of the alleged abuse that caused their placement in foster care as because of the rootlessness, confusion, and lack of stability in the foster care experience.

Patricia Wood, a nationally-recognized expert on dealing with abusive families, directs a residential facility whose goal is to provide each child a permanent home. At the 1985 Conference on Child Abuse and Neglect, Ms. Wood estimated "conservatively that three-fourths of the parents who have been through her program themselves were once in foster care."[14]

But emotional harm, as you have already seen, is only part of the picture. Foster care can be *physically* dangerous. In Kansas City, a study conducted by federal court judges found that *57 percent of foster children were at high risk of being abused or neglected in their foster homes.*[15]

I asked a man who has been working with abused children for a decade and a half, "Is this true in your experience?"

"It's horrible," he replied. "Of the children I have seen, over 90 percent of the girls are raped in foster care by the time they are sixteen, and also a large percentage of the boys. For one thing, children are bounced about so much in foster care. When you've been in ten homes, you're likely to have landed in at least one that's very bad."

"But how can you be sure these children are telling you the truth?" I asked. "You've just told me about one particular girl who was sexually molested by three or four foster fathers. How do you know she wasn't making it all up?"

"Well, for one thing," he responded quietly, "the girl next door to where I live was molested at the age of six by one of the same foster fathers."[16]

Gelles and Strauss, in their first book on family violence, note in passing that "for children placed in foster homes, the risk of further abuse (especially sexual abuse of girls) is very high."[17] I personally have encountered this. A foster care graduate in our church in New York had been raped and impregnated by her foster brother, the foster parents' son. (She subsequently miscarried.) At the time, I hardly knew anything about foster care, but even so I could see that theoretically this kind of behavior was entirely possible: defenseless girl living with pubescent and post-pubescent males not related to her by blood. If incest is a "taboo" (the term of choice for social workers), foster rape certainly is not.

Tearing a child from his natural family because of "emotional neglect" or "inappropriate punishment" or other trivial reasons and putting him in the hazardous environment of state care (perhaps for the rest of his childhood) is like taking him away because there is flu in the family and putting him in a leper colony.

And that is only what happens to the children who actually end up in foster homes. Allegedly abused and neglected children often end up in *jail* while social workers try to arrange foster placement. Of the half million juveniles detained in jails across the country each year, only fifty-five thousand have committed crimes.[18] Who are the rest? Many are children removed from their homes because of alleged abuse or neglect.[19]

This is what happens to kids in jail:

> Statistics show the suicide rate for jailed youths is five times higher than that of unconfined youngsters. . . . Youths confined in jails are raped and beaten by the adult prisoners. . . . If separated from older inmates in jails, younger prisoners are often in solitary confinement or otherwise isolated. They are deprived of nearly all human contact.[20]

And the lot of those in children's homes and detention centers is no piece of cake, either. A piece glowingly entitled "County well equipped to handle children with problems" in the Bloomfield, Missouri *Vindicator* described one day in the life of an abused child:

> The facility is operated around the clock, with at least one person on duty. There are two secure cells and five non-secure bedrooms. When a youth is brought in, he or she is placed in a secure cell. From that point on, each item and privilege they get is earned. This includes bedding, TV, and others.

"You'd be surprised how uncomfortable it is sleeping without a pillow if you're used to it," [the center director] said. . . .
All bedroom doors are locked at night. . . .
There's a red line at each doorway, and students must ask permission from a supervisor to cross any red line. This way the youths are controlled at all times. . . .[21]

The center, according to the article, was specifically designed to handle "abused and recalcitrant youth." So children can be removed from their families (for some "crime" like paddling) and then put in this delightful facility, where they will be cheek by jowl with those who have committed offenses like "assaults, drugs, and alcohol."

What a terrific double standard! Can you imagine parents depriving their children of bedding, forcing them to ask permission every time they walk through a doorway, and locking them in their bedrooms at night? Wouldn't child protective workers whisk those children out of that "abusive environment" in a flash? If the parents tried to plead that the children were wild and recalcitrant, all they'd get is a compulsory invitation to classes in permissive parenting. But when the *state* does it, it's thought of as a model program: "Both Governor John Ashcroft and Lieutenant Governor Harriet Woods express interest in coming to an open house [at the facility]."[22]

Jail. Detention. Rape. Murder. Prostitution. Is this "erring on the side of the child"?

The only conclusion is that the state is not only failing to protect "its" children, but making matters *worse*.

A Canadian has put his finger on the problem: the crusade for perfection, and a religious belief that the state, and only the state, can provide perfection.

It [a proposed Canadian law] says a child will be apprehended [taken from his family] if it is in immediate jeopardy. "In immediate jeopardy" means a child's life or health is seriously or imminently endangered. Sounds good until you remember that health is interpreted by some in the World Health Organization definition which says health is complete physical, social, and mental well-being [e.g. perfection].[23]

However, the standard of perfection only applies to natural families, not to the State. If a child is hurt, traumatized, raped, or killed in foster care or a state institution, child abuse industry advocates never take responsibility. When Elene Humlen's little sixteen-month-old daughter, who was taken from her in perfect condition, was found a week later sick, dirty, and covered with bruises, the people in charge dismissed this outrage with the lame excuse, "Some other child must have gotten to her."[24] (And we ask—if a hotlined mother excused her baby's neglected and abused condition in this way, wouldn't she stand a good chance of losing custody? But if the state abuses or neglects a child, nobody talks of the state losing custody.) When children have been murdered, raped, or neglected to death in state "care," this is exploited as an excuse to plead for *more* money for the bureaucrats! No matter how much evidence mounts that *state "care" is dangerous,* the myth persists that state "care" *can* be perfect, if only we'll spend enough on it.

Can dangerous care be made safe with more money? Of course not. The more money the state provides to foster parents and institutions, the greater the likelihood that purely mercenary individuals will be drawn into foster care. The fact is that blood *is* thicker than water and that, criminals aside, people are far more unselfish towards their own flesh and blood than toward strangers. Jesus Christ, addressing a generation he called "evil," said, "Which of you if your son asks for bread, will give him a stone? Or if he asks for a fish, will give him a snake?" (Matt 7:9-10). Jesus never flattered his hearers; in fact, he called them "evil" in the next sentence. Yet his verdict was that even imperfect, sinful parents "know how to give good gifts to [their] children" (Matt 7:11).

I've worked in a foster home and listened to others who work with foster children. They all say the same thing. Even when the foster home is better in some respects than the original one (a by no means universal phenomenon), the children almost always want to return to their own parents. As the social services director of the Annie Malone Children's Foster Group Home rather touchingly reports, "Some of our kids are still very attached to their own parents and they will not attach themselves to anyone else. They do not wish to be placed in foster or adoptive homes."[25]

State "care" is no panacea. As in all real-life situations, there are trade-offs. A natural home will be imperfect, but so is a state substitute, with the important difference that the latter lacks natural bonding and permanent commitment. The state cannot guarantee children protection, let alone perfection. Only in the absolutely worst cases can there be any justification for subjecting children to the high risks of state care.

However, the child abuse industry continues to act as if it *can* provide perfect protection. The public is fed propaganda, not facts, about foster care and state institutions. Children are removed for trivial or contrived reasons from homes where they have never been harmed and are placed in this very dangerous environment, where they are at high risk of being abused, neglected, raped, or murdered. And all is sanctimoniously justified by the claim that child advocates are "erring on the side of the child."

The choice, though, is not between the "side of the child" and the "side of the parent." It's between family care and stranger care; the side of the family or the side of state agencies. Child advocates, in erring on the side of stranger care, are erring on the side of danger.

But even worse than the child abuse industry's failure to protect children is its emerging campaign to actually *harm* children, in the name of "the best interests of the child." The story is in the next chapter.

"IN THE BEST INTERESTS OF THE CHILD" 9

To do evil a human being must first of all believe that what he's doing is good . . .

Ideology—that is what gives evildoing its long-sought justification and gives the evildoer the necessary steadfastness and determination. That is the social theory which helps to make his acts seem good instead of bad in his own and others' eyes, so that he won't hear reproaches and curses but will receive praise and honors[1]—Alexander Solzhenitsyn.

The six-year-old sidles up to his four-year-old sister. "Give me some of your ice cream cone," he demands.

"No! It's mine! Besides, you already had one," she replies, clutching the cone and eyeing him with distrust.

"You're too little to have a whole cone. It'll make you sick," he mutters, grabbing it out of her hand.

And while anguished wails of "Mommy! Jason stole my cone!" fill the air, we can meditate on how true Solzhenitsyn's words were. How much easier it is to commit crimes against men and God once one has a good excuse. And what better excuse is there for a crime than the plea that it was all done "in the best interests of" the victim?

Ideology! That is what justifies tearing children from their families, against the will of both parent and child. Ideology! That is how bureaucrats justify expanding their intrusions into non-criminal families. "We speak for the children," child advocates claim. "We are acting for the best interests of the child." Ideology!

As demonstrated by the Russia of the Gulag Archipelago, that great system of slave labor camps dedicated to the "brotherhood of man" and the "liberation of the oppressed classes," if you press ideology too far you find it has a flip side—usually the opposite of its stated claims. There is a dark side to this force. The child abuse industry that claims it needs uncontrolled power in order to help children actually uses it to *harm* them—all in their supposed "best interests."

CASE 1: OHIO THROWS DAUGHTER IN JAIL

A retarded daughter told contradictory tales of sexual abuse by her step-brother and other male relatives. Medical exams showed that she had never had sexual intercourse. All family members denied the charges. However, based on a psychological exam, an Ohio county prosecutor decided she had in fact been abused. So the girl was placed in juvenile facilities in Ohio. She ran away *three times*, trying to get back to her mother in Florida.

So here we have a girl who probably made up the story in the first place, and who definitely wants to be with her mother. What did the compassionate friends of children do?

> When Judge Page mentioned sending the girl back to Ohio, she became hysterical in the court and had to be physically restrained.
>
> "That (staying with her mother) is what she wants, but you don't let a 14 or 15-year-old make that decision when a psychologist says she needs institutionalization," Ohio prosecutor Vanderkarr said. . . .
>
> The mother said her daughter already has announced she will run away again if she is returned to Ohio. She said she is very worried the child will be hurt by someone who finds her along the road. On one occasion when she ran away from a juvenile facility in Ohio, the girl said, she was raped.
>
> "She can try to run from anywhere, but we're going to try to deal with that," Vanderkarr said. "We'll have a facility with a person assigned to be around her, in essence, 24 hours a day."
>
> He said he expected the girl to remain a dependent of the state for "a long period of time." Vanderkarr said a psychologist would decide when and if she would be allowed to see her mother.[2]

Are you wondering where that poor girl ended up while her compassionate friends mediated what amounts to a long prison sentence for her? Perhaps they wanted to get her emotionally prepared: they threw her in jail.

CASE 2: CALIFORNIA ALSO THROWS DAUGHTER IN JAIL

It's not easy to get a journalist mad. But this California case, written up in the St. Paul, Minnesota *Pioneer Press*, got newspaperman John Camp angry.

> The California case involved a 12-year-old girl who allegedly was molested by her physician stepfather. The incident occurred

last summer, and in July, the entire family—the girl, her stepfather, and mother—voluntarily sought counseling to handle the problem.

Although they were in treatment, the state decided to file charges against the stepfather. A state attorney argued that because the man was a physician, he might have opportunity to abuse other children, and so should be prosecuted.

The girl, however, refused to testify against her stepfather. Because she refused to testify, the state locked her up for contempt of court. Locked her up, to be precise, in a barren 4-by-8-foot cell.

So she not only suffered the trauma of sexual abuse by a parent, but was put in jail for it.

On Monday a judge dismissed the case against her stepfather saying that the girl had shown that she would not talk and that further efforts to make her talk would be pointless.

Nevertheless, the judge said his action was "an abrogation of justice and denies the state an opportunity to prove its case."[3]

What aroused Mr. Camp's ire was the realization that "Even in the end, the judge acted as though the main offended party in the whole hassle was not the little girl, but the state."

CASE 3: MISSOURI COVERS UP FOR IMPOSTERS

What would you call it if individuals posing as state-employed social workers came to your home, took your children into another room, stripped them, invaded their body cavities (i.e., raped them according to the legal definition), and tried to take them away? Not exactly a day at the beach, is it?

Starting in August of 1985 and continuing through spring of 1986, this is what was happening in Missouri. (Similar incidents occurred in Michigan and other states.) The Division of Family Services failed to notify the public or the police that this was going on, and only made it public when a confidential memo was leaked to the media.[4]

This means that for *six months* imposters were allowed to invade homes, sexually molest children, and threaten kidnapping with *no action taken* to allow parents to protect their children.

Finally the case was cracked. As this book goes to press, it appears that workers from private social service agencies that had contracts with the government were the perpetrators. They used the supposedly confidential child abuse files to obtain information about the families they invaded, then presented this information to the families to prove they were genuine DFS workers. Now that these illegalities have been found to be committed by the establishment, "our gang," the whole thing is being soft-pedaled.[5]

CASE 4: DOCTOR MOLESTS CHILD FOR STATE

Perhaps the reason the imposters case is being soft-pedaled is that so often state investigators do the very same things. As Donna Whitfield reported in a February, 1985 article in *Fidelity* magazine,

> One of the most distressing aspects of this problem is that during the investigation your child can be stripped naked, examined, and even photographed. One female pediatrician referred to as a child abuse expert described the type of things professional investigators can do to children. "We can actually use the child's body," said the doctor on a TV program. "I actually put my finger in a little girl's vagina and ask her, 'Is this what he did to you, and do you think that it went in that far, and did it bleed?'" She said she deals mainly with children three, four, and five years old.[6]

If *you* did this sort of thing to your child, you would be nailed for sexual abuse: no ifs, ands, or buts. But if a state investigator molests your child, that's O.K. It's "in the child's best interests."

The "in the child's best interests" ideology can be stretched even further than this, as the next case shows.

CASE 5: CANADA DECREES CHILDREN DON'T NEED LOVE

Bob and Norma Maycock Germaney were the only parents tiny Jacqueline had ever known.

They worshippped the handicapped toddler and she adored them.

But the ministry of human resources pulled the rug out from under all three of them after Jacqueline, then three and a half, had lived with the foster parents for three years.

The deputy minister admitted yesterday that it should never have happened.

The admission came too late to help the Victoria couple, who had planned—with the ministry's encouragement—to adopt the girl.

The ministry yanked the child away after ruling that the Maycock Germaneys were too old to adopt and didn't have the extra skills necessary to deal with a special-needs child. Bob is 46, Norma, 42.

The ministry sets 40 as the maximum age for adoptive parents.

The couple was called into MHR offices one day and told to have Jacqueline's things packed and have her ready to move by the next day.

The Maycock Germaneys, who cannot have a child of their own, eventually persuaded the ministry to review the case.

But three weeks before they heard the results, Jacqueline was adopted by a family in the Lower Mainland.

The adoption took place despite evidence obtained by the Maycock Germaneys in support of their case.

Dr. John Gossage, head of the child-protection service at Royal Columbian Hospital in New Westminster, strongly recommended that the child remain with the couple.

"My own assessment of the couple revealed them to be deeply concerned foster parents bringing total devotion to the only child they have ever had," Gossage wrote. "Would that other special-needs children that I encounter in my work could experience such unquestioning love!"

But the ministry refused to budge.

Regional director Ivan Carlson agreed that their love was obvious, but said, "Love is not enough, and overwhelming love can be detrimental to the growth of a child."[7]

There you have it, folks: the official word from those acting "in the best interests of the child." The official word is that love is *bad* for children. As Human Resources Minister Grace McCarthy said, "This is not an example of where a child falls through the cracks." McCarthy claimed the decision to tear Jacqueline from the foster parents she loved and who loved her was "best for her."[8]

This whole line of reasoning—that love and a great home environment can be *bad* for children—first came to my attention over five years ago in a *Presbyterian Journal* article. It seems that in England, a country which has traveled farther down the bureaucratic road than we have, a Christian couple asked to adopt one of their foster daughters. The state refused, on the ground that the parents never quarrelled or fought and that their home was a haven of love and serenity. As the worker in that case put it, a good home life is not "in the child's best interests" because the real world is unpleasant and children need to learn to prepare for it.

Of course, that line of reasoning, if strictly followed, would destroy the entire child abuse industry's present excuse for existence, because then abusive parents would be *better* parents than loving ones. Rape, attempted murder, and fun things like that all occur in the real world, and isn't it "in the child's best interests" to prepare them for the real world? After all, "overwhelming love can be detrimental to the growth of the child."

What we are seeing is a policy shift towards *favoring bad homes* and *downgrading good ones*. If social workers can think a good home is not in the child's best interests, what protection does any family have? Hasn't state intervention then become a licence to *harm* children?

The next case shows how the state does just that.

CASE 6: SOCIAL WORKERS SPONSOR CHILD PROSTITUTION

"I'm not hot," a 16-year-old girl on her way to party with friends announces to Constable Serheniuk.

"I'm living in a group home. You can't touch me."

She's so high on speed she's bouncing.

Constable Al Arsenault gets out of the car to talk to the girl's friend, a tough-looking fellow in his thirties who heads quickly off down the street.

"He's a pimp," says Serheniuk.

Later, while Arsenault is talking with another girl, a well-muscled man in his twenties climbs off the back of a bus stop bench and confronts him.

"What are you doin', man?" he asks as he struts up to the plainclothes policeman, tensing some muscles for effect. "She's my girlfriend."

After a few words with Arsenault, the shirtless pimp goes back to his bench.

"The pimps offer the girls protection when they first come down here," Arsenault explains later over coffee. "Then they end up using intimidation to take their money and keep them on the street.

"Part of the problem is that the social workers don't have the authority to keep the kids in the Ministry of Human Resources home," Arsenault says. "There's not really much we can do. . . . Even if we see they're killing themselves with drugs, it's not enough to hold them."[9]

Most of Vancouver's street kids are in the care of the ministry of human resources. The MHR agrees to provide 24-hour-a-day care, but when a child runs away, the absence is often not even reported to police.

Street social workers, police, and older prostitutes say almost all the kid hookers and drug addicts are runaways from MHR foster homes or group homes.

Street worker John Turvey says some of the kids even work right out of the MHR-approved group homes.

"I've seen tricks [patrons of prostitutes] actually in the homes, having a shower." . . .

A veteran prostitute says the fastest way for a kid to end up as a hooker is to go to a MHR home.

"MHR homes are a joke," says the 21-year-old, drug-addicted prostitute who's been on Vancouver streets since she was fourteen. . . .

A North Vancouver couple say they were seeing a lot of progress with a 13-year-old adopted daughter until MHR stepped in.

They said social workers "wrecked her life" during the month it took the family to successfully fight a child abuse allegation.

"We turned a problem child into a decent human being," the mother says. "They turned her into a monster."[10]

CASE 7: KANSAS BATTERED WIVES—THE TIP OF THE ICEBERG

You may remember the story of Sarah from Canada, told in Chapter One. Sarah's children were taken when she reported they were accusing her ex-husband of sexual abuse.

In the months since I first heard of Sarah's story, I've been hearing more and more like it. The plot goes like this:

1) Battered wife/mother of battered children seeks help.

2) The state takes her children to "protect" them.

So far, not wonderful, but marginally justifiable. However, the real kicker comes next.

3) The state then begins proceedings to *give custody to the father who battered and/or sexually abused the children.*

I've heard far too many of these stories to believe any longer that they are isolated occurrences. Too many social workers from too many states and provinces have been reported practicing the same behavior: taking children from the innocent mother and striving to reunite them with a brutal or rapist father. It can't be a coincidence.

A most illustrative example of this new movement to protect "the best interests of the child" by handing him or her over to a criminal was told to me in person. (Documentary evidence is available, if any reporters care to follow up on this story.) It's a harrowing experience to look into another woman's eyes while she tells you how they stole her children.

Lisa C. had been battered for twelve years by her husband. At one time, he had dislocated her hips. Towards the end of this period, she found that he was raping their children. She moved out and took steps to obtain a divorce. However, in the meantime, her husband got together with the doctor who had treated her hips over a year ago, accused her of being crazy, and got her temporarily committed to a mental institution.

Naturally, the kindly social workers came, took away her children, and placed them in foster care. The father, who was now about to go to jail for sexually abusing both his daughter and a twelve-year-old niece, was allowed frequent unsupervised visits with the children. However, the mother was allowed no contact.

At this point, social workers began working to get custody for the father. They openly admitted that this was their plan.

Does this make sense to you? It does not to me.

The children, in the loving hands of the state, have developed severe personality disturbances. The daughter has split personalities; at times her behavior is so bizarre she can't even attend school.[11] The daughter has also made drawings for a therapist showing a man's hands and penis and saying, "This is how Daddy hurt me." She is presently in the home of a foster family whose oldest son is about to be released from jail after serving a sentence for killing his foster brother. But *in the best interests of the child,* social workers have made up their minds, not only to traumatize the children by taking them from their mother and placing them in a dangerous environment, but to give these helpless children to a proven rapist.

Along the same lines, in the same state, another woman whose daughter was being molested on visitation by her ex-husband was told that she could go along on visitation, but had to stay *downstairs* while he was allowed alone with the girl *upstairs.*[12] Still another story along this line is that of the little baby girl, given back to her rapist father at the age of five, who called her mother to say, "We've moved into a new house and don't have any furniture, so Daddy and I have to sleep in the same bed."[13]

It seems lately that every battered wife I hear about has either lost her children to the state already or is being threatened with removal. The new twist is that, instead of taking the children and putting them in foster care, the social workers are moving heaven and earth to give the children to the batterer.

Confirmation of this comes from a surprising quarter: from men falsely accused of sexual abuse. As a Utah State Legislature subcommittee was told in summer 1985, "because of the way the laws are being enforced . . . men who plead quilty usually don't go to jail, while a man . . . who maintains his innocence faces huge legal costs and a possible jail sentence if he cannot prove his innocence."[14]

As one man put it,

"I was promised that if I pled guilty I would get no jail time.
"I spoke with Families United (a non-profit counseling ser-

vice that deals with child sexual abusers) and was told that if I pleaded guilty I would be seeing my children now."[15]

This is how it works. Social workers have taken up *plea bargaining*. If you will sign away your right to a hearing, they will promise you something. In the case of a sexual abuser (innocent or guilty) this takes the form of *promising visitation or custody if he will just say he is guilty*.[16] Naturally, the guilty jump at this offer, and then the social worker has to follow up by arranging visitation or custody against the best interests of both the innocent mother and the victimized child.

What happens to the innocent? Those who maintain their innocence get *threatened with removal*. Plea bargaining is designed to punish the innocent and reward the guilty. As a *Woman's Day* article about a little girl who was removed after she slightly fractured her leg stepping on a pencil reveals,

> One of the most offensive tactics used by child-abuse personnel came to light the day after Kristin was taken. In the presence of witnesses, a supervisor candidly told Kathy, "If you admit guilt, you'll get your daughter back immediately, and you'll only have to go to a few parenting classes. But if you stick to your story, you could lose her for up to six months—maybe even permanently."[17]

As the *Woman's Day* writer commented, "Understandably, such high-powered maneuvers force many parents into submission." And that is *all* they are good for. Is this protecting children—to promise to give them back to accused abusers if they will just say they did it? Is this civil rights—to tell innocent parents the agency will persecute them and try to permanently terminate their rights if they maintain their innocence? Obviously, child abuse workers and supervisors who use these tactics want *control* and are not at all concerned about the children they are supposedly protecting.

The public hears horror tales of children sexually abused or severely battered and then hears child advocates begging for support so they can "do something" about it. What the public does not know is that the child abuse industry will gladly let a perpetrator off the hook if only he will confess. Not only that: in cases where the perpetrator's guilt is so obvious that there can be no possible excuse for plea bargaining, the child abuse industry's stated goal is to *reunite the victim with the perpetrator*. As Tom Kirkwood of the Johnson County Mental Health Center in Olathe, Kansas says, "The last treatment step is to put the father and daughter, or perpetrator and victim, together."[19] Mr. Kirkwood, echoing the current social work consensus, "[says jail doesn't solve] anything and prefers treatment for first-time offenders."[18]

How much public support is there for keeping rapists together with their victims? Why even bother intervening if all that happens is counseling? If we applied this thinking to extra-familial rape, every rapist would merely have to show up for counseling appointments, and his victim would be required to live with him for a while to work out her problems.

The excuse for forcing children into the harmful situation of living with a person who has already raped them is, of course, "the best interests of the child." As a county director of Missouri's Division of Family Services put it, "Children worry that their parents, if they are the perpetrators, will get in trouble." Really? Raped children are terrified that the rapist will get in trouble? The county director continues, "We need to get across the idea that our staff will be there to try to work out a solution, to *try to maintain the family intact,* less the abusive act."[20] (Emphasis mine)

As you have seen, social service agencies have no real compunctions about breaking up families. The rate of placement outside the home is *increasing.* Yet, in the case of sexual abuse, the agencies' supposed deep desire to keep families together excuses failing to protect children from rapists.

Nobody has ever shown counseling to be effective in dealing with rapists of any stamp. So the theory that social workers actually can eliminate the abusive act while keeping the family intact is sheer wishful thinking. The only possible case in which counseling could perhaps make any difference is the case where the perpetrator turns himself in: which as you saw in the case of the stepdaughter from California is effectively prevented by law. In all other cases, counseling occurs under duress, and is just an excuse for the perpetrator to cry on a counselor's shoulder about how he was abused as a child and is not responsible for his actions.

The real bottom line, as revealed by the Missouri county director's testimony, is that the child abuse industry wants lots of hotline reports to keep it going. They want children to turn in their parents, so the children must be told that no harm will come to the parents. They want the public to be up in arms about the crime of sexual abuse, and anxious to let the child abuse industry "deal with" the perpetrators, which would never happen if the public knew that once a genuine sexual abuser was caught practically nothing happens to him. They mainly want control of the family, which is why they offer alleged sexual abusers the plums of visitation, or even custody, for their cooperation.

A COLORADO ADOPTIVE MOTHER'S STORY

If one picture is worth a thousand words, one story that reveals the hidden motives of the child abuse industry is worth a thousand pages of explanation. I ran across this amazing letter in a newsletter for adoptive families with five or more children. The letter was written in response to previously published letters dealing with the problems foster and adoptive parents have in working with social service agencies.

This is a beautiful state with lots of fun things to do that don't cost a lot. We have ponies and riding space. . . . Have 13 acres and place to camp, ponderosa pine trees. Are building a large 10 bedroom home. Four bio children (two boys, two girls), eight adopted (seven boys, one girl). . . . Have raised or helped raise dozens of others. Some married (nine grandchildren) . . .

We have hurt with you who have suffered the cruel, unnecessary, severe pain of totally untrue false accusations. . . .

When these precious needy children can bring such joy to us who love and want them so much, I really cannot comprehend how anyone with any heart can do the things too many of us have experienced. There has to be more we can do to stop it. For over thirty years we have known harassment but it became more severe after the first of 1963. At this time, after prayer, we were led through extremely unusual circumstances to choose lawyer D. for a private adoption.

At the first appointment it came up about a pending Child Welfare bill that had passed the Senate three months earlier. Mr. D. was a senator and tried to fight it knowing it had bad intents. It should have been before the House of Representatives long before. The sum of it was that any child left without parental or relative support should automatically become a ward of the child welfare department so that no child would be left alone, helpless, without anyone over them. Suspect all laws they make, as they make them sound good but there's usually a hidden bad motive! D. told us and said how he wished he had known of our present problems before the bill had passed the senate. I said that the Lord was never too early or too late and that He intended to help now. D. said he and friends in the House of Representatives could still try to fight it. Could I come down when it came before the House in Denver?

We had a boy (Brent) that child welfare had caused awful trouble over and kept pressing us to give him to them. (His mom was ill and we were raising him unpaid, nonrelative and unadoptable, placed with us by her.) Only two days later I was called down before the House voted. As a result an amendment was attached to the bill. The sum of it was—except in cases where some nonrelative was willing to assume all responsibility, financially, etc., for the care of a needy child when parents or relatives couldn't or wouldn't. The bill and amendment passed. The latter protected our Brent and any we could or would adopt privately.

However, the child welfare department only knew the bill passed. They fired off a terse letter to us saying give Brent up or we'll take him by force if necessary. Now we knew the intent of the bill. I sent the letter to our lawyer D. upon his request. He dictated a letter for them to leave us alone since we intended to continue giving Brent a home. They called him, blew up about us breaking the law. D. said we were not. They asked vehemently, "Aren't you aware we just got a bill through the legislature that gives us the right to go take Brent by force if necessary?" He informed them of the amendment, which they were unaware of, then furious over. . . .

The aim of the child welfare department, as has been demonstrated through countless large adoptive families, is to tear up the homes, to help get children out of control through the public schools (we have ours in a Christian Academy), to further discredit us parents in all ways, ruin our good names by false charges and accusations to stop us from adopting . . ., for each child we take out of the system takes a large monthly Federal grant check which they no longer receive. It jeopardizes their jobs and that of countless child welfare workers, psychiatrists, psychologists, etc. Why shouldn't they hate you and me? We are upsetting their security. . . .

To keep the letter as brief as possible and still relate some necessary harassment tactics and reasons, so much is omitted naturally. . . .

For your help and understanding get the book *Child of Rage* by Glenn Hester. He was a boy growing up in the child welfare system. Each time foster parents and he learned to love each other and adoption was mentioned he was yanked out and his foster parents were blackballed as no good and their home shut down. Glenn went from tender love to hate and finally almost murder and felt no regret.[21]

This, friends, is how the "child protective" system really works. This is why foster children continue to be removed unnecessarily and, once in the system, are literally abused by the state. Just like the Organs of State in Soviet Russia, which Solzhenitsyn so aptly remarked *need* victims in order to justify their existence, our child abuse industry needs a continual supply of confused, mistreated foster children who are endlessly passed from one hand to the next. Children with a stable home of their own, whose natural or adoptive parents receive no state or federal money, mean unemployment for child abuse workers. Miserable foster kids mean *jobs*.

The child abuse industry has not protected children, but is actually harming children; and, if its current treatment of sexual abuse victims and foster children is any indication, it will do even worse in the future. It cannot successfully replace parents, although it is striving to eliminate parents' authority and the parent-child relationship. It does not help children: rather, it harms them. It serves its own interests first, last, and always, to the detriment of the families it is supposed to serve. To say the very least, it does not act in the best interests of the child.

The next chapters will explore the fascinating origin of the child abuse industry, and its terrifying vision for the future.

Outrageous Facts III

INSTITUTIONS
VERSUS
THE FAMILY

YOURS, MINE, & "OURS" 10

Everyone is alarmed when a child is kidnapped. Take, for example, the case of little Inamae Harper of North Las Vegas, Nevada.

On April 27, 1985, five-year-old Inamae was kidnapped while walking to a fast food restaurant five blocks from her home. After an intensive search by authorities, including a campaign of leaflets carrying Inamae's picture, someone finally responded to the $20,000 reward offered for information leading to Inamae's return. The little girl was discovered in a filthy $85-a-week motel in California.

Inamae's story ended with an unusual twist. When confronted with arrest for kidnapping Inamae, the neighbors who had snatched her claimed they were being "good Samaritans" rescuing Inamae from parents whom they disliked. As one of those involved put it, "All we were doing was loving her."[1]

As Inamae's case shows, would-be child savers don't always have their heads screwed on straight. Snatching a child off the street, cutting her hair, dying it another color, carrying her away from everything familiar in her life into another state, and depositing her in a filthy environment is *not* the way to help. In Inamae's case, this behavior was treated as a crime, and rightly so.

Unhappily, the unthinking desire to "save children" at any cost is not confined to a few unbalanced civilians in North Las Vegas. What Inamae's neighbors did against the law is being preached to government workers as their legal *duty*. With apocalyptic rhetoric, a campaign has been launched to "rescue" children from their parents. As a well-known lawyer and child advocate from Texas pleaded at a Missouri conference on child abuse and neglect,

> "There's an assignment on the nation's billboard and it reads, 'Save the Children.' ...
> "The fear is we are possibly losing ground ... the hour is late. It's 11:59 on the clock of children's destiny. We only have a minute. It's just a tiny little minute, but our children's whole future is in it.
> "Save the children."[2]

Of course, she did not mean that the conference attendees should save *their own* children—by, for example, staying home and looking after their children instead of consigning them to day care. The "our children" whose "whole future" and "destiny" she wanted the conference-goers to control are *yours*.

We hear about the elite's plans for "our" children all the time. Missouri's Governor John Ashcroft, who we are told is a Christian and who should therefore know better, has said, "Children are Missouri's most precious natural resource."[3] But when did Missouri discover how to get pregnant and deliver children? When did children become, like gas and oil, a "natural resource"? Isn't "exploitation" the very word that means "to make use of a natural resource"? If children are "natural resources," then aren't they there just for the State to exploit?

Childless Gloria Steinem declares, "By the year 2000 I hope we will raise *our* children to believe in human potential instead of God."[4] Homosexuals hang out banners at Democratic Party conventions telling us they want a nuclear freeze in order to save, they say, "our" children. Representatives of the Court-Appointed Special Advocates program write anguished letters about "our" children which reveal that they actually have other people's children in mind: they claim we need anonymous accusations of child abuse "if we are to protect *our* children and sustain *their* families."[5] Apparently it's OK to use "our" children as cover for one's own social plans, but one doesn't want to go so far as to insinuate that "our" families have any problems. These people claim your children as their own, but refuse to associate themselves with you.

We have already seen that outlandish rhetoric about the horrible danger to North American children is not justified. We have also seen that when government agents rush in to "rescue" children they very often make matters worse. Now we are going to see why, in spite of the facts, so many people fervently desire to make your children and my children into "our" children—meaning *their* children.

HISTORY IN THE HANDS OF A MODERN FAD

First, we must clear up one thing.

The child abuse industry *is* a recent innovation.

In their otherwise ground-breaking work *Defining Child Abuse*, the first book to try to look at the big picture of child abuse and how it is handled, Jeanne Giovannoni and Rosina Becerra argue that removal, like the poor, hath always been with us, and that in fact it has always been a response to the problem of poverty. They cite the English Poor Laws, which did separate poor families and send them to the workhouse, and the colonial laws based on that model.[6] They also refer to the practices of indenture and apprenticeship,[7] and summarize with a look at two state laws that required government supervision of families.[8]

Giovannoni and Becerra base their analysis on the assumption that the English and colonial laws were primarily materialistic, based on economic reasoning. This is simply incorrect: all law of that age had a religious base, as even the most cursory appraisal of history reveals. They also attempt (probably unawares) to superimpose a bureaucratic ideology on the sixteenth and seventeenth centuries. As they say,

> In the hierarchy of values, the community's interests were prima-ry. Parents were essentially community surrogates charged with raising desirable citizens.[9]

In order to justify this thesis, they confuse the colonial system of indenture and apprenticeship with our current program of anonymous accusations and termination of parental rights. They also confuse the voluntary accountability of members of a congregation (who submit themselves to the discipline of their state church) with our modern system of unwanted government harassment. They fail as well to distinguish between colonies with state churches, where some kinds of intrusion did take place, and those without, where every man's home was entirely his castle. Finally, and I'm sure this is accidental, they tend to make it sound like the laws regarding destitute families applied to *all* families: as if the mayor of the city back then could have his children forcibly removed, as can and has happened today.

The question of whether we have always had a system that took children from unwilling parents is important. If the system has always been there, then for us to only start crying out against it now would seem strange. Also, if we had always had such a system, then it would be impossible to compare the way things were with the way things are, to see if the new system is any worse than the one it replaced. Even those who despise tradition the most (I'm not accusing Giovannoni and Becerra of this) like to invoke it in their favor, if at all possible: wrapping new oppressions in the colonial flag makes them seem so much less threatening!

Let's look at the Poor Laws first, because the poor, as always, had it the worst. Keep in mind that the only people affected by these laws were the totally destitute, those who would have starved or frozen to death without help. Unlike our current "poverty level," a standard of living higher than that enjoyed by the middle-class in many countries, the colonial poor were *really* poor. How to help them without turning them into state dependents: that was the question.

And here is the answer. The authorities wanted to make sure each poor person was working hard for his keep. Children of destitute families were taken from their families and apprenticed or indentured to masters until they reached their majority or, in the case of girls, until they married. The colonial authorities preferred this system, where every able-bodied person had to work for his keep, to a system of subsidizing poor families, thus keeping them permanently dependent.

This system, while not liberal, at least did not include baby-snatching. No employer wanted an infant or young child, so the parents got to keep those. Also, the parents had some say in selecting their children's new master. And since removal was based on poverty, if things went better for the parents, they could possibly redeem their children, unlike our system which does not guarantee under any circumstances that children will be returned. Furthermore, poor parents did not always consider even compulsory apprenticeship to be child-stealing. Remember the stories about babies in baskets deposited at orphanage doors? Parents then, as today, would prefer to see their children alive in someone else's care than dying in their own home. As an alternative to starvation, the apprenticeship/indenture system did work.

We need to understand the seventeenth and eighteenth centuries from the inside before we start likening apprenticeship to foster care. Many families voluntarily apprenticed their children to teach them a trade, much as modern-day Americans send their eighteen-year-olds to college. True, the children were younger, but life was also shorter and children grew up faster. Parents had no real fear of their children coming to moral harm in a master's household (as the parents of today's foster children have reason to fear) because of the community's very strict moral code. Sodomy, for example, was punishable by death, thus making it unlikely that a boy would be approached sexually when in the master's home. The same went for adultery, making life safer for girls. Also, unlike our current system which sucks in children of all ages, the colonial system left infants and young children with their parents. Mothers, even the most dissolute, were free to keep their babies, since no other women were standing in line to breastfeed the children of "unfit" mothers.

In spite of the strictures against all sort of misbehavior, community feeling was generally sympathetic to keeping families together. The beloved evangelist George Whitefield, the friend of Benjamin Franklin and founder of a major orphanage in Georgia, found he had shot himself in the foot when he tried to remove some younger children from their older siblings who were raising them. Though it was true that the older children were not raising the younger ones in Christian piety, the community became outraged when Whitefield forcibly (and legally) removed the youngsters to his orphanage. This one act of tyranny, arising though it did from misguided piety, cost Whitefield enormously in popular support and was the beginning of the end of his control over that institution.[10]

There really was no such animal as a colonial "child advocate," dispensing counseling freely to unwilling clients under the threat of removal. Serious crimes against children, like incest or attempted murder, were punishable by death, as were similar crimes against adults. In fact, all crimes against children had some kind of penalty attached for the perpetrator. Removal was only an option for the destitute or those who showed no interest at all in raising their children according to Christian standards, and it was hardly ever exercised. If the family was doing any kind of reasonable job, the authorities left it alone. Nor did they resort to stealing the children of Jewish parents or other non-Christians then resident in the colonies. You could be a nonconformist without losing your children. And, finally, you did not have to fear anonymous accusers, nor was malicious slander encouraged by the state.

FRUSTRATED MOTHERS UNITE TO SAVE "OUR" CHILDREN

The first real child-saving movement in America began in the 1800s. Colonial child advocacy had been at best a sporadic affair, hampered both by public sympathy for families and a lack of institutions to house the "rescued." When "saving" a child meant taking him into your own home, this put a damper on any outbreak of crusading zeal.

Only institutions and organizations stood to gain anything by expanding the numbers of children "saved." Private agencies led the way.

> A major movement in the second half of the [nineteenth] century, founded by Charles Loring Brace, resulted in the wholesale transportation of children from Eastern cities to homes in the Midwest. The Children's Aid Society, which Brace founded, "rescued" homeless children and children of morally decadent or cruel families by awarding them to farm families. . . .[11]

Mr. Brace didn't feel it necessary to get the parents' permission to send their offspring across state lines, even though some of the parents had been forced to surrender their children in the first place merely because of poverty. His fellow child-savers agreed that parental knowledge and permission was totally unneeded. When Dr. Thomas P. Norris, president of the Board of Commissioners of Kings County, New York, proposed that a conference on the needs of children adopt a resolution that children should not be taken out of the state without the consent of their natural or legal guardians, "his was the only affirmative vote."[12]

Another wing of the private child-saving movement, according to Giovannoni and Becerra, "is best viewed as a distinct kind of social agency with police powers" as well as "a social movement." This was the Society for the Prevention of Cruelty to Children, the forerunner of our modern American Humane Association.

From the beginning, the SPCC was involved in "seeking out mistreated children" and placing "agents in courts to investigate cases and to advise as to the proper handling of the children and the enforcement of any legal penalties that could be imposed on the perpetrators." The SPCC's "focus was on removal of children from their parents or guardians" as well as "on punishment of the parents as a deterrent to others." "The Cruelty" became a common household term.[13]

At this point, the child-savers were halting between two opinions. One side, exemplified by the SPCC's insistence on punishing perpetrators, held to the old standard of legal justice: defining crimes and punishing perpetrators. The other side, symbolized by the SPCC's equally vigorous child-removing efforts, took up the banner of "the best interests of the child." The latter side prevailed.

The victorious side, the juvenile justice movement of the 1890s, was first, last, and always a frustrated mothers' movement. As D. D. Randall told a national conference on charity in 1884,

> "Whenever and wherever we find [woman], she is always the fearless and uncompromising apostle and the inspired prophet of a higher and better humanity."[14]

This corps of "uncompromising apostles" and "inspired prophets" was overwhelmingly composed of wealthy females with few or no children, lots of time on their hands, and large egos.[15] The group included radical feminists whose litany sounds remarkably like the modern version—"the patriarchal family and the housewife are doomed, capitalism is decaying, socialism is the answer," and so on.[16] It also included those striving to trade their *anomie* for a fulfilling career in taking and raising other women's children. This latter group, including such luminaries as Louise Bowen, Ellen Henrotin, Julia Lathrop, and Jane Addams, sought only a modified female role. Child-saving, they argued, was a reputable task for women seeking to extend their traditional housekeeping functions into the community. As Mrs. Bowen told the Friday Club of Chicago, "If a women is a good housekeeper in her own home, she will be able to do well at larger housekeeping."[17]

George Orwell was wrong: Big Brother was really Big Mother. And Big Mother's first goal was "to decriminalize juvenile procedures entirely."[18] Besides bringing a more motherly tone to the courtroom proceedings, this meant a total absence of constitutional rights for the objects of the investigation.

Although it took the name of the "juvenile justice movement," the new movement was not concerned at all with justice, but with "health" and "happiness," which its proponents felt were perfectly attainable for all children in some kind of government-controlled environment.

Almost immediately this maternal system began to open its arms wide to *all* children, not just the depraved or deprived. As Miriam Van Waters wrote way back in 1927, in her book *Parents on Probation*,

> Hardly a family in America is not engaging in the same practices, falling into the same attitudes, committing the same blunders which . . . bring the court families to catastrophe. . . .[19]

It is "only a question of time," she said, "before the parent's psychological handling of his child" would come under the scrutiny of the state. She looked forward to a day when Juvenile Court would become a humanistic environment, when children would no longer be "separated from parents who violated traditional moralities: they would be severed from parents who violated the right of the child to sanity and integrity of mind and body" as defined by Ms. Van Waters and her friends.

> On that great day, the parent would throw himself into the therapeutic arms of social work, "willingly cooperate in a plan for his own welfare," and then face "the superparent, which is mankind," with a "face stained with tears," saying: "Sure, I'll make good."[20]

This brave new world would not be possible if the superparent lacked the organizational means to pressure parents to tears. So the next stage of child-saving, predictably, was the bureaucratic.

INTRODUCING THE CHILD ABUSE INDUSTRY

In 1909 the White House Conference on Children, called by President Theodore Roosevelt, brought the message that "children should not be removed from their parents for reasons of poverty alone."[21] This noble call was quickly transformed into the Mothers' Pension Laws, the precursor of our own Aid to Families of Dependent Children. A widow of insufficient means could now keep her children with her at government expense—if she was "a fit person, morally and physically, to bring up her children" and it was "in the best interests of the children" to remain with her.[22] This immediately led to "the constant intrustion of home inspection and judgments about [her] child rearing practices."[23]

The private agencies, who had pioneered the child-saving movement, "bitterly opposed the public laws as socialistic."[24] Well might they complain: through their efforts, private charity had completely replaced public welfare programs in many Eastern cities.[25] Now they were being pushed aside, in favor of a system which considered its very intrusiveness as a form of "help" for families.

The private agencies feared that government agencies would engage in empire-building at the expense of the children. The maternal kindliness of private charity would be replaced by calculating bureaucracy, they warned.[26]

In the intervening years, this was certainly true for poor families. Dick Gregory, for example, in his autobiography recalls how the social workers humiliated and harassed his mother by their inspection visits. But it was not until the 1970s that the child abuse industry really began to balloon.

We now have a system of "child protective services" in every state which consumes somewhere between ten million and a billion dollars per state. Psychologists demand and get more than a quarter million dollars per year apiece for their "expert" testimony in child abuse cases.[27] As Allan Carlson of the Rockford Institute points out,

> Psychiatrists testifying for the prosecution on vague concepts such as "the Child Sexual Abuse Accomodation Sydrome," have pulled down $1,000 a day for their efforts. In the Jordan, Minnesota case, therapists grilling the children for weeks on end earned $100 an hour for their efforts. As one renegade psycholgist, W.R. Coulson, admits: "Therapists love child abuse because it makes more work for them. There hasn't been a lot done on the fact that the growth in statistics on child abuse comes from people in whose advantage it is to discover it."[28]

The United Way now allocates over ten percent of its funds to "child care/child abuse prevention."[29] And in many states, citizens can check a box and donate to organizations dealing in "child abuse prevention" right on their tax form. Michigan raised two million dollars last year this way.

Private and public organizations holding children removed from their families can get ridiculous sums per child. One such Children's Home in our area sent out an urgent plea when government funds ran short, saying they needed $70,000 to $100,000 immediately or they would have to "end services to eleven children."[30] Quite a tidy sum per child.

> Child-saving has become quite a lucrative business. In Sweden—always "a decade ahead" of America in the evolution of social policy—an investigative magazine recently discovered that that nation had *ten* times as many children in foster care, on a per capita basis, as neighboring Norway and Denmark. The reason? Foster parents, commonly trained in social work, could earn 7,000 *kronor* (roughly $1,000) per month, or more, for every child they took in. Moreover, half of this income, called a support allowance, was tax-free, the hardest kind of income to find in tax-happy Sweden. In one case, a couple annually earned $50,000 for caring for three foster children. Crudely put, legalized child-snatching in Sweden pays well.[31]

Nor does legalized child-snatching pay badly here in the good old U.S.A. "Special needs" children are popping up everywhere now that it's been discovered that it is possible to charge ten times as much for the care of these youngsters. I know of one woman who provides "medical care" for "special needs" infants taken from their families. She leaves them propped all day with bottles in front of the TV, and gets $1,000 per child per month for her efforts.

And of course the numbers of child protective workers, court employees, statisticians, clerks, managers, researchers, trainers, and so on have swelled tremendously. The gravy train for those "helping" children grows ever longer, with no end in sight. There does seem to be some squabbling at the trough, though. As one of the conferees at the National Institute on Child Sexual Abuse Victims told the press, "The system is loaded with turf battles. Everybody is trying to protect their own damn job."[32]

So this is what it all comes down to: protecting somebody's job. We have created a system that has all the incentives working in the wrong direction. Bureaucrats need child abuse to be a huge, intractable problem so they can embellish their budgets. If they actually succeeded at reducing it, they would lose their cushy jobs. Social workers are liable for damages only if they leave children at home and those children are subsequently harmed, not if they take children for trivial reasons. If they are sued, they could lose their shirts as well as their jobs. Legislators protect their jobs by kowtowing to the bureaucrats, who can tap their employees' union dues for campaign funds, and who have the perseverance and government-paid time to lobby legislators endlessly for their programs.

All of this is short-sighted: you can only push the people so far before they push back. Nor are those "damn jobs" necessarily worth all this extraordinary effort. Front-line social workers, for example, make puny wages, and about half leave the profession voluntarily inside of a year. But in the upper echelons the call of self-interest rings loud and clear. And what will people not do for self-interest?

In the next chapter, we will see how the leaders of the "helping" professions are now networking together to gain themselves clients by planning to bring every North American child under the control of at least one participating bureaucracy from birth, or even earlier.

BRINGING
IN THE THIEVES *11*

"There once were two cats of Kilkenny
Each thought there was one cat too many
So they fought and they fit
And they scratched and they bit
Till, excepting their nails
And the tips of their tales
Instead of two cats, there weren't any."

"Little drops of water
Little grains of sand
Make the mighty ocean
And the pleasant land."

Nursery rhymes tell us something about the world. From the Two Cats of Kilkenny we learn that infighting is counterproductive. From the Litle Drops of Water and Little Grains of Sand we discover that cooperation can build something bigger than we dream.

Let nobody say that North American bureaucrats are slower of wit than nursery children. Child abuse industry leaders quickly recognized that they had nothing to gain from infighting, and everything to gain from networking.

As early as August of 1977, one of HEW's consultants approached the North Carolina Divison of Health Services to

prepare a plan and develop an initiative to "regionalize child health care" in response to the emerging national priority toward developing a child health strategy.

Take note: at this point, neither the legislature nor the public had requested any such plans or initiatives. All we have is one lone bureaucrat making suggestions. Considering this, the N.C. Division of Health Services response is suspiciously overenthusiastic:

The Division of Health Services responded to this challenge by calling a statewide meeting of persons interested in such an approach. Interested individuals from pediatrics, obstetrics, social services, public health, health systems agencies, and other fields met in Raleigh to discuss forming a Steering Committee. Its mandate was to develop a plan and *prepare a proposal to the federal government* which would demonstrate that a comprehensive, locally developed service delivery system could be put in place. . . . Eventually, as a result of this *demonstration* project, the system would become statewide and *embrace all children.*[1]

Don't you wish the government responded with this much zeal to *your* suggestions? One bureaucrat suggests that North Carolina ought to "prepare a plan and develop an initiative," and immediately there's a statewide meeting. Experts from every conceivable child-related field converge, zealous to produce a "demonstration project" designed to "embrace all children." Nor was this meeting another huff 'n puff round of go-nowhere talks. No, all of a sudden, without consulting the legislature or the electorate, we have a "mandate" to develop a plan not only for the state of North Carolina, but that can be presented as a "proposal to the federal government." Absolutely eveyone interested in children had a part in this plan . . . except parents.

Leaving parents off the Steering Committee apparently was no oversight. The *Child Health Plan*, when revealed in all its glory, included

- a compulsory "health care home" for every child. Children had to be registered in one such "home" at birth. [2] If parents refused, they would be turned over to child protective services and threatened with losing their children. As the report said, "in some cases aggressive outreach and even governmental intervention may be appropriate."[3]

The report doesn't mince words about what it means to be involved with a health care "home." As the report says, it will *require*

1. Continued acceptance and contact—the child and his family *will* accept one principal source of primary care. They *will* make contact with that source often enough to provide continuity.

2. Conformance with recommendations for prevention and promotion—the child and his parents *will* arrange for examination, education, counselling, immunization and other "well child" services rather than only episodic treatment.

3. Adequate information flow—records will be transferred

between health care homes in case of relocation. Further information will be furnished the health care home of significant episodes as well as treatments from other sources. [What they mean is that you will not be allowed to escape the system by moving from place to place, or by obtaining care "outside" the system.]

4. Compliance with administrative requirements—registration, qualification, and communication requirements will be met . . . [They mean you will comply, or else.]" [4]

- Even before birth, parents would find themselves entangled with the state. One of the health care "home's" so-called "services" is "organized instruction and individual counseling throughout the parenting cycle," including "the decision to have the first or an additional child." Genetic counseling seems to be mandatory for high-risk parents, in the minds of the planners, with mandatory abortion not too far behind.[5]

- "At risk" mothers could have their children removed at birth and placed in "crisis nurseries."[6] "Prenatal care" includes "screening for potential medical and psychosocial problems."[7] The "at risk" category included cases where "no current problem may exist."[8]

- *All* children, with no exceptions, would be forcibly trained to reject Judeo-Christian moral and ethical teachings, and instead to embrace "values clarification" and promiscuity.[9]

- In those compulsory "health care homes," teenagers would receive counseling designed to encourage them to rebel against their parents' authority.[10]

- Abortions and contraception would be available through these compulsory "homes" without the consent of the parents.

- Health care "homes" would be exploited as "screening sources" to "detect possible problems" such as "suspected child abuse or neglect, nutritional problems, emotional trauma, or any one of any other clues."[11]

- Compulsory psychological testing and therapy would be another "service" of these "homes." Families could not refuse this "service" if offered.[12]

- Kiss your Twinkies good-bye department . . . Under the title "nutritional supplementation" we discover that the health care "homes" not only would prescribe particular foods for their compulsory "clients" but also "ideally, appropriate measures are taken to ensure that the right foods are actually consumed."[13]

That's just what we need: a social worker under every kitchen table.

- Health care "homes" also would concern themselves with every child's *social* life. One of the "handicaps" which bring down the full range of "services" is "social handicaps."[14] The "homes" then decide which "services are designed to meet the need for wholesome physical activity, stimulation of self expression, and artistic pursuits." The list includes disco dancing (because staying up to the wee hours, flattening your eardrums, and flattening your feet is *healthy*) but not any form of physical labor in the fresh air, such as gardening.

Not surprisingly, the great "barrier to service" listed in every one of the six priority areas was the attitude of parents and the community. This barrier was to be overcome by "parent education." The need for parent education (to persuade the public to accept this totalitarian agenda) ranked as "problem #1."[15] More on this in a minute.

Throughout the report, its writers kept stressing how each group of professionals would benefit from this kind of compulsory program. Under each "service" a handy list of "possible providers" was appended. The list included:

- "schools, other institutions of learning . . . social service agencies, other community groups such as the International Childbirth Educaion Association and La Leche League";[16]

- every kind of health worker, including private physicians and surgeons, county health departments and other public health facilities, hospitals and their employees, health educators, nutritionists, dentists, and clinic personnel;

- specialized public programs such as WIC, the Food Stamp Program;

- private adoption services, community agencies;

- law enforcement and family service agencies;

- developmental evaluation clinics, child psychiatrists and psychologists, etc.;

- public and private day-care centers, nursery schools, developmental care centers;

- schoolteachers, health educators, staffs of children's institutions.[17]

Parents, relatives, and volunteers did get a few nods, but almost every one of the forty categories of "services" was exclusively reserved for institutions and their agents.

The North Carolina plan was endorsed by the Governor, James B. Hunt, Jr., and copies of it were sent to every state in the Union.

Not long after this great leap forward, another Governor, this time Christopher Bond of Missouri, was calling another conference. This Missouri Governor's Conference on Children and Youth met in Jefferson City on December 7 and 8, 1981. Funded by the federal Department of Health and Human Services,

> the stated goal of the conference was to develop "networking partnerships," to create interdependence among all governmental health agencies, and to implement these plans in the public schools.[18]

The first speaker at the Education Workshop was Dr. Burton White of the Center for Parent Education. In one conference participant's words,

> White said that to be effective, educators must reach the child at birth. He felt that ill-informed parents ought not be allowed too long a time to pass their value-system on to their children. He recommended management of the child by what he called "professionals" at age zero, with the parents acting as caretakers under the direction of the professional from age zero to two and one half. And then at age two and one half, he thought the approach should change with BOTH the management AND the service of the child being in the hands of those whom he called "professionals."[19]

As Dr. White condescendingly put it in another conference a year later, "Sending a new parent home with a six day old baby as we do now in this country is insane."[20]

Dr. White's ideas were implemented in the public schools of Farmington, Independence, Ferguson-Florissant, and the St. Charles County District of Francis Howell. This pilot program would serve as the model for a later, compulsory program,[21]

> using the public schools to do what he calls "brokering" wherein he introduces his experimental "parenting programs." . . .
> During the question and answer session Dr. White . . . said that one objective of those who wish to implement networking partnership should be to get "the biggest bang for the buck."[22]

A year later at the Governor's Conference on the Young Years, Dr. Edward Pino spoke in the same vein, explaining why schools and other institutions are getting so interested in preschoolers. For the child's "best interests," right? Only if you spell that M-O-N-E-Y. . . .

> The five to eighteen year old market is dead. We should have learned that a long time ago. Basically, we're in the two to five year old market.[23]

The second day session was introduced by Dr. Eva Schindler-Rainman, who pointed out, "The dollar is more 'gettable' when you collaborate than when you compete," and, "We must become more interdependent." This was followed up by an array of speakers who opened up the concept of "networking."[24]

> The schools were to be viewed as "facilitators" and "brokers." We were told that human service agencies, private organizations, mental health services, foster care service, even various business concerns would like to, and should be able to, use the public schools to dispense their various products and services. . . . A resolution expressing the desire to use the public schools as a broker was presented to Governor Bond.[25]

At the closing session, Dr. Prentice A. Meador, Jr., demonstrated how this kind of networking might work. Dr. Meador

> called for another "mandate" that all junior and senior high schools have classes in parenting and family planning. Dr. Meador stated that implementation of these mandates should begin with an immediate inclusion of a section on health in the present Basic Essential Skills Test. When low scores were demonstrated on this health section, there would be justification for bringing in new parenting programs.[26]

So every agency would funnel in to the others. Abortion clinics could use the schools to publicize and promote their services. Social workers could gain "clients" by schools turning youngsters into informers on their parents. Conversely, social workers could force home schoolers and those with children in private school to enroll their offspring in public school. Doctors would require all births to be performed in hospitals, psychiatrists could have a steady stream of clients referred by the schools and social workers, foster parents would have no shortage of children, institutions would have plenty of residents, and on and on. As a report on the Governor's Conference summed up:

> The fact book handed out for conference participants specified exactly how a child enters the system. The child can enter through:
> 1) The Department of Family Services
> 2) The Department of Mental Health, or
> 3) The Division of Youth Services. The Juvenile Justice System, the public schools, and all human service agencies would be participants in the networking partnership. . . . Networking partnership is the agent whereby the State of Missouri, with tax monies, creates an interdependence of agencies which would assure that no child would escape the net of management by professionals.[27]

Here's how it would have worked, if twenty thousand copies of Laura Rogers's report on the conference had not been distributed to legislators, the media, and the public:

> The system assumes management of the child at birth through the parenting programs designed to reach all first time parents. Other children are gathered in by developmental testing which begins at age zero and continues all through the school years. This testing, coupled with a complete data system, ensures thorough surveillance and control of all children by state approved professionals. This can all be accomplished through the "health programs" set forth by Dr. Meador. These . . . programs would be required by law in all public schools, and would be interfaced with the Missouri State Health Plan which is also supported by Dr. Meador.[28]

Are North Carolina and Missouri the only places where institutions have discovered the joys of networking and the power of a State Health Plan? No. This very week I received an outline of the Florida Prevention Task Force Report, yet another Governor-sponsored program for total control of children. As the outline states,

> The goals are alarmingly similar to the International Year of the Child, North Carolina's "Child Health Plan for Raising a New Generation," Michigan's and Missouri's Conferences on Youth and Children AND Sweden's state control of the family![29]

Theoretically, the Florida task force was supposed to produce a "State Plan for the the Prevention of Developmental Disabilities in

Florida."[30] But here we go again! Among the many objectionable goals of the Prevention Task Force are:

1. the implementation of a state health profile for ALL Florida's children beginning at birth

2. the networking of persons who have regular contact with children (such as school personnel, physicians, social workers, law enforcement, etc.) so no child escapes the oversight of a state approved professional

3. the implementation of a complete data system to track Florida's children who are "at risk"

4. mandating a physical health, mental health, and family living [meaning bureaucratic propaganda] curriculum for K-12 for all Florida's public and PRIVATE schools . . .[31]

Nor is Florida the end of the road. Every time you read the newspaper you see some new scheme aimed at helping children. Mandatory kindergarten and all-day kindergarten are hot right now, though studies have shown, in the words of one headline, "young kindergarteners may have trouble."[31] And what do you think of Tennessee School Boards Association rep Dan Tollett's inspired idea of forcing children who are not in government schools to undergo private interviews with social workers four times yearly in the hopes of securing incriminating information about their parents?[32]   Or how about "health care visitors" to inspect your very own home periodically to make sure you're still entitled to keep your own children (a doctor suggested this)?[33] North Carolina suggested it, but Kansas already has it: a program for detecting "high risk" maternity patients and stealing custody of their children before birth.   And who is high risk? "A first time unwed mother, or a mother who shows no parenting skills in the hospital" among others. Also "parents with a history of abusing other children," which includes those with a history of *suspected* abuse.[34] Even the most insufferably tyrannical suggestion of all, that the state should license parents and only allow its favorites to breed, was seriously suggested at the 1979 Dallas Child Abuse Conference by a HEW official and, more recently, by a state Supreme Court judge.[35]

PARENTING OUR WAY TO DESTRUCTION

How in the world can bureaucrats expect us to put up with this takeover bid? The answer is simple: parenting education.

Parenting is not only, as Joyce Taylor has pointed out, "a rank example of faddist nouning when they should be verbing."[36] It is an avowedly humanistic system, which as its main proponent Thomas

Gordon of Parenting Effectiveness Training (P.E.T.) fame admits, "differs dramatically from tradition."[37] Contradicting and even ridiculing biblical methods of child discipline, and in fact *all* traditional methods of child rearing, parenting education is an attempt to abolish "all kinds of punishment, not just the physical kind."[38] Thus it dovetails nicely with the current open-ended definitions of child abuse in forbidding *all* disciplinary measures.

Joyce Taylor describes "the three common characteristics of all Parenting Programs:

> 1. Don't be the kind of parent you have [e.g. reject all the weight of human history and your own experience]
> 2. The family is a democracy; children should have equal rights in decision making
> 3. Children should never be subject to physical punishment[39]

The idea is to, as in Sweden, "subject the child [or in some cases, the new parent] to compulsory educational programs . . . which are consciously and with ideological bias intended to counteract the child's values derived from parents within the family."[40] The whole thing is a naked power play designed to obliterate traditional Jewish, Christian, Mormon, Muslim, you-name-it families. Here comes the new law from Mount Sinai, the Three Commandments of Parenting. Take warning: in Sweden dissenters from these Three Commandments are jailed.[41]

Who is Thomas Gordon and why should he dictate who gets to keep their children? The question is worth asking, because although "there are literally hundreds of Parenting Programs and you will probably be told the program was 'developed locally,'" one such supposedly locally-developed program "contained more than 200 pages directly from P.E.T. although the title was different."[42]

The main thrust of parenting education is that only "experts" know enough about children to raise them properly. Average citizens are incompetent, and should meekly allow themselves at all times to be overruled by "experts." No religious authority can overrule parenting experts; God need not apply. It is indoctrination in dependence—the means of turning free North Americans into a herd of sheep.

BIG BROTHERHOOD IS GLOBAL

The child abuse industry and its parenting programs didn't start in North America. The mother country was probably Sweden, though some parts of it could have been imported straight from Russia or China. But from here it is spreading with alarming speed.

In an Associated Press article of May 19, 1985, we find that, right now, the United Nations is hard at work putting forth a convention that "for the first time would define the rights of children under a recognized document of international law."

> The convention was proposed by a Polish [i.e., Soviet bloc] delegation to UNICEF in 1979 during the International Year of the Child. It has been under study for five years and is being formed article by article in annual sessions lasting one week by a subgroup of the U.N. Commission on Human Rights. . . .
>
> The articles of the Convention on the Rights of the Child deal with education, nourishment, health care, citizenship and drafting children as soldiers.
>
> Under international law, nations that ratify a convention are saying they agree to abide by its covenants.[43]

So the child abuse industry wants to be enthroned as an *international* organization. Nor is this all. Our friends at the United Nations have also come up with a definition of the rights of women that calls, not for full *opportunity*, but full *employment*.[44] This, dear friends, means the *death* of freedom of choice. If the U.S. and Canada ever ratify this, our national policy will *demand* that all babies be deposited in day care and that all mothers, even those of infants, be employed. If you don't comply, the child abuse industry stands ready, as in Sweden, to accuse you of abusive tendencies and *take your children*.

It's time to step back a bit, and ask, "What is going on here?"

What is going on is a push to *institutionalize all kids at birth* or even sooner, if possible, in order to *create government-controlled jobs*.

- Get kids in school earlier. This creates more jobs for teachers.

- "Screen" preschoolers. Creatively done, this can produce some kind of professional referral for just about *every* child.

- Threaten to take newborns, if parents don't conform to state expectations.

- Control who even gets to have children, both by threatening to remove children if they are born and by (eventually) making it illegal to have children without a permit.

The bottom line of all this is not so much some grandiose scheme of social adjustment (although that kind of ideology helps justify tyranny in some people's minds) as it is power for the elite and JOBS.

As I pointed out in an earlier book, in spite of all the pro-choice rhetoric today, we don't really have any more choices than we ever had.[45] The steady stream of men, and now women, out of the home is creating a boom market for institutions. Instead of family-based living, we are witnessing a push for *compulsory* institutionalization from womb to tomb.

Where's the "freedom of choice" in state licenses to bear children; compulsory day care for infants; compulsory Early Childhood Education programs for toddlers; compulsory government-controlled schooling for schoolkids; a job (for both men and women) in some mega-corporation; followed by institutionalization in a nursing care facility, and solitary death?

The child abuse laws are just one extremely popular excuse for institutional control of every citizen. By calling all nonconformity "child abuse," nonconformists can be martyred without any public sympathy. The rest, in order to retain custody, surrender their right to impart their own values to their children. The state becomes that Superparent, and 1984 arrives just a year or two too late.

That's the child abuse industry's vision for your family's future. But you don't have to accept it. Find out why in the last chapters.

IV
Everyday
Rebellions

WHAT
WE CAN
DO

IF THIS 12
BE REASON

"If we really care about the sufferings of innocent children in North America, we would not for one moment consider turning loose the swarms of muggers and child molestors who the system has already caught. . . . As the Marquis of Halifax said, 'Whenever a knave is not punished, an honest man is laughed at.' . . . Our continued refusal to do the right thing can only be the result of cowardice and a callous indifference . . . By turning over the entire business to social workers and psychologists, we think we have discharged our responsibility, when all we have actually done is wash our hands."—After Thomas Fleming[1]

Today parents feel out of control, and no wonder. What is "right" and permitted today may be "wrong" and forbidden tomorrow. What is the trend of the week? we all wonder. What infallible new expert will write the book that will tell us how to raise our children this year? The experts duly appear, announced by trumpets, but instead of *help* they thunder *orders*.

Increasingly, these self-anointed "experts" manipulate the government to back up their theories with force. If today's trend is permissive parenting, then everyone who believes that God requires spanking will have to do it in the closet, and hope to heaven that Junior doesn't tell his teacher. If tomorrow's trend is strictness, then mellow folk who like to give their children the freedom of the neighborhood will get phoned in for neglect. If, as is actually the case, *both* strictness and permissiveness are frowned on, nobody wins and bureaucrats get to play house with our children.

Why are today's parents losing control? Not because children are different, or because our outward circumstances are different. It's because, without even realizing it, we have stepped out of the protective circle of law based on unchanging *justice*, and stepped into the chaos of law based on fads and theories about what is "healthy" for us all.

THE NEW STATE RELIGION

Every tyranny requires its very own state religion so the rulers can feel justified in their oppression. In our case, the religion is Health.

Today in North America, Healthism enjoys almost total acceptance. Who doesn't want to be healthy? Who doesn't think that sick people should be cured? You can hear the "health" message from fundamentalist pulpits and evangelical platforms almost as often as from New Agers and the frankly atheistic. Conservatives and liberals alike vie to get the other side declared "sick" instead of slugging it out fairly on the grounds of right and wrong. Literally anything can be justified as "healthy," literally any crime can be forgiven as "sick."

We are heading towards *exactly* the same social structure as Soviet Russia: a piggish elite ruling over the servile masses, whose entire lives are under the sway of the elite. All this can be accomplished without ever invoking the names of Marx or Lenin or subscribing to their doctrines. All we need is a good enough reason to believe in the omniscience of the elite, and a willingness to let them make the decisions—"for our own good," of course. And, just to insure our compliance, we will be suffocated with tax-supported bureaucracies, and be surrounded by anonymous accusers. This *is* the definition of the child abuse industry.

Christians who drool over the latest psychological fads and revel in the "new reformation" of self-esteem delude themselves. Pop psychology *is* the religion of Health, and is fundamentally hostile to any absolute authority besides its own infallible dogmas.

If you would like to find a source for totalitarian theories of social oppression, try looking through back issues of *Psychology Today*.

At its very beginning, *Psychology Today* announced it was here to wipe out the old religions (Judaism and Christianity) and bring in the New.[2] But still this was hailed as the voice of Objective Science, not a raw power grab. The more the new priest-kings announced, "We will bury you," the more reverently they were obeyed—and the more obedience they demanded. As *Psychology Today* in 1969 denounced those family patterns "that lead to dogmatism, traditionalism, authoritarianism, and dependence on the older generation,"[3] it went on in 1973 to demand "political control over the economic institutions that shape our society."[4] In 1978 it boasted, "Psychology and politics are converging."[5] Too true.

There's a lot to be said for objectively observing human responses and recording those observations. Although this pastime, called psychology because it deals with the ultimately unobservable human psyche, is more of an art than a science, it can yield valuable results. But this new push to control you and me has nothing to do with real psychology. Or real health. Or the best interests of our children. Or anything else but the lusts of a selfish, arrogant, lawless elite. Stalin could have written the lyrics and Hitler the tune.

CONTROL THROUGH "HEALTH"

Under the law of Health, all of life becomes politicized. The most powerful man simply declares his personal prejudices to be society's new norms, and that is that. We all must conform or lose our children. We are even denied the dignity of resisting our oppressors, because they are supposedly tyrannizing us out of *love*, for our own good, and, "in the best interests of the child."

Whoever can ascend the pedestal of Health controls everything, and there is no way to predict what he will demand. Nor is there any theoretical limit on what can be demanded in the name of Health. Right now, in the Soviet Union, dissenters are being tortured in psychiatric hospitals in the name of Health. Or, since Soviet-style tyranny seems to be gaining respectability nowadays, let us consider the example of Nazi Germany, where dissenters were castrated so as not to bear "unfit" children, and Jews and Gypsies were massacred to "purify the race." Nobody can justify Stalin or Hitler's behavior by any traditional standard of *justice*, but they both found it easy to persuade a majority of the population that these measures were necessary for "social health."

LIFE BEFORE "HEALTH"

In North America, we have no cultural tradition of oppression as existed for centuries in tsarist Russia. Nor have we suffered the economic devastation that flattened the Weimar Republic and paved the way for Hitler. From its very beginning North America was founded, not perfectly but substantially, on absolute standards of justice. To consider a return to these absolute standards is not some fanatical theory, but an option that can be weighed against the historical facts.

Let's ask and answer some questions:

- Was there *more* juvenile delinquency and child abuse or *less* before the child abuse industry was established?

- Was there more sexual abuse, or less, before the new campaign of sex education and "helping professionals"?

- Were we overrun with murderers, rapists, and child molesters before the courts started trying to "rehabilitate" these kinds of offenders?

- Did half of all marriages end in divorce before we decided that marriage vows were an empty joke instead of a binding contract with penalties for those who broke them?

- Did children grow up illiterate before God was banned from the classroom and the schools began undermining children's values?

- Was a large percent of the population chronically unemployable, with no real prospect for their children but poverty, before we formed an army of bureaucrats (inaptly calling this the Great Society) and declared a War on Poverty?

The answers: no, no, no, no, no, NO! Juvenile delinquency is up 11,000 percent since 1950.[6] Incest was estimated at one in a million or less in 1940.[7] Murder, rape, and other violent crimes were a tiny fraction of today's reality before the religion of Health replaced the justice of law. Child molesting was almost nil. Few couples divorced, and few children had to suffer through this major childhood trauma.[8] Literacy was at the 99 percent rate in 1910.[9] Immigrants, uneducated and totally poverty-stricken (far below our current inflated standard of "poverty level"), saw their children wealthy and successful.

The difference is that North America used to be governed by *law based on unchanging absolutes*, and today we are governed by the dictates of special interests and the fads of the elite. No security or progress is possible while our laws oscillate madly this way and that. All that the child abuse industry and our related social change agencies have accomplished with their faddish programs is to make us a contender for crime capital of the world.

Our old standard, of "justice for all" instead of Health for all, is simple and time-tested. It requires no elaborate, self-interested bureaucracy. Most of all, it is fair. As you will now see for yourself.

A REALISTIC DEFINITION OF CHILD ABUSE AND NEGLECT

Under our old, fairer laws there was no special category called "child abuse." The same laws applied to those committing crime against children and adults. Because there were no double standards, no special rules were needed and also no special bureaucracy. The only difference between the rights of adults generally and those of parents in particular was that parents were recognized as having the biblical right to apply the "rod of discipline" to an erring child's backside—e.g., spanking.

Murderers of either children or adults received the death penalty. So did those attempting murder, but failing. This made the question of what to do with a murderous father or mother who has been released on parole or probation irrelevant.

Rapists also received the death penalty. There was no question of getting an incestuous father back together with his tiny victim "for the health of the family."

If a parent knocked out a child's tooth, or blinded an eye, or cut off an finger, or some other atrocity, he did not get free counseling and the chance to sob on some therapist's shoulder. Following the spirit, if not the letter, of the biblical injunction to require "eye for eye and tooth for tooth," he was soundly horsewhipped.

Nobody got too excited about "emotional neglect" or the forms of so-called "neglect" that go along with being poor. Poor parents were more likely to beg for the privilege of placing their children in charity institutions than these institutions were to steal the children.

Deliberately neglecting a child physically by starvation or other means was considered attempted murder. Since the penalty for murder was death, hardly any of these cases occurred.

Children who ran away because they were being mistreated (like young Benjamin Franklin, who ran away from his brother) were generally not forced to return. This community feeling had a basis in the Bible's "Fugitive Slave Law," which prevented an Israelite from returning a runaway slave to his abusive foreign master. A small number of children ran away out of sheer rebelliousness, usually only overnight. Remember the classic cartoons of small boys with a bundle of belongings on a stick? People who tried to alienate children from their families could be sued.

All this adds up to: punishment for genuine perpetrators, and very little actual perpetration. Parents were presumed innocent until proven guilty, as provided by the United States and Canadian Constitutions. In *no* case did the State assume custody. Orphans went to their next of kin or (failing that) to those willing to help. We had no "search and destroy" squads on the lookout for children to increase bureaucratic caseloads. We also had no network of foster parents who were paid for their services. There was absolutely no financial incentive to set up a Children's Archipelago.

The sole exception to the rule that the State never took custody occurred in the colonies with state churches. It seems an infallible rule that a state church ends up threatening nonconformists. However, our modern State Church of Health makes any of the Puritans' efforts pale by comparison.

Busybodies were not encouraged. Instead of thinking vile thoughts about each other, under the rule of justice North Americans occupied themselves with their own business. Thus, parents didn't have the stress of trying to prove to every community member every day of their lives that they were worthy of keeping their children.

Those were the days when families stuck together, when fathers were respected, and mothers were all but worshipped. I'm not saying that things were perfect—they never will be in this world. But at least the laws didn't *cause* problems.

You might think this sounds like misty-eyed nostalgia, wistfully (and unrealistically) wanting to return to the dear old days. We constantly hear our self-proclaimed leaders saying, "You can't turn back the clock." By this they mean that we should accept their theories on blind faith, rejecting what we know about the past. But actually, they have already turned the clock back—to barbarism and dictatorship.

As it says in the book of Ecclesiastes, "There is nothing new under the sun."I question whether the values of sexual anarchy and institutionalized living compare favorably with the equally ancient values of family fidelity and home life. The first shot down the Roman Empire in flames; the second civilized this continent.

A NEW VISION

We need a new vision of the future. Instead of planning for defeat by establishing a massive, self-perpetuating bureaucracy based on the assumption that North American family life can only get worse, we should be planning for *success*. Government should be encouraging families who do what is right, instead of impounding their children. Government should trust experienced parents and grandparents, churches, and private-sector institutions to train families, instead of making all families bureaucratic dependents under the guise of "parenting education." And, instead of pampering criminals, government should punish those who commit crimes against children.

What incredible hypocrisy to gush about how it is "better to err on the side of the child" to the point of being willing to remove children from their families unjustly, only to swing around 180 degrees when it comes time to decree justice for the criminal. At the moment of sentencing, our legal system declares that its sympathies lie more with the criminal than with his victims.

The biblical penalty for rape, murder, and attempted murder was death. This was completely fair. The only alternatives are to after a while allow the criminal to go free and to tolerate the risk he will again commit the same crime, or to punish the taxpayers by forcing them to provide free lodging and food and supervision for this criminal for the rest of his life.

When society fails to exact the capital penalty for these horrendous crimes, what we are saying to the criminal is this: "There is no justice for victims and their survivors, or for your future victims. It is O.K. to murder and rape. In fact, soon we are going to let you go do it again." When we allow judges to hand out lenient sentences or even put these terrorists on probation, we are saying, "Go ahead and rape and bludgeon children! *Their* rights don't matter. We are only concerned about you."

Judges have handed out longer sentences for bombing an abortion clinic (a crime in which nobody was hurt—only property of a very dubious nature was destroyed) than for raping children.[10] This must stop.

As for the case of those who attack children physically without raping or killing them—the biblical penalty of eye for eye and tooth for tooth is most appropriate. You can bet a violent man would think twice about beating his children if he knew he would receive a beating himself. This kind of man (or woman) is a bully, and it is a long-established psychological fact that bullies *only* respect force.[11] As to the threadbare argument that penalties do not deter crime: haven't you ever seen a person who was drunk or otherwise under the influence sobering up (or at least trying to) when he feared the heavy hand of the law? It's amazing how people who seem completely out of control struggle to sober up when a policeman is standing next to them. Yet those lost in an alcholic or drug-induced fog are the very people that have least control of their actions, and who the experts try to tell us are totally incapable of controlling their short-term desires. Nonsense. Even drunkards at least marginally try to protect their own self-interest.

People don't commit crimes against children because they are "sick": one thing Drs. Strauss, Gelles, and Steinmetz do well in their book *Beyond Closed Doors* is debunk this argument. As these authors point out, "Those treatment programs which base their efforts on 'curing' the pathology which afflicts the violent individual have had minimal success—probably because there are no clear pathologies which make people violent."[12] Another way of saying it is that people who harm children *are* responsible for their actions. They are not sick; they are criminals. And most of the excuses why people commit crimes, whether they are Jack the Rippers or Qaddafis, boil down to one fact: they think they can get away without serious punishment. Although obviously it is better to escape the temptation to commit crime, in some circumstances (like unemployment or marital upsets) tempers run short. The fear of punishment is a necessary control in those situations: it can mean the difference between life and death. But when the temptation to seriously harm a child is accompanied by the knowledge that the most likely outcome is that you will receive lots of sympathy from friendly counselors, or at the very most a judicial slap on the wrist, the so-called "penalties" can actually be an *incentive* to commit the crime.

Recently I read in our local paper about a woman who stabbed an eight-year-old girl, critically wounding her although she didn't even know her. The woman's reason? She wanted to be readmitted to a mental hospital, but the authorities had refused. What a moral: stab a perfectly innocent kid and get *rewarded*.

Under our present antique system of jail sentences for serious crimes, criminals know they are unlikely to get sentenced for the crime they actually committed. The financial stress of keeping people in jail effectually prevents prosecuters from taking a hard line. Not only that, but our jails, although not a lovely environment, are not exactly the last word in punishment. Criminals get thoroughly fed, have libraries, watch TV, engage in illicit sexual acts, and can perform most of their other "outside" functions while in jail. Further, the tendency towards work release and early parole keeps most criminals hoping for early release. The most disgusting press clipping in my file records the trial of a child molester who *strutted and smirked about the courtroom even as he was receiving his sentence.*[13]

It is an empirical fact that if child molesters were executed, each one would be unable to claim the thirty to sixty additional victims that are now the norm. A government that is afraid to apply this degree of force to solve the problem has no business whining about violence against children.

Even the mildest forms of punishment, such as overnight incarceration, have been shown to have a dramatic effect in curtailing future acts of family violence.[14] Directing society's reaction at the offender, rather than removing the child, also relieves the social tensions which are making parents so legally uptight.

As the U.S. Attorney General's Task Force on Family Violence pointed out, it is surely inappropriate to cling to a "mediation" model of psychiatric counseling for all family members, when the victim is genuinely *not* to blame.[15] Family counseling presupposes that all parties are somewhat guilty. What this does to the soul of a child who has been viciously attacked I don't like to think.

CIVIL RIGHTS AND RULES OF EVIDENCE

Some people, including some victims of the child abuse system, become alarmed whenever strong penalties for child abusers are proposed. In some cases, they have good reason.

A Congressional wives organization headed by Nancy Siljander, for example, wants all those accused of child abuse denied bail (i.e., considered guilty without a trial). The group also thinks "consideration should be given to a proposal to *mandate* fingerprinting and photographing all children for the parents to keep."[16]

Obviously, this is going too far. Tactics like these smack of the Spanish Inquisition more than they do of democratic freedom. But where do you draw the line? Should we throw out all serious punishment for child molestors and those who severely injure children for fear of harming some innocent person's civil rights?

Right now we have a system that both denies the accused their civil rights, *and* fails to punish or restrain the perpetrators it catches. Neither of these faults are necessary.

Civil rights: what is the problem? The problem, if you think about it, is obvious. People are held guilty on *insufficient evidence*. If all the evidence necessary to convict a person of child abuse is the uncorroborated word of a child who might have been coached by an adult into making the charges, then obviously we can't dare to sentence a "convicted child abuser" very heavily. Deep down we know we have no *real* proof he is guilty. That is why those falsely accused of child abuse are so upset by Nancy Siljander's suggestions. Having already been falsely accused, and maybe even found "guilty" *without* proof, they know how easily a system of severe laws could be used to put away all nonconformists and dissenters, and to cover up the illegal actions of state agents.

In contrast, biblical law (upon which, it should be remembered, our countries' laws were originally based) requires that no person be found guilty "except on the testimony of two or three witnesses." More: the accused has his right to face his accuser in court. If the witness's accusation is found to be a lie, then the judge is supposed to "do to him as he intended to do to his brother" (Deut 19:15-21).

With these kind of safeguards, if a molester is found guilty, he *is* guilty. Now it makes sense to talk about stiff penalties.

We need *rules of evidence* in abuse and neglect cases. That means we need *police investigations* instead of "investigations" conducted by some social worker who may have had only fifteen hours of training,[17] and who may have *no* experience at all with children or rules of evidence. We need *multiple witnesses*. We need to stop allowing the unsupported testimony of children who are of an age where they can barely distinguish fantasy and reality. If children's testimony is to be allowed, then *every interrogation and interaction with those children by state agents* should be videotaped. It's just too easy to rehearse a child until he finally says what the prosecutor wants him to say, put that on tape, and call it "evidence."

We also need to stop prosecuting cases for which *there can be no evidence*. Day-care workers should not have to fear "fondling" charges because they must change diapers; parents should not be made afraid to hug their children. If there is no physical evidence of rape or injury and no eyewitnesses, what on earth is the state doing trying to build a case? Cases like these *must* violate the defendant's civil rights. Such a case could be fabricated against any person in the world, including each and every reader of this book. Yet, at the moment, the state prosecutes these cases, even in instances where the suppposed victim claims abuse never occurred.

How can people cry out against establishing standards of evidence because they are afraid children will "slip through the cracks" when they know very well that, under their system, perpetrators are often allowed to keep right on harming children if they will just plead guilty? A system that will leave a man the state knows is guilty of sexual abuse right in the home has *no business* pretending it needs to bypass civil rights in order to "protect" children.

We *can* have laws that provide both civil rights and serious punishments. The laws are not the problem. The problem is our *corrupt justice and penal systems*.

WHY REFORM OF THE LEGAL SYSTEM IS ESSENTIAL

Why do people like Nancy Siljander, who undoubtedly have their hearts in the right place, want to deny bail to anyone merely *accused* of child abuse? Because they know that it could be a whole year before the accused ever comes to trial—and they don't want to give him a year to keep molesting his victim, or to interfere with her testimony. But the answer is not to destroy your and my civil rights in order to maintain the present system. The answer is to *reform the system*.

Judges are swamped with trivial cases that should never have come to court. Get rid of these cases, and child abuse cases can move faster. Why, for example, must a judge preside over a divorce case when the two parties have already agreed on a settlement? And this is only one example of hundreds of judicial cases that could just as well be handled outside a court.

The prison system is swamped with people who ought to have either (a) made restitution (through cash on hand or by "working out" their thefts), (b) been physically punished and let go, or (c) been executed. Because the prison system is swamped, judges have an excuse for handing out weak sentences. Judges know that for each child abuser they put in jail, some other criminal must come out. This bias towards probation can create some bizarre instances of "justice." For raping an eight-year-old girl, a man in Missouri recently got *two years probation*.[18]

Judges claim they need complete freedom in sentencing so they can be "flexible." Wrong. Complete freedom in sentencing makes each judge a tyrant, able to act completely on his own prejudices. We need the rule of law, not the rule of lawyers.

All these reforms, though they seem radical at first, are really far more simple than our current confusing, often contradictory, system of "justice." Nor can our families survive for any length of time without them. Why? Because the threads all weave together.

Because the courts won't punish proven rapists and murderers in a way that guarantees they will never commit that crime again, the only way they can claim to "protect" children from such a perpetrator is by removing the children. Since the courts won't deal properly with the perpetrators, they take the victims. This, as you have seen, creates a whole industry around the victims: child protective workers, foster homes, institutions, juvenile court personnel, administrators, scholars, mental health "experts," and so on. Self-interest then dictates that as many children be removed as possible. To justify leaving perpetrators at large, the ideology of "rehabilitation" is invoked. Crime then becomes redefined as mental illness. At this point there is no way to draw a clear line: the definition of "mental illness" becomes ever broader to include everyone whose beliefs threaten the industry. Tyranny in six simple steps.

You may think I am overstating the case. If anything, I am understating it. Once crime is not punished because it is *wrong*, once we abandon the ideal of justice and replace it with the ideal of Rehabilitation and Mental Health, it's open season on anyone who irritates the elite. Consider this diatribe:

> I am arguing for more than a separation of state and church; I am arguing for a separation of fantasy and reality as a necessary precondition for producing *mentally healthy* and responsible citizens. . . .
>
> There are laws in most states which prevent the insane and the feeble-minded from having or raising children. Since no one but a moron or a lunatic can believe . . . the Christian religion . . . is the indisputable truth, one wonders why believers are excluded from such prudent legal restrictions. . . . I am for keeping religion out of the churches and the home; in fact, I am for abolishing religion altogether. . . .[19]

If you should happen to, like the author of the above jeremiad, dislike Christians, think how his speech would sound with the word "Jew" or "atheist" or *whatever you are* substituted for "Christian." Once the ideology of Mental Health becomes the accepted background for discussions of right and wrong, the prejudices of whoever is in charge will dictate whether you are allowed to marry, to have children, or to keep the ones you have. No such campaign to eliminate unpopular families could possibly exist under the law of Justice.

Capital punishment or physical punishments for physical violence are messy, and therefore out of style in our sterilized society. Lifetime imprisonment for rape and murder (the only reasonable alternative for these crimes) is expensive. But consider the alternative—unrestrained power for the child abuse industry to, at any time, "discover" *your* values are anti-social and "sick." Are you willing to lose your children to defend murderers and rapists from punishment?

BEYOND THE CHILD ABUSE INDUSTRY

We have never needed the child abuse industry, and we don't need it now. Police are far better qualified to investigate crimes than are social workers; and social workers have no business forcing themselves on families that have committed no crime. Coercive social work simply has no right to exist. We need to get rid of coercive social work and replace it with justice and *voluntary* help.

Our future should not hold an ever-increasing, parasitic bureaucracy whose main job is meddling in families. Although many good people work in this bureaucracy, good people have worked in other industries that time has left behind. The smart ones voluntarily left. Those not so smart continued to clamor for government to prop up their antiquated jobs instead of realistically accepting the need for change. This cycle, which has occurred again and again in outmoded or overpriced industries such as steel, will naturally occur if we seek to replace the child abuse industry with more humane responses. In spite of the screaming about "jobs being lost," we should press forward to cut back this industry. Any job the taxpayers no longer have to support liberates more than enough money for a corresponding, more honorable job somewhere else.

The world needs statisticians, clerks, typists, office managers, and those with compassion for families.

We just don't need them as our masters.

COUNTERFORCE *13*

For every action, Sir Isaac Newton said, there is an equal and opposite reaction. This law does not hold true in politics. For every action of the child abuse industry so far, there has been almost no reaction at all.

Nothing in the nature of things guarantees that the child abuse industry will not continue to expand. If you don't like the vision of the bureaucrats' Brave New World spelled out in this book, it's up to you to do something about it.

Most people, once they find that the law threatens their families, want to know how to defend themselves. The reaction is natural, but no permanent relief is available this way. Appendix I lists strategies which have been somewhat successful.

For permanent protection, we need permanent changes. First, become acquainted with the *real* roots of child abuse hysteria, which you will see are identical to the real roots of child abuse. This will both help you see through the so-called "prevention" programs, whose actual purpose is to make kids distrust their parents and all other adults, and give you an idea of what kinds of political action *really* help children. Next, we must band together to squeeze out the child abuse industry. We need to replace the "experts" with our personal friends and relatives, to regain responsibility for our own families, and to develop a sense of community. And finally, it is time to take a step above and challenge the materialistic view of our age that increasing government control is a necessary part of life in the twentieth century.

Some of the most urgent strategies to accomplish these goals are outlined below.

KNOW THY ENEMY: THE COMMON ROOT OF CHILD ABUSE HYSTERIA AND CHILD ABUSE

The reason child abuse hysteria took such immediate hold is that we have become an anti-child society. As Marie Winn suggests persuasively in her book *Children Without Childhood*, there is a dark undercurrent of resentment towards children in our society. Mrs. Winn pointed out the rash of "child-monster" movies and books, beginning in the Sixties with *Rosemary's Baby* and *The Exorcist*, and wondered if these books and movies revealed a desire to see children as powerful enemies (thus justifying hating them).

The longer I've pondered Mrs. Winn's thesis, the more valid it appears. Child-monster movies may be the most flagrant case of adults casting children in the role of a powerful enemy, but all our media are loaded with images of powerful children, sexual children, intimidating children. Even the Sears catalog has swung away from the open-faced child models once featured in those pages to a more decadent, hostile, and come-on look.

The media shift to debunking childhood innocence and helplessness reveals sinister things about us adults. If preteens' fannies sell jeans, as Norman Lear has noted disparagingly, it's only because someone out there *likes* that image of children.

Which brings us to a new thesis, and a new strategy for preventing child abuse. The thesis is that *child abuse hysteria is a self-righteous coverup for anti-child attitudes*. People who don't want to have children and don't want to raise them themselves even if they do have them find the child abuse issue a convenient way of proving their love for children. By crusading loudly against wicked child abusers, child advocates both establish an unclouded image as lovers of children and get a chance to point the finger at someone more anti-child than they. It's the "at least I don't" part of human behavior bubbling to the surface. "Sure, I had ten abortions, but at least *I* don't abuse children." "Yeah, I put my child in day care at birth, but at least *I* am not an abuser."

As Allan Carlson notes in his excellent piece on child-saving,

> The constant media focus on abusive parents from intact, suburban families belies the fact that a greatly disproportionate number of the serious physical abuse cases are found in the otherwise celebrated "female-headed families," commonly involving the illegitimate father or mother's current boyfriend. The attack on the middle-class and traditional values also cloaks the growing problems of real neglect caused by a spiraling divorce rate and working mothers with "latch key" children. As [psychologist W. R.] Coulson suggests, the concentration on child abuse allows these categories of child abandoners to "steer attention away from their own sin by pointing at this awful thing which others do."[1]

Now the parents of day-care children can self-righteously condemn mothers who stay home instead of feeling guilty because parents in circumstances similar to theirs are willing to make the sacrifice to put their children first. Now the parents of children in public school can feel superior to those who spend the extra money to enroll their offspring in private school, or the extra time to homeschool them, because "who knows what goes on in those places." How clever this is. Spending time with one's own children and taking extra responsibility for their spiritual upbringing, instead of being the epitome of parental love, has been transformed overnight into a symptom of abusive tendencies! Now the compulsory institutionalization of all children can proceed apace.

The thrust of child abuse hysteria has *always* been to separate children from parents and remove the parents' influence. Family life controlled by state "experts"; *total* control, beginning with deciding who gets to have children and continuing right into mandating a new state religion, the religion of Health—these are the "solutions" the hysterics invariably propose as the only way to combat the so-called epidemic of child abuse: an epidemic that appears to have been invented *solely to give credibility to the proposed "solutions."*

If the new thesis is that child abuse hysteria arises out of anti-child attitudes, the new strategy for countering both child abuse and child abuse hysteria is to *recognize and challenge those basic anti-child attitudes.*

MODERN ANTI-CHILD ACTIVITIES

- Abortion tortures babies to death. It also leads to anti-child attitudes. If you can legally murder your child before birth, it's hard to understand why you can't slap him around afterwards. Those who scoff at this linkage may be interested to know that the Canadian provinces which forbid or limit abortion have vastly lower child abuse rates than those which do not.[2]

- Pornography is inherently anti-baby—it divorces sex from reproduction. As I pointed out in an earlier book, this leads quite inevitably to departing from normal man/woman sex.[3] If having sex has nothing to do with having babies, you can have sex with anyone or anything. Including children. Which just happens to be the current pornographic trend.

- Sexual infidelity, so much glamorized by the media, is present in the vast majority of sexual abuse cases.

- Drunkenness has been shown again and again to be a factor in serious crimes against children. This is common sense—doing a dreadful deed is easy if one's conscience is thoroughly sedated.

Common sense should also lead us to look for ways to reduce drunkenness.

● Age segregation increasingly alienates children and adults. Children are the "new niggers," a term I absolutely hate, but that is the only one to convey the force with which adult society rejects them. Not only are children barred from almost all adult activities (up to and including the worship of God), but the idea that the society of children is actually *bad* for their parents, and vice versa, is gaining ground.

In our brand-new set of World Book *Childcraft* volumes, a set designed specifically for loving parents who willingly spend large sums on enhancing their children's educational environment, we find that the "move away from family ties" will be the "major task of [a child's] teen-age years."[4] According to *Childcraft* "most preteens want to be as far away from the family as possible."[5] This is hailed as necessary and normal, and parents are supposed to willingly allow *all* family ties to be supplanted by "the most important thing in the child's life . . . to be in line with the code of his peers."[6]

And for the parents, *Childcraft* shares the advice that parents need, not only an "evening out," but "days away from home, free from the demands made on them by their child."[7] Actually, *Childcraft's* prescription is fairly mild compared to the fervent anti-baby pleas so common in literature for new mothers. I've seen some that practically order parents to get a babysitter at least once a week to prevent the allegedly unavoidable mental breakdown caused by too much association with their own child.

This is simply family Marxism, pitting the parents (bosses) against the proletariat (children). Family life, instead of being a source of love and enjoyment, is presented as a trap. Children are seen as *enemies* who both resent their parents and who parasitically suck up their parents' energy, wealth, and time.

Until we stop feeding this largely public-school-and-media-created hostility between children and parents, the war will continue, of which child abuse victims are the casualties.

● No-fault divorce has been a disaster for children. Not only does the median income of the children of divorce fall over 70 percent, putting more and more children into poverty,[8] but the whole mindset of no-fault divorce treats children as objects. Children supposedly have no feelings at all. What matters are the feelings of the *adults*.[9] If the adults, or even one of the adults, decides he wants out, the state lets him break his vows to his spouse and children. The man who has sworn to provide for his family, and on whose goodwill the woman has trusted by giving birth to children, is not even required to continue to support them (beyond some kind of token, unenforced effort). Thus doth single-mother poverty make mockers of us all.

Remarriages are also a fruitful source of sexual abuse. In today's sexually overcharged world, where men are trained from youth to regard all women as sexual objects, what's going to make a forty-year-old restrain himself from releasing his lusts on the body of a ripe young twelve-year-old, not even related to him, who is living in his house? Or even, if he indulges in pornography and the growing cult of equally offensive best-selling literature that endorses incest and child molesting, of attacking his three-year-old stepdaughter? Some men marry women just to gain access to children. But again, who tells us about this? Who warns women to check out their hot dates or new fiancees for sexual inclinations toward their children? Who cries out that serial marriage is not just as nice as for-real, monogamous marriage? Who?

It's time to speak out against the *real* roots of child abuse: abortion, pornography, sexual infidelity, drunkenness, no-fault divorce, age segregation, and the growing enslavement of both fathers and mothers in the corporate-industrial workforce. It's also time to speak out *for* having babies, for raising one's own children, for the joys of large family life, for home business, for sexual fidelity, for clean entertainment, for life, for God!

MOVING OUT

Now, a few modest proposals. These are essential for cleaning up child abuse hysteria and providing justice for North American children and their families. The footnotes indicate responsible individuals and groups who have made these suggestions.

- A definition of child abuse that includes genuine crimes against children but does not allow a government elite to dictate what is permissible child-rearing practice.[10] This definition should not only be enacted into law, but should be publicized so that every mother and father knows what is and what is not allowed, and what the penalties are for child abuse. See the appendix for a sample definition.

- No more anonymous accusers. Abolish the child abuse hotlines. North America doesn't need the KGB.[11]

- If a child ever must be removed (due to abandonment or some other reasonable cause) he should be placed with relatives, friends, church members, or others who know him and who he trusts. The state should not be in the business of competing with families for children.[12]

- Even under our current system, removal should never even be considered except in cases of demonstrable life-threatening harm. The child should never be removed and the perpetrator left in the home when evidence exists sufficient to make an accusation.[13]

- Our present system of liability encourages social workers to take children needlessly. This is because social workers can be sued if a child dies who is left in the home, but not if he is taken wrongfully, except in unusual circumstances.

First, as long as social workers are allowed to remove children the liability laws should be balanced so social workers have no incentive to misuse their authority. Douglas Besharov's suggestion of "good faith" immunity for social workers (which would *not* protect them from lawsuits in cases when they acted contrary to the law) is excellent.[14] Social workers aren't God: it's ridiculous to hold them guilty for cases in which they would have had to infallibly predict the future. Then, we should return to a (dare I say it?) scriptural doctrine of liability, which limits the plaintiff to receiving only reimbursement for actual expenses incurred. We would not have a plague of multi-million-dollar lawsuits if all you could get out of suing was a reimbursement for your medical bill and lost work time.

Parents should not have to go bankrupt fighting false charges. Let the state and its agents take some responsibility for the expenses its victims incur.

- The whole facade of psychological examinations and evaluations should be scrapped. What matters is a parent's *behavior*, not somebody's theories. Forget about psychiatric courtroom "experts" and their $1,000 per day fees. Get rid of child protective agencies' "pet" doctors whose interest lies in finding child abuse in each and every case they see. Let any necessary medical examinations be done by a doctor or clinic of the parents' choice. If it turns out negative, let the state pay the fee.[15]

- Let the police be the police. Criminal investigations are their proper work. When social workers investigate cases that, if substantiated, can add to their caseload, thus protecting their jobs, this is a glaring conflict of interest.[16]

● Crimes against children should be prosecuted. Swiftly. Effectively. Regardless of the criminal's relationship to the victim.[16] Suggested penalties are outlined in the previous chapter.

REAL AND PHONY CHILD ABUSE PREVENTION

The list above addresses the legal shortcomings of our present system. It does not cover the question of "how should we prevent child abuse?" That question has perhaps the farthest-reaching consequences of any political decision of our day, yet average parents have been squeezed out of the discussion.

To date, the proposals for child abuse prevention have been submitted by those who had their ideas in hand even before the "problem" was labeled as such. These are: eliminate corporal punishment and all forms of parental authority, teach four-year-olds about incest, put all children in day care, give the government control of private schools, and so on. They want to eliminate child abuse by eliminating parents.

Particularly obnoxious about all this is that, since the child abuse industry networks with the public schools, children are being propagandized in a phony "prevention" strategy at taxpayer expense. For example, Kansas recently declared April as Stop Violence Month.

As part of a month of domestic violence and child abuse issues activities, more than 30,000 children are expected to release helium-filled balloons imprinted with the message, "Up, Up and Away With Violence," at 1:30 p.m. April 25 from the school yards of more than 100 Kansas elementary schools. . . .

Children write slogans on a piece of paper that is attached to the balloon.

The day before, April 24, has been declared "No Hitter Day." [The founder of the Kansas Committeee for the Prevention of Child Abuse, SuEllen] Fried expressed a desire that that day become to non-violence what the smoke-out day has become to the American Cancer Society.

The Stop Violence Campaign, in conjunction with the Menninger Foundation, will sponsor a second National Conference on Violence in the Family. There experts will examine what may be done to prevent abuse. Last year more than eighty-five people attended.

"What we're talking about is changing the value system of our country," Fried said.[17]

We are all against violence. But this newspaper report is disturbing because

(1) Public school children are being indoctrinated that corporal punishment is violent and wrong *when the law does not so state*. Public schools, in fact, have a Supreme Court-upheld right to apply corporal punishment, and by analogy so do parents. This public-school-sponsored event is coercive propaganda.

(2) As the article indicates, eighty-five men and women are supposed to meet for a national conference and decide our private family decisions for us.

(3) As the article also states, the views being foisted on us are *not* consistent with the behavior of most of us. "Changing the value system of our country" through rational discussion and persuasion is one thing. Using the public school to broker these attitude changes, and exploiting children as propaganda-pumpers, is another.

(4) Lastly, the people choreographing this razzle-dazzle aren't even aware of the most basic facts about child abuse. Ms. Fried, for example, elsewhere in the article says, "They say one out of four young girls is sexually abused . . . They also say one out of six young boys is sexually abused." *Who* says, we ask? Not even the eighty-five experts who are going to single-handedly eliminate child abuse in America. Both the National Center on Child Abuse and Neglect and the National Committee for the Prevention of Child Abuse deny originating those statistics. *Nobody* knows where they come from!

Ironically, the article itself contradicts Ms. Fried's assertion. As it says,

A total of 23,595 incidences of child abuse were reported in Kansas last year. Of that number, 6,564 were confirmed [which means false reports were almost 3/4 of the total]; 310 children were hospitalized and 11 children died.

It's sad that eleven children (out of a population of two million plus) died in Kansas last year of alleged child abuse. But writing slogans on paper and flying balloons won't help.

In return, here are some proposals that I believe cut to the *real* roots of child abuse. You may take them or leave them, although I hope you will find them convincing. *Real* child abuse prevention comes from an inward change of heart reflected in outward behavior, not through a coercive government program dreamed up by Washington experts without the input of the people and imposed monolithically without their consent.

- Abolish no-fault divorce. Reinstate the penalties previously attached to breaking the marriage vows. Spell out what these penalties are, and before the wedding have couples sign an agreement that if contested will stand up in court. Then *hold them to it.* If a man wants to promise he will forsake all others and provide for his wife, let him *in advance* agree to penalties if he fails to uphold his vow. Same for the woman. It's outrageously dishonest to let starry-eyed couples make wedding vows in church as if the vows meant something, without any social sanctions against those who faithlessly break their word.

For starters, how about agreeing to forfeit the children and one's share of the mutual property if one commits adultery or deserts one's spouse? How about signing a marriage covenant which specifies that alimony *would* be paid in the above cases? That would bring the herd of mid-life males divorcing their wives for some young thing to a neck-snapping halt.

Every parent who commits adultery or who files for what would have been a contested divorce if marriage vows still meant anything is *rejecting his children.* He (and it usually is a he) is saying, "The space twenty-five centimeters below my waist matters more to me than you do, children dear." How can we encourage this and claim to be concerned for children?

If a man or woman intends to commit adultery and live like a single while married, let them spell this out in their marriage contract. Then see who'll take them. Let's have some honesty in advertising here.

- As long as pornography is a big part of American macho culture the laws against it will never be enforced. Isn't it about time to enlist some peer pressure? Responsible married sex, which includes willingness to have children, is wonderful. Other kinds of sex are not. That is why those who practice them are, as the title of Marilyn Chambers' movie puts it, Insatiable.

  Pornographic sex is not macho. It is childish. Any dog can do it—it takes a man to show restraint. If women, who are the biggest victims of porn to the tune of several hundred thousand rapes per year, started morally boycotting men who feast on the stuff, wouldn't this accomplish something?

  The existing laws against pornography should be enforced. But even if they are not, those who are morally opposed to porn have a right to make their feelings known in the society of others. Let's promote self-control and the beauties of fatherhood in our conversation and lives (*not* with balloon campaigns forced on captive children). Every woman alive has something to gain from this.

- Intergenerational togetherness. The homeschool movement is a giant step toward a pro-child society. Homeschooling parents not only spend considerable time with their children, but create a host of family activities that the generations enjoy together, such as field trips. Homeschooled children regularly participate in community events, not having received the school prejudice against people outside their age group.

  In general, children benefit from being sent into institutional school settings later, rather than earlier. See Dr. Raymond Moore's books on this, and my own *Big Book of Home Learning* (Crossway Books, 1986) for a catalog of home school products and methods.

- Networking. We have got to short-circuit the monopoly of "experts" on child-rearing theory. Younger parents and experienced parents need to get together and find out what *really* works. The biblical structure of the Christian church, with older families instructing the younger, is ideally suited for this. The bureaucratic model presently so much in favor is not. See my book *The Way Home* (Crossway Books, 1985) if you'd like to look into this.

These are just suggestions, but I believe they demonstrate the difference between a genuinely pro-child child abuse prevention program and the phony, paranoid "prevention" programs presently being pushed.

If we aren't willing to confront our anti-child prejudices and treat babies as a blessing and children as people who deserve to be brought up by their very own parents, then why waste time complaining about child abuse? If we aren't willing to punish those who do it, why ask them to stop?

We don't need the child abuse industry, as this book has shown. Nonetheless, we will be ruled by their schemes if we don't get our own houses in order. The child abuse industry is something, and you can't fight something with nothing. We must fight fire with fire. If we want less government intervention, we must accept the responsibility for self-government. If we want the freedom to raise our children according to our beliefs, we had better find out what they are. If we don't want to see children exploited as sex objects, we had better make sure that we have our thinking straight about sex.

Our danger is also our opportunity. Maybe now that our own

children are being attacked by the elite, we will finally find enough energy to analyze and reject the elite's ideals. Perhaps this grave threat to our personal liberties will alarm the Sunday morning worshippers enough to put their faith into practice the other six days of the week.

DEUS EX MACHINA

Many have written about the dangers of bureaucracy in our age. Now, with the invention of a child abuse "epidemic," bureaucrats have the tools to wield unprecedented control over us. As a UPI Bureau Chief accused of child abuse said, "I've lived through two totalitarian regimes, but I've never seen anything like this."[18]

At such moments, our tendency is to feel weak and helpless. Which is just fine. We *are* weak and helpless. None of us is God, to right all wrongs with a judicial "Let there be justice!"

George Roche, in his insightful book on the bureaucracy entitled *America By the Throat*, and Alexander Solzhenitsyn in his writing about the Russian state system, have both pinpointed the only ultimate cure for a state that tries to play God: God Himself.

When the forces controlling our lives seem irresistible, it is well to remember that God is not controlled by those forces. Rather, He is controlling them.

The history of our century is that of man rejecting God and trying to create his own utopia. It is also the history of the Holocaust, of the deliberate starving of millions in Russia by Stalin, of the massacre of millions more by Mao, of the Pathet Lao, in short, of totalitarianism. Historian Paul Johnson has said that totalitarianism is the most important movement of our times.[19]

So where is God in the midst of this? He is letting us have the fruit of our own stubborn schemes. Russia wanted a man to worship, and they got Stalin. Germany got Hitler. China got Mao. We North Americans prefer to worship ourselves, so we got the child abuse industry. We don't want to take the responsibility of raising our own children, as God requires? All right, they'll be gone. We don't want to sacrifice ourselves for our children? Fine, there'll be no more children for whom to sacrifice.

Don't ever say God is harsh and unloving because of this. *We asked for it.* Now it's time to start asking for something a bit more sensible: like mercy.

14 THE SECOND NORTH AMERICAN REVOLUTION

Trust in God and keep your powder dry—Oliver Cromwell (1599-1658), leader of a successful revolution in England against the tyrannical King Charles I.

The Revolution had its beginnings in the hearts and minds of the people—John Adams (1735-1826), great American patriot, a leader in the American Revolution, and second President of the United States of America.

O, Canada! Glorious and *free* . . .—from the Canadian National Anthem.

Oh, say does that Star-Spangled Banner yet wave
O'er the land of the free, and the home of the brave?—from the U.S.A. National Anthem.

You and I were brought up to be led. In school we were taught that government experts alone had the answers to the problems of our countries. Social studies texts praised every government program and idolized those who had led the movement towards ever-stronger government and ever-weaker citizens. Never did these texts suggest that everyday people like you and me could or should shake the world.

American Constitutional lawyer John Whitehead has written an excellent book on the bureaucratic takeover called *The Second American Revolution* (Crossway Books, 1984). It explains how U.S.A. bureaucrats have overthrown most of our Constitutional rights. This, against only feeble protests. In the U.S.A., as in Canada and the rest of the Western world, the population has allowed its rights to be stolen in return for government promises of peace and safety—promises which have not been fulfilled.

Mr. Whitehead's message is excellent, but his book's title is misleading. We have not had a Second American Revolution; we have had an American Counter-Revolution. Everything for which the founders of the United States pledged their "lives, fortunes, and sacred honors" is either lost or in immediate danger of being swept away. In Canada and elsewhere it's the same.

Judges now rule with no regard for the Constitution. Legislators allow government agencies to break the law without penalty. Governors endorse plans for total control of your and my children. Could this be the end of the rule of Law, and the beginning of anarchy or dictatorship?

No! History is not like a children's slide, where countries start at the top and then plummet to the bottom. Under God, average people can change history. It's happened before.

Not everyone has remained silent. When God was banned from the public schools, parents began private schools and home schools. Today in the U.S.A. one out of every four children is enrolled outside the public schools. When the spurious "right to privacy" was invented as an excuse for legalizing abortion, pro-lifers began picketing and sitting in at abortion clinics and founding crisis pregnancy centers. Today in the U.S.A. there are more crisis pregnancy centers than abortuaries. When zoning boards started quietly zoning all new churches far out of town, some people began worshipping in their homes. One zoning board in Colorado tried to ban a home Bible study that created no noise or parking problem. But instead of crawling away in defeat, the pastor in question is *fighting*. When Canadian legislators were considering issues of state, a Christian position never used to be mentioned. But now a preacher friend of mine and his students are preaching on the Capitol steps!

Some people don't like this. Grass-roots movements aren't predictable and bland, like toothpaste. But where they are, there is liberty.

So far the bureaucracy has concentrated mostly on economic affairs, with the predictable result that the rich get richer and the poor get poorer. Now it's baring its fangs, attacking both God and our children. If the present trend continues, as documented in this book, you will not be allowed to have, raise, or keep your own children if you disagree with the government in any way.

If you are willing to give bureaucrats total power over your family, there's nothing more to say. But if you love your children enough to fight for them, come join the real Second North American Revolution.

We have just now begun to fight.

REVOLUTION, NOT REBELLION

If, as the Bible says, "rebellion is as the sin of witchcraft" (I Sam 15:23 KJV), then standing against oppression is as the virtue of godliness. Rebellion is attempting to overthrow legitimate authority, usually because of envy and selfish ambition. But unlimited bureaucracy is *not* a legitimate authority by either the laws of God or the constitutions of man. As the Bible also asks, "Can a corrupt throne be allied with you [O God], one that brings on misery by its decrees?" (Psalm 94:20). The answer, obviously, is "No, it cannot."

Thus, believers and non-believers alike may feel free to ignore the dictates of public policy which contravene our Constitutional rights.

Here is a list of suggested activities. All are more or less subversive of the Established Order. The child abuse industry will tear its collective hair out if you do them. Enjoy.

EVERYDAY REVOLUTIONS

(1) Have a baby. Don't let the buzzards get you down. Getting too scared to have kids is total surrender.

(2) Stay married. Divorce makes your children the property of the state. Every one of the really messy child abuse cases I've encountered, where bureaucrats were playing hopscotch with a family, involved the children of divorce. The buzzards pick on *dead* families.

(3) Help to kill the market for institutional care of children. Stay home if at all possible. Spend more time with your kids. Take responsibility for raising them. Instead of Mom and Dad fighting to be first out the door and into an outside job, consider home business.

(4) Don't become a foster parent—*especially* if you have children of your own. I've heard too many sad stories of foster parents losing their own children because of some spurious accusation from the foster child or his natural parents. Our goal should be to eliminate foster care entirely and replace it with "clan care" where every needy child is taken care of by relatives or friends. Most kids in foster care right now ought to be returned. Don't both support our present corrupt system and set yourself up as a sacrifice to it.

(5) Organize a parent support group, preferably in your church. Seek out older, experienced parents and grandparents to lead this group. Learn from the wisdom of experience instead of the theories of "experts."

(6) If you're a grandmother or grandfather, have some pity on the younger generation. Be willing to share your experience. Why not write a book?

(7) Pull your kids out of public school. That will hit the child abuse industry where it hurts. While you're at it, vote against all school bonds. We do *not* need compulsory Early Childhood Education and the other grandiose schemes for which new school bonds inevitably earmark a significant amount.

tion and the other grandiose schemes for which new school bonds inevitably earmark a significant amount.

(8) Demand that La Leche League and any other organizations to which you may belong stop labeling corporal punishment and other forms of traditional discipline as child abuse. Even if you personally disagree with these forms of discipline, you have your own lifestyle to defend, which could just as easily be labeled abusive.

(9) Give no support whatsoever to universities whose social work and psychology programs incorporate the doctrines of the child abuse industry. Do not enroll in those programs. Let these schools know why you are not supporting them.

(10) Give no support whatsoever to hospitals that support removal of newborns into "crisis nurseries" and that routinely phone in parents for suspected abuse. Your parents' group or, even better, childbirth education group should demand *as a group* that local hospitals reveal their policies on these matters. Childbirth groups have been successful already at getting hospitals to be more customer-oriented. Each hospital is hungry for your dollars. No hospital would like the public to know that they turn in their customers for child abuse. If the hospitals in your area prove uncooperative, home birth is a viable alternative. In any case, your group should support the midwifery movement, which can demonstrate many benefits for those it serves.

(11) Your parents' group should sound out local doctors and try to gain their support for a revival of laws favoring medical confidentiality. The present laws create unnecessary tension between families and their doctors and create incentives for denying abused children necessary medical care.

(12) *Don't hotline anyone.* If you see evidence that a crime has been committed against a child, *call the police.* Cases where the police perform the initial investigation have a much higher chance of actually making it to court, where they belong. If, as a mandatory reporter, you feel you must call the hotline, call it well *after* the police have come and gone. The law does not specify that you must call the hotline immediately. As for reporting your "suspicions" if you are a mandatory reporter: any law that meddles with your *thoughts* is innately wrong. Ignore it.

(13) Stay in touch with your friends and family. Isolated families are the ones who get picked off. Covenant with your friends, and possibly your church, that you will defend each other if attacked by the state. You'd be amazed what the presence of four or five friends can do for the tone of an investigation or a courtroom hearing. Financial help may also be in order. The child abuse industry, with unlimit-

ed government resources, often wins its cases by starving the family out, making the case drag on until their finances are exhausted. Let your church minister to the needs of these truly needy victims of the system. You don't have to believe every sob story you hear, but you should consider lending a hand in cases where the state was obviously abusing the family.

LEGISLATIVE REVOLUTIONS

(1) Find out who is representing you at the state level. Look in the phone book for the Republican or Democratic Committee for your area and call them up. They can tell you what you need to know. Right now, state government is where the action is. Most people also don't know anything about state government. That is why you can make a big difference.

(2) Join a political action group. You will find pro-family groups listed in the appendix. This need not be a heavy commitment. One or two letters or phone calls a year at appropriate times can really influence your legislators. But you won't know what or when to write unless you're in touch with a group that can keep you informed. Do it.

(3) First things first. Plug for a *solid definition* of child abuse (like the one in the Appendix), for *abolishing the hotline* or at least *abolishing anonymous accusations*, for *criminal penalties for perpetrators*, for *court trials with rules of evidence*, for *removal limited to life-threatening situations*, for *preferential placment of removed children with family or friends*, for *automatic firing of government agents who transgress the law*. Don't get distracted with lesser issues until these are settled. If the political climate in your state is ripe, introduce the idea of letting the police investigate and handle child abuse cases. Plant the seed.

(4) Never vote for a non-repentant bureaucrat. Never vote for a candidate whose campaign promises include "doing more for children," meaning more government takeover of families. One way the child abuse industry expands its control is by nominating and electing its own in-house bureaucrats. Oppose this with all your might.

(5) Your political group should start a Judge Watch. Once in, judges tend to stay in forever because nobody knows what kind of justice they deal out. If you have an elected judge in your district who believes that child molesters should be given probation and innocent families should be broken up, spread his record around to the voters.

(6) Never vote for increasing government revenues. The more money, the more oppression. Smaller government would have to concentrate on serious cases; big government needs to create problems to justify its existence.

(7) Take your family to the Capitol and introduce them to your legislators. Keep in touch with them. Get this book into their hands. Most of the time, the only input legislators have is from special interest groups. Yet most legislators are very interested in serving their constituents. Know your legislators personally, if you have time for this. Help the good ones with their campaigns. Nothing keeps social workers honest like knowing they are dealing with someone who "knows someone."

(8) If you're a well-organized, attractive person with a history of success in leadership, you may want to go for the big time and start a Families Union in your state. The Union could provide for its members such things as legal insurance, free flowers and meals when a new baby arrives, a Grandparents Club of volunteers to help younger families, group outings that *include* children, local support groups, a newsletter with political news affecting families and ads for items families (especially large families) might have trouble finding in stores, maybe even a political arm to represent the Union. The churches of a state could start such a Union, whose membership should be open to all, as a ministry. Or you could do it on your own. New parents should have somewhere to turn before the child abuse industry grabs them and indoctrinates them into fearing to be in the same room with their child.

ACCURACY IN MEDIA

(1) Challenge every false statistic or slogan you see in print or hear on the air. Ask the reporter where he or she obtained this statistic. Make them think. You might want to present the reporter with a copy of this book.

(2) Participate in call-in shows. Tell your story, if you have one, or the story of a friend, or share the facts.

(3) Your group may want to consider presenting awards to the local media that provide the most responsible coverage of the child abuse issue.

ACTIVISM IS JUST THE OPPOSITE OF FLABBINESS

As you see, protecting your children from the child abuse industry can actually be fun. Outings to the State Capitol; trips to the Zoo with your Families Union group; making new friends in your local support group; award dinners for responsible journalists; these are all enjoyable as well as profitable. All we need is a few dedicated individuals to get it started, and the blessing of God.

Picture a future where each generation respects the other, where families are no longer isolated in the suburban ghetto or inner city but part of a loving circle of friends, where parents enjoy their children and children their parents, where child abuse is a thing of the past! It can happen.

Please, help make it happen.

APPENDICES

HOTLINE PREVENTION, AND WHAT TO DO IF YOU ARE HOTLINED

Your children are not safe in your home, and never will be until the laws are changed. However, there are some things you can do to make your family less vulnerable, and some actions you can take to defend yourself if you are falsely accused of child abuse or neglect.

HOTLINE PREVENTION

Any family can be hotlined by an anonymous accuser. Your personal chances of getting hotlined, however, are decreased if you take care to cultivate friendly relations with others. Fighting with the neighbors is one of the best ways to invite a nasty hotline call. On the other hand, those who try to "do unto others as you would have them do unto you," who mow the grass of the widow lady next door and help out when others need help, are much less likely to be hotlined.

Avoid isolation. Reach out and make a few friends. Join a good church. Families who are unknown and isolated are prime targets.

Try to dress your children nicely whenever you go out in public—but not *too* nicely. Also, impress on them the importance of politeness and quiet good manners. Loud, rowdy kids irritate people, and irritated people make hotline calls.

Buy a portable cassette recorder and a good supply of cassettes and batteries. You will need it if you are ever investigated. A video camera, for those who can afford it, is a good thing to have around the house.

If your child is injured, take him to your own private doctor if at all possible. Emergency room personnel are trained to be oversuspicious of child abuse in all child injury cases.

Line up a good attorney before you are ever hotlined. You want one who will fight for your rights, not one who undermines you. Contact the pro-family groups in your state for leads on which attorneys have a good record of winning child abuse cases. Get the names of several attorneys, if possible, so if one is on vacation or otherwise unavailable when you need him, you have a backup.

Of course, the best defense is a good offense. Join with others in changing the child abuse laws, and you will have the best support network around.

IF YOU ARE HOTLINED

The social worker is at the door. Now what?

First, make sure the person at your door *is* a child protective services worker. Ask for identification, then excuse yourself, go to the telephone, and call the county office of child protective services to verify that a worker has been dispatched to investigate you. Do not open the door; tape-record the exchange between you and the worker. You have a right to make sure that an imposter is not attempting to gain access to your children.

Next, call your lawyer. If he's not willing to hurry over to your house to be there at the interview, call another.

If your husband is not home, call him home. If you have relatives in town, ask them to come over. If you have time, call a few friends and neighbors and collect them as witnesses to what happens next.

Now, take the tape recorder and go back to the door. In some states it appears that policemen are allowed to break your door down and take your children; in others they aren't, but a policeman or social worker may threaten to nonetheless. Try to keep things cool. Tell the worker that she can see the children through the screen door to see that they are O.K., and that you will be glad to make an appointment with her at her office at some convenient time.

If the caseworker can see that the children are all right, she has no reasonable cause to object to an office interview. However, most caseworkers are virtually untrained, and according to a number of lawyers and judges I have talked to, the newer ones are often arrogant. She may demand entrance. You do not want to let a social worker in, because once inside she has a "fishing license" to build a case against you. She may poke in the refrigerator to see if it contains any spoiled food; take notes about the unswept kitchen floor or the cracked window pane in your study; look through the family photo album for pictures of bare babies; and worst of all, take your children off alone, with no witnesses, and then swear in court that she heard them accuse you of abuse. Everything you have ever said or done can and will be construed as evidence against you, no matter how innocent.

What you want to find out is what you are accused of, so you can disprove the charge. You do not want to give a social worker the opportunity to snoop around your house inventing new charges.

Obviously, if a policeman breaks down your front door and snatches your children, you can't do much about this. But if the social worker is alone, she can't take your children. So be polite; don't panic; negotiate; and try to assemble your witnesses.

The minute the social worker leaves, it's time for you to start building your case. The state will not do this for you. It will expend no energy whatever on uncovering evidence that proves you are not guilty. The first step is to have the children thoroughly examined by your private physician, no matter what the charge. Charges of physical or emotional abuse can easily turn into charges of sexual abuse once state doctors get their hands on your children. Document everything. If the social worker acted rudely or strangely, report this at once *in writing* to the head of the division in your state.

Keep in close touch with your lawyer. You need to understand what is happening so you can make the correct legal decisions.

Under no circumstances sign anything or agree to anything that abridges your rights. Some social workers will tell you that "if you don't sign this paper you will never see your children again." If you can get this on tape, that's great. Pass it around to your state legislators. In any case, don't sign. You will be pleading guilty and waiving your right to a court trial. Too many families have desperately agreed to a child protective division's "plan for reuniting the family" only to be put through hoops for years with no chance of getting their children back.

If your children were taken, either from your home or (more likely) directly from school, daycare, or put into protective custody at a hospital, don't panic. You will be tempted to agree to anything to get them back. But your best chance of getting them back is to show some backbone and willingness to fight. Resolve that, if necessary, you will picket the hospital or school where this happened; write letters to the editor; appear on talk shows; visit your legislators; spend your family fortune on lawsuits; write magazine articles; and make yourself such a grade-A, number-one nuisance that the state will be sorry it ever thought of meddling with you. Be polite, but relentless.

I heard of one mother who, threatened with losing her newborn, ran screaming through the maternity ward, "They're stealing my baby!" She got the baby back. Although the screaming-in-the-halls method is not choice number one, that mother put her finger on the message you'll want to convey: "They're stealing my children!"

APPENDIX II
A SUGGESTED DEFINITION OF CHILD ABUSE AND NEGLECT

The following definition is suggested as a starting point for child abuse reporting laws. Based on a formula created by Missouri Parents and Children, it seeks to define abuse and neglect in a clearcut fashion. Mild bruising and scrapes, such as every child acquires in the course of normal living, are not defined as injury; bruising severe enough to cause incapacitation, such as an inability to walk or eat, is. Neglect is defined as *wilful* failure to provide the essentials of life, which are spelled out in order to avoid spurious courtroom interpretations. Emotional maltreatment is not included, since (a) it is impossible to define satisfactorily and (b) the state can't guarantee an adequate emotional environment for the children in its own custody. Sexual abuse is no longer assumed; it must be proven that the contact was sexual, thus relieving parents, family members, and child care workers from paranoia. Affection and diaper-changing are not to be viewed with suspicion.

This definition could be improved. For one thing, it would be a good idea to explicitly declare in the law that midwifery, chiropractic, and other forms of alternative medical and surgical care do not constitute neglect. However, it is a starting point for a bill to submit right now to the legislature in your state.

(1) "**Abuse,**" any physical injury or sexual abuse inflicted on a child other than by accidental means, except that discipline by those responsible for his care, custody, and control including spanking, administered so as not to cause physical injury shall not be construed to be abuse;

(2) "**Child,**" any person under eighteen years of age;

(5)"**Neglect,**" wilful failure to provide, by those responsible for the care, custody, and control of the child, food, clothing, or shelter sufficient for life, or essential medical or surgical care; and

(6) "**Those responsible for the care, custody, and control of the child,**" those included but not limited to the parents or guardian of a child, other members of the child's household, or those exercising supervision over a child for any part of a twenty-four hour day.

(7) **"Physical injury,"** any damage to bones or teeth, brain damage, damage to organs, or other internal injuries; poisoning, burns, cuts, or permanent skin disfigurement; or any injury resulting in permanent or temporary incapacitation;

(8) **"Sexual abuse,"** rape, sexual assault, sodomy, indecent exposure, or promoting prostitution as defined by law; or non-accidental touching of genitals, buttocks, or breasts for which no non-sexual reason can be found. Non-sexual reasons include, but are not limited to, normal physical expression of affection and necessary hygienic or medical care.

APPENDIX III
PRO-FAMILY GROUPS AND ORGANIZATIONS FOR HOTLINE VICTIMS

Contact these organizations at their listed national addresses for information on state or local chapters near you.

EAGLE FORUM
Box 618
Alton, IL 62002

This pro-family group is best known for its founder, Phyllis Schlafly, and its winning fight against the Equal Rights Amendment. Eagle Forum's motto is "Leading the pro-family movement," and you can expect these savvy ladies to get involved with the child abuse issue at both the state and federal level.

Functions: education, lobbying, media work, meetings, conventions, state groups, special interest groups (such as Eagle Forum's Education Committee).

MISSOURI PARENTS AND CHILDREN (MoPaC)
Box 16866
Clayton, MO 63105

MoPaC, founded by the redoubtable Laura Rogers, is a single-issue group, and that issue is the child abuse laws. MoPaC's specialty is research and offering improvements to the law—i.e., "where should we be going and how do we get from here to there?" For people in Missouri, MoPaC offers a channel through which they can personally affect their state laws for the better.

Functions: education of the membership (including printed instruction on how to lobby by phone or letter), lobbying, media work, research, legislative proposals.

PRO-FAMILY FORUM
P.O. Box 8907
Fort Worth, TX 76112

Pro-Family Forum is a state-by-state lobbying group concerning itself with a wide variety of pro-family issues, ranging from sex clinics in schools to the child abuse laws. Members are trained in lobbying techniques and put to work.

Functions: education, lobbying, media work, meetings, conventions, state groups.

VOCAL (Victims of Child Abuse Laws)
P.O. Box 8536
Minneapolis, MN 55408

VOCAL is *the* group for those victimized by child abuse laws. With an efficient administration, a good media presence, and a fast-growing membership, VOCAL will be going places. When the organization was new, it functioned mainly as a support group for those crushed by their experiences with the state. Now the media are taking note, and we hope legislators will be following suit.

Functions: newsletter, some lobbying in some states, media work, support group meetings, conventions, state and local groups.

NOTES

Introduction

1. Remark delivered at the first VOCAL (Victims of Child Abuse Laws) National Conference, held November 14-16 in St. Paul, Minnesota. Reported in VOCAL Newsletter, Nov/Dec 1985, p. 2. Dr. Besharov made a similar remark in his article "An Overdose of Concern: Child Abuse and the Overreporting Problem," *REGULATION: AEI Journal on Government and Society*, Nov/Dec 1985, p. 28.

Chapter 1—You Are the Target

1. The figure for one million falsely hotlined families per year comes from government statistics. In the U.S.A. alone, 1,024,178 families were hotlined in 1984 (*Highlights of Official Child Neglect and Abuse Reporting 1984*, American Humane Association, Denver, 1986, p. 2, hereafter referred to as *Highlights 1984*). Of this number, 58 percent were unsubstantiated. Of the remainder, less than 10 percent involved anything serious enough to deserve the title "child abuse" (See Chapter 2). This means in the U.S.A. alone, close to a million families who were not guilty of battering, molesting, starving, or otherwise actually harming their children in any objectively verifiable way were hotlined in 1984. Canadian national statistics are unavailable, but what I hear from the provinces tends to confirm that Canadian families are, if anything, treated worse. The Canadian laws are certainly as vague and the social workers' powers as broad.

> • Re those "cleared" by investigations and found unsubstantiated: consider this comment from New Jersey Division of Youth and Family Services head Thomas Blatner (a man who personally "changed the division's policy from guidelines dictating 'least obstrusive' investigation to a philosophy that urged caseworkers to 'err on the side of the child'"—i.e., abandon objectivity and go in with the bias that abuse occurred):

Blatner concedes there are many parents who have been wronged by the division's policy and the state's laws. But he does not deny that *even those whose alleged abuses cannot be proven remain under suspicion.* ("Parents Battle Pain of Child-Abuse Allegations," *North Jersey News*, January 13, 1986.

This includes retaining the "cleared" family's name on central computer records, which are supposed to be deleted after a number of years. Every state has some such law. However, I know of no state with an actual procedure to delete these names. What actually happens is that the "cleared" family gets networked onto national computer systems.

- Re the incredible things the state can require of those accused (and not even proved guilty) of child abuse:

What "intervention" means in practice might come as a shock to some parents.

It came as a shock to Harold and Carole Kanter.

So also to Judy Nokes and Kathleen Zylstra and other parents whose children or foster children were removed without prior notice by workers from the county's Child Protective Services and kept at least forty-eight hours at a place unknown to the parents. In some cases, the children were permanently removed from their homes.

These couples and single parents were ordered by Ventura County Juvenile Court judges to take parenting classes, see psychiatrists, take up a new residence, or send their child to a special school—a situation Kanter likens to life in the Soviet Union. (Lori Schweitzer, "The difficult art of protecting children," *Sunday Star Free Press* (Ventura, CA), p. 1.)

- Re your lack of rights and the financial hazards of being hotlined:

"They (the division) may claim they use a 'preponderance of evidence' standard," says [New Jersey] Public Defender James Louis. "But in fact the only measure they use is whether the caseworker says the abuse took place. The parent's best bet is to get taken before a real judge."

But few of the accused ever see their day in criminal court. Instead, members of the state's advocacy groups spend an average of $8,000 defending themselves against the division's charges. Nearly three-quarters lose at least half their income during the fight, and most report serious physical and emotional damage. ("Parents battle pain.")

- Re losing your children: Among cases opened for "protective services," the rate of children removed from their homes continues to climb. As *Highlights 1984* says, "The 17.7 percent receiving placement services is suggestive of a higher rate than was reported in 1982 and 1983." The laws *do not require evidence that a child is in physical danger* in order for social workers to remove him. There are *no controls* to prevent social workers from removing children from perfectly harmless homes. Even agency heads like New Jersey's Thomas Blatner (quoted above) admit it.

2. The reason our state laws on this subject look like they come from the same cookie cutter is that they do.

On January 31, 1974, Public Law 93-247, the federal "Child Abuse and Prevention Act" became effective. This legislation defined "child abuse and neglect" as "physical or mental injury, sexual abuse, negligent treatment, or maltreatment of a child under the age of eighteen." . . .

Soon thereafter a rash of similar legislation began appearing in state legislatures in order to bring state laws into compliance with the federal law, and *to assure the federal funding provided by the federal law.* [Emphasis mine] (Barbara Morris, *Change Agents in the Schools,*

P.O. Box 756, Upland, California, 91786, The Barbara Morris Report: 1979, p. 91. This book is "must" reading.)

What *is* "mental injury" or "negligent treatment" or "maltreatment"? Nobody knows. However, the states went even further in making "abuse" mean everything or anything. The Missouri law of 1985, for example, instead of requiring "mental injury" to have taken place, loftily speaks of "emotional abuse" (which category includes scolding and belittling) and defines neglect as

> failure to provide, by those responsible for the care, custody, and control of the child, the proper or necessary support, education as required by law, or medical, surgical, *or any other care necessary for his well-being*. (Sections 210:110:1, 5 of the Missouri Statutes, emphasis mine)

The kicker here is the "or any other care necessary for his well-being." All of a sudden, the judges and social workers find themselves in the heady position of being able to define what constitutes "well-being" for a child and threaten parents who do not agree with removal. Does well-being mean four weeks at camp, or a small family size, or designer jeans, or a middle-class house? Who knows? It can mean anything the person enforcing the law wants it to mean.

You might also notice that the law does not recognize the possibility that a parent might wish desperately to provide for his child, but not have the resources, due to ill health, unemployment, or other reasons. I have heard of cases from around the country where parents who couldn't afford to keep the heat or electricity turned on lost their children to the state.

3. This was part of the same model federal statute. As Barbara Morris reports,

> in order for states to obtain the funding provided under P.L. 93-247, the abuse or neglect need only be "suspected." Furthermore, the federal law stipulates that state legislation must provide "immunity for persons reporting instances of child abuse and neglect from prosecution. . . ."(*Change Agents*, p. 91)

The way this worked out in Missouri (which prides itself on being a leader in "the fight against child abuse and neglect") is especially interesting. In defiance of the fact that Missouri law requires hotline workers to obtain the reporter's name and address, plus other relevant information, the Division of Family Services placed an ad in papers all over Missouri which said, in part:

> Callers do not need proof of abuse or neglect to make a report and the name of the caller will be kept confidential. Callers may remain anonymous if they desire. [See, for example, *Jefferson City Post-Tribune* of September 17, 1985.]

Callers "*do not need proof*" (in other words, feel free to use the hotline for slander) and "*may remain anonymous*" (i.e., there's no way you can ever be prosecuted or sued for slandering a family via the hotline).

When we pointed out to the appropriate legislative committee that it was in fact illegal for DFS to take anonymous calls under current law, those particular legislators (Kaye Steinmetz, D-Florissant; Sue Shear, D-Clayon; Steve Banton, R-Manchester; Doug Harpool, D-Springfield; Marion Cairns, R-Webster Groves; Mary Kasten, R-Cape Girardeau; Pat Dougherty, D-St. Louis; Gene Lang, R-Warrensburg; Chris Graham, D-Jefferson City; Judy O'Connor, D-Bridgeton) responded by proposing a bill that would allow DFS to accept anonymous calls. The committee made no effort whatever to restrain DFS from their illegal actions or to rebuke them.

Missouri is an anomaly in that our legislators apparently intended to allow anonymous reports, as the model Federal statute required, but somehow were clumsy in failing to enact anonymity into the actual law. Most states explicitly allow their "Child Protective Services" or "Division of Family Services" to solicit anonymous (i.e., false and malicious) calls on their child abuse hotlines.

4. "Mandated reporters" are in every state. However, some states go further than others.

> Delaware requires not only that doctors and other medical workers, social workers, school personnel and medical examiners report cases *suspected* of being child abuse and neglect, but also "any other person" with reason to believe it has occurred. And Michigan law makes any person who fails to make a report liable for civil damages. (Sally Bixby Defty, "States' Efforts to Fight Child Abuse Discussed," *St. Louis Post-Dispatch*, March 31, 1985, p. 10D. Emphasis mine.)

It's just too bad they can't advertise it honestly: Every Citizen A Gestapo Agent! Be Suspicious Or Get Sued! What a law—requiring people to be suspicious or face legal penalties. What a way to dredge up extra "clients" (totally innocent ones) for state bureaucrats.

5. See Stephen Chapman's excellent op ed, printed in papers around the nation, that I clipped from both the *Jefferson City Post-Tribune* of April 5, 1985, and the *St. Louis Post-Dispatch* of March 28, 1985.

Mr. Chapman says in part,

> If you are a parent living in Illinois [and his column applies to almost every other state as well], be warned: On the basis of nothing more than an anonymous phone call by someone falsely accusing you of child abuse, your home and your children may be subjected to the most invasive kind of search by agents of the state government.
>
> That is the result of a March 12 decision by U.S. District Court Judge John Nordbert in a lawsuit brought by several parents who had been investigated and cleared. . . . It upholds the existing procedures of the Department of Children and Family Services for reports of child abuse. For these cases, it essentially renders the Fourth Amendment null and void.
>
> The framers of the Constitution guaranteed protection against "unreasonable searches and seizures." If you're suspected of murder or rape, the police may not search your home without a warrant issued by a judge, based on evidence showing probable cause of your guilt.
>
> But the ruling says that if you're suspected of child abuse, no matter how flimsy the grounds, the state has a nearly absolute right to search your home and conduct a nude inspection of your child. . . .

The judge basically argued that (1) the division didn't need to obtain a warrant, because the parents consented to the searches (ignoring the fact that the caseworkers didn't tell parents they could refuse to let them in, and actually threatened to get an order to remove the children if the parents refused to allow them in) and (2) that searches to investigate child abuse are all "reasonable" (in spite of the extremely high percent of unsubstantiated hotline calls). So out the window go Constitutional rights and in the door come the police.

6. Once accused of child abuse, you have no due process rights. Why? Because *you have not been charged with a crime! Child abuse is not a crime.* Your children were not arrested, but taken into "protective custody" (or threatened with same). You were not arrested. You find yourself in Juvenile Court, where proceedings are confidential "in order to protect the child." The judge does not have to hear your evidence unless he feels like it. If you actually know enough to appeal his ruling, this may not help you, because *only evidence that was allowed in the previous hearing is heard in the appeal.* You have no right to a trial by jury, no right to cross-examination of witnesses, no right to face your accuser, etc., etc. Furthermore, your child may be represented by a "guardian ad litem" who is supposedly protecting the child's best interests, *in opposition* to your interests. (Your child, in other words, cannot be represented by your attorney.)

If a parent is brought to trial with *criminal* penalties, such as rape or murder, he is entitled to a fair trial. But there's no fair trial for those accused of scolding or spanking or thwarting Junior's tender will.

7. Remember, the federal statute required state legislatures that wanted their bite of the federal funds to provide "immunity for persons reporting instances of child abuse and neglect from prosecution." See footnotes 2 and 3, above.

8. Naturally, being so solicitous to protect informers from any civil or criminal penalties, the states did not neglect to also protect their own employees.

The state does not have to show irrefutable evidence that you were harming your child in order to remove him or her. You have to provide infallible proof that you have always complied with state child-rearing guidelines (which are not stated explicitly anywhere), and that you always will in the future. The state has infinite discretion in how it decides who shall or shall not keep their children. This discretion extends not only to removing children from families unfairly, but also to putting abuse victims back in the hands of genuine perpetrators, as is shown elsewhere in this book. In all such cases, the bureaucrats are immune.

This is all, of course, totally unconstitutional. A promising lawsuit has been filed in Washington state against the governor, director of family services, and assorted lesser bureaucrats for infringment of the Constitutional rights of a number of families who lost their children to the state. We'll have to see how it goes.

9. This figure comes from Douglas J. Besharov, the first director of the National Center on Child Abuse and Neglect, as reported in an AP article of December 17, 1985, "Expert Says Two-Third of Abuse Reports Unfounded" by Sandy Johnson. As you'll see in subsequent chapters, that two-thirds figure is really much too low. Only a tiny minority of child abuse reports concern anything that the general public would seriously consider child abuse.

10. These categories are all taken from the Missouri Statewide Child

Abuse and Neglect Statistics for 1984, and listed under the "Incidents Substantiated." "Threatened Harm," for example, accounted for 6,949 "substantiated" incidents of child abuse and neglect in Missouri in 1984.

11. Most people don't realize it, but when your local Family Services office reports that "X cases of child abuse were substantiated this year," what they mean is "we were suspicious of the parents when investigating X cases." Substantiation does not mean that *evidence* has been found. It means that the social worker is *suspicious* of you. As this ingenuous quote from an article in the *Columbia Missourian* reports:

> "The sexual abuse complaints have a higher rate of substantiation than neglect cases," [Mack] Abernathy [social services supervisor] said. "We find a *reason to suspect* sexual abuse in 70 to 80 percent of the reports we get, compared to only half of the others." (Jospeh Pryweller, "Agency Helps Curb Child Abuse," August 12, 1985. Emphasis mine.)

It's not hard to see why sex abuse has a higher rate of "substantiation" when all substantiation means is that a social worker finds it possible to stretch her mind to entertain evil suspicions of you. When children are well dressed and look well-fed it's hard to suspect neglect. When children have no scars or bruises it takes an effort to suspect physical abuse. But it takes no effort at all to suspect any father (or mother) of sexual crimes, especially when the definition of sexual abuse is conveniently fluid enough to not require physical evidence of rape or witnesses, and when social workers have been trained to believe that children deliberately cover up these crimes.

12.

Many assume that since child abuse and neglect are against the law, somewhere there are statutes that make clear distinctions between what is and what is not child abuse or neglect. But this is not the case. Nowhere are there clear-cut definitions of what is encompassed by the terms. (Jeanne M. Giovannoni and Rosina M. Becerra, *Defining Child Abuse*, [New York: Free Press/Macmillan, 1979], p. 2)

Giovannoni and Becerra's book includes eleven pages listing the condensed results of a survey of lawyers, pediatricians, social workers, and police. The survey was conducted to discover what these professionals felt about various scenarios of parental conduct. Respondents were asked to rate the scenarios on a scale of 1 to 9, with 1 being the least serious act and 9 the most serious. Respondents labeled each act individually (they could give more than one 9 or more than one 5, for example).

Looking through the survey the significant thing is that *some* social workers considered *every* scenario "abusive or neglectful" (there wasn't a single perfect 1.00 score). These same social workers have unlimited power to impose their conflicting standards on your family.

Social workers rated "spanking with a leather strap (leaving red marks on the skin)" as a 6.15, and even spanking with the hand that left red marks received a 3.21. On the other hand, the scenario of parents who "regularly left their child alone outside the home during the day until almost dark" (which, by the way, is the way most American school-age children have always been allowed to play), received a 4.42, and got a 5.33 if "neighbors have spotted the child wandering five blocks from home." If "parents regularly left their child alone inside the house after dark" social workers gave the parents a 6.33, and when "on one occasion the child started a small fire" this graduated to 7.64.

If "the parents are constantly screaming at their child, calling him foul names," social workers rate this as a 5.19. If, on the other hand, "the parents ignore their child most of the time," this rates a 5.57.

If "the parents never see to it that their children do any homework. They let them watch TV all evening. One child is failing in school," those folks rate a 4.23. (Ibid., pp. 111-121)

Along the same lines, Christian Liberty Academy reproduced a bit of written correspondence received by one of their member families, the Kenneth Eicheldingers, on April 26, 1984, from the child welfare bureaucracy in New York State:

Dear Mr. and Mrs. Kenneth Eicheldinger,
     I am writing to you regarding the report of alleged maltreatment received concerning your daughter, Robin. . . .
     I would like to discuss your views on raising your children in general, as the report also mentioned that you do not allow your children to watch television or listen to the radio. While these actions do not necessarily constitute abuse or neglect on your part, I do feel that it might be beneficial to discuss these matters with you.
     With this in mind, I have scheduled an appointment to meet with you in my office . . . (Mike McHugh, They Can Take Your Children, a pamphlet published by the Christian Liberty Academy of Illinois, a well-known Christian day and correspondence school.)

So the bureaucracy in New York State is willing to consider that not allowing TV and radio might be abuse or neglect. "Necessarily" is the key word here. Is living without the constant din of the electronic media abuse or neglect? The bureaucrat wouldn't say it was not.

13. Foster Family Care in Missouri: An Assessment (Missouri Coalition on Foster Care, October 1981), p. 101.

Black children enter foster care earlier and stay in care longer . . . much longer. The median length of stay in foster care for white children in this sample is 21 months, but for black children it is 51 months. . . . Most children enter care at the younger ages.

This same report revealed that, as seems to be the case nationwide, Missouri had no standards requiring children to be returned in cases where they were wrongfully taken. The law does not even recognize this possibility.

14. Jesse Tinsky, "Girl's size spurs suit by parents," Rocky Mountain News, n.d.

15. Patricia Lakes, "Battle for custody of seized children becomes nightmare," Nelson (British Columbia) Daily News, Nov. 7, 1985, p. 1.

16. "Workers acted appropriately," a letter to the editor, Nelson Daily News, Dec 3, 1985.

17. Lakes, "Battle," p. 5.

18. Frank Jones, "Families destroyed by charges of abuse," Toronto Star, Page C1, n.d. The story is about a Minnesota family.

19. See the address for VOCAL in Appendix 3.

20. Kenneth and Donna Wilkerson, both accredited public school teachers, withdrew their twelve-year-old son, Christopher, from the Hazelwood, Missouri school district at the start of the 1983-84 school year to educate him at home in the Christian Liberty Academy Satellite Schools program. In an article appearing in the *St. Louis Globe-Democrat* of March 16-17, 1985, page 1, we find

> Now the parents face charges of child abuse. . . .
> In November, district officials, conducting the investigation to determine whether there was educational neglect, found indications the program was "too religiously centered," attorney Arnold T. Phillips Jr. said. . . .
> On Jan. 31, Susan Goodwin, attorney for the juvenile office of St. Louis County, filed a petition in the court alleging that Christopher needed care and treatment because "the behavior or associations of Christopher were injurious to his welfare."
> The court ordered Christopher, now in seventh grade, to undergo psychological testing and appointed a state guardian to represent him at a court hearing. . . . (Steve Zesch, "Court again orders child tested because of education at home.")

Local papers took up the Wilkersons' cause and so embarrassed the bureaucrats who had ordered the psychological testing that they backed down. Indeed, they had reason to be embarrassed. The Wilkersons had fully cooperated with the school district, allowed numerous school officials in their home to review Christopher's program, and Christopher had done superbly on *educational* tests.

But notice what happened here. A Christian family, whose educational program had received *academic* approval from school officials, were accused, not of truancy, but of *child abuse*. Why? Because their program was *"too religious."* And the state didn't back down until the papers started plastering the story all over page one.

I cannot too highly commend the *St. Louis Globe-Democrat* for not only featuring the Wilkersons' story, but publishing an editorial, "Child Abuse or Family Harassment?" on April 27-28, 1985, rebuking the state for bringing charges in the first place and calling upon the court to drop the charges. Which the court eventually did.

21. Testimony of Laura Rogers, *Missouri House of Representatives Report to the Speaker on the Child Abuse Reporting Law*, by the Interim Committee on Children, Youth and Families, December 1985, pp. 83-86.

22. *Ibid.*

23. *Ibid.*

24. My husband Bill heard this testimony at the legislative committee hearing in St. Louis, September 30, 1985. The foster father in question was quite bitter about his experiences. He had been told, "These poor abused girls just need love," and found he had taken in what amounted to an unpaid prostitute. She hotlined him and he spent thousands clearing himself. His final comment was, "I'll never take in one of those kids again."

Also, the summary of witness testimony from the Sept 11, 1985 Jefferson City hearing states,

> A foster child who is "street wise" may use the hotline to get away from an unsatisfactory foster situation. The child will be removed with few

THE CHILD ABUSE INDUSTRY

or no questions asked. The child quickly learns to manipulate the situation. (*Missouri House Report*, p. 5.)

25. Testimony, *Missouri House Report*, pp. 15-18.

26. *Ibid*. Jack Anderson did a radio expose (featuring a different case) in which the mother also miscarried. "Jack Anderson Confidential," Show 11, air date 11/27-28/82, p. 5. The parents had taken the baby to Cardinal Glennon hospital in St. Louis for a checkup to find out why she was spitting up a lot. The hopital tests showed nothing, so the hospital arbitrarily decided to call the undiagnosed case "emotional neglect."

27. Alida Gookin, "Delusional Religious Beliefs," *Jackson Journal*, September 19, 1985, p. 3. Jackson, Tenn.

Associated Press carried a much less detailed writeup of what happened to Gary and Judy Ann Cordie under the heading "Aid Urged For Mentally Ill" as seen in the *Memphis Commercial Appeal* of August 3, 1985. This article confirmed the major facts of the case. You can also write directly to the Cordies for a copy of their testimony (I'd enclose a dollar or two to help with postage if I were you). The address is: 505 W. Lincoln, Fergus Falls, MN 56537.

28. Schweitzer, "The difficult art of protecting children," p. A-5.

29. Nov 11, 1985, p. 25.

30. Frank Allen at age twenty-eight was the youngest mayor ever elected in Spartanburg, South Carolina. His record was outstanding in all areas. Appointed to several White House and national committees, his future looked bright. Then he got a divorce.

According to a pamphlet Mr. Allen put out, the following events now occurred.

The ex-wife accused him of legal malpractice. The Bar dismissed this accusation. After Mr. Allen obtained full custody of their daughter, the wife accused him of child abuse. He obtained full custody nonetheless. The wife now filed a police report, likewise dismissed as false. Now the child abuse allegation was revived. The daughter was taken and given into the wife's custody. When Mr. Allen's case finally came to court, the jury acquitted him after only a one-hour deliberation.

During this entire process, Mr. Allen says all his requests for visitation (by himself or his pastor) were denied, as were his requests that his daughter be examined by a physician or psychiatrist. Although none of the charges ever were proved, they ruined his career, and he lost his daughter. (Pamphlet: *An Attorney Accused*, Frank Allen.)

31.

Government intervention into child-rearing comes in any number of forms. On the county's legal record books [Ventura, CA] is a case where a court took custody of an unborn child because the mother was ruled unfit.(Schweitzer, p. 1)

Also see the lengthy section on "crisis nurseries" and other devices planned to remove children at birth in Chapter 11.

Chapter 2—The Plague That Isn't

1. Just one of the million repetitions of this dogma, which has been broadcast over the whole world: "Child abuse does not belong solely in the

domain of the poor. Child abusers come from all economic, racial, ethnic, and religious groups." (Polk County Child Advocacy Program, Advertising Supplement to *Bolivar* [MO] *Herald Free Press* and *Humansville Star-Leader*, October 23, 1985.) Another: "Family violence is just as prevalent in wealthy homes as in lower class homes. It occurs in all socio-economic, ethnic, racial, educational, and age groups." ("Domestic Violence Group Needs Help," Eldon [MO] *Advertiser*, September 12, 1985.) Note the concern to break down our "prejudice," i.e., the informed testimony of history, that places abuse chiefly among down-and-outers and other social outcasts.

2. As reported in the *Ozark Beacon* of September 18, 1985, in an article addressed to dentists (believe it or not), entitled "Watch For Child Abuse": "The National Center on Child Abuse and Neglect has estimated five of every 1,000 children in the United States may be abused each year." This is the only place I have ever seen this statistic, which comes far closer to reality than those much more widely publicized.

3. I have many sources for the "1 in 45" tag, which seems to be based on the current nationwide average of 27.3 *reports* per 1,000 children. This statistic, of course, assumes that all reports are true (when most of them are not even substantiated) and that no reports are duplicates (when, according to national statistics, "roughly 40 to 50 percent of the children reported have been a part of the data file since 1979"). (*Highlights 1984*, pp. 2, 9.)

4. Special supplement to *The Mountain Echo* (MO) of August 14, 1985 produced by Camp Penuel, a Christian camp for children. This supplement contained more statistical untruths than any other single publication I have seen.

5. Quoted in local papers and magazines everywhere. One example: the small town *Lawrence County Record*, serving a circulation of 3,196. "TEA Studies Child Abuse," November 28, 1985. Even the smallest papers have been fed these figures, which have been labeled "utterly ridiculous" by Douglas J. Besharov, former director of the National Center on Child Abuse and Neglect, and disclaimed by both the National Center and the National Committee for the Prevention of Child Abuse. ("Parents Battle Pain of Child-Abuse Allegations," *North Jersey News*, January 13, 1986.)

6. Camp Penuel supplement.

7. Only 82,088 rapes were reported in 1980. Even the number of rapes that people claimed that happened, including those *not* reported to the police, was only 192,000 in 1980. (Andrew Hacker, *USA: A Statistical Report of the American People* [New York: Viking Press, 1983], p. 222.)

8. "Animal Character Helping Kids Recognize Sexual Abuse," *St. Joseph* (MO) *News-Press*, September 18, 1985.

9. Douglas Besharov as reported in AP article, "Expert Says Two-Thirds of Abuse Reports Unfounded."

10. "Statewide Child Abuse and Neglect Statistics for Calendar 1984" (the most recent year available as of this writing, *Missouri House of Representatives Report*, p. 72).

11. "1984 Child Abuse and Neglect Reporting Totals and Rates," *Highlights 1984*, p. 6.

12. "Type of Maltreatment," *Highlights 1984*, p. 16.

13. The perpetrator can be a parent, other relative, babysitter, teacher, neighbor, member of institutional staff, or even "other" or "unknown" and it all counts as "child abuse." Even worse: the category "Parent" in our national statistics includes

"a. Natural
b. Step
c. Adoptive
d. Foster
e. Unspecified/mixed parental relationship."

(*Highlights 1984*, p. 45.) This means that FOSTER PARENT ABUSE is lumped in with natural parent abuse! The abuse *caused* by the state removing children is listed to prove that they need to remove children!

14. "On a day-in, day-out basis, we don't deal with extreme cases of child abuse," [says Detective Karen Sullenger of the Cape Girardeau Police Department.] "Cases where children are put into an oven or scalded to death may happen every five or six years, or hopefully they may never happen again in our area." ("'Safety Net' to promote awareness of child abuse," *Southeast Missourian*, December 31, 1985.)

15. "Communication Needed to Combat Drug Abuse," *Salem* (MO) *News*, December 10, 1985.

16. "Statewide Child Abuse and Neglect Statistics for Calendar 1984," *Missouri House of Representatives Report*, p. 72.

17. *Nevada* (MO) *Daily Mail*, June 27, 1985.

18. "Statewide Child Abuse and Neglect Statistics . . ."

19.

In a recent column, Nicholas von Hoffman questioned an estimate given by Jay C. Howell, executive director of the National Center for Missing and Exploited Children, that 1.5 million children turn up missing each year.

He pointed out that such a figure means that 3 percent—3 out of 100 kids younger than 17—in the United States would be listed as missing. That would mean that a school with an enrollment of 500 would have 15 kids missing each year. "Wouldn't that mean," Mr. von Hoffman asks, "that everyone would know someone whose kid is missing?"

Noting that a California expert says fewer than 1,000 people of all ages are missing more than 30 days, Mr. von Hoffman theorizes that perhaps 7,500 kids a year turn up seriously missing in the United States—and it's likely that a good percentage of missing kids are runaways, and another hefty chunk consists of children who have been snatched by divorced fathers or mothers.

A CBS News report this week confirmed Mr. von Hoffman's views and claimed that the "missing children" problem has been blown out of all actual proportion. ("Child kidnapping and abuse blown out of proportion," *Nevada* [MO] *Daily Mail*, July 8, 1985, p. 4.)

20. Saf Lerman's Parenting column, *St. Louis Post-Dispatch*, May 1, 1985, p. 6W.

21. Murray A. Strauss, Richard J. Gelles, and Suzanne K. Steinmetz, *Behind Closed Doors: Violence and the American Family* (Garden City, NY: Anchor Press/Doubleday, 1980), p. 13.

22. *Ibid.*, pp. 53, 21.

23. *Ibid.*, p. 243.

24. *Highlights 1984*, p. 5.

Chapter 3—Home, Horrible Home

1. "Violence in the American Family," *Journal of Social Issues*, 35, 2, 1979, p. 15. Murray A. Strauss travels about with the message that the family is a "school for violence" (Jennifer Bolch, "A Slap on the Hand Starts Lessons in Violence," Living section, *Dallas* [TX] *Times Herald*, March 20, 1979.) His definition of violence includes all forms of corporal punishment. Thus he makes his case for eliminating corporal punishment by begging the question (and meanwhile tagging millions of perfectly innocent North American families as child abusers).

2. "Child Abuse: the Facts", Advertising Supplement to *Bolivar Herald-Free Press* and *Humansville Star-Leader*, October 23, 1985. Unlike so many of the other "facts" in this supplement, the 1,000 child abuse deaths per year figure is born out by our national statistics (*Highlights 1984*). Page 28 says, "Over the nine years of reporting, 1,491 children have died in connection with deprivation of necessities." Page 30 notes "500 fatality cases available in the data" for 1984, gleaned from twenty-three states and possessions, or about half the country. Compare these FACTS to the typical journalistic statement "Abuse and neglect are believed to be the leading causes of childhood deaths" (Schweitzer, "Difficult Art of Protecting Children").

3. Andrew Hacker, *U/S A Statistical Portrait of the American People*, p. 30.

4. *Ibid.*, p. 67.

5. Jan Paul, "Study Cites Failures on Child Abuse," *St. Louis Post Dispatch*, October 30, 1985. The study of thirty-three fatal cases of child abuse found "Paramours, or live-in boyfriends, who were involved in 15 cases, are especially dangerous to toddlers. They were identified as the abuser, or helper in the abuse, in 10 cases. Five of these children died. . . .

Most of the children came from single-parent families . . . Ten of the mothers were employed or attending school. . . .

Nine families had a history of violence. In five families, at least one parent was mentally ill. In eight families, drug or alcohol abuse was considered to be a problem. . . .

Those cases in which boyfriends were involved . . . The five who were identified as abusers in fatal cases had an average age of 25. Three had criminal records. . . .

Three of the live-in boyfriends had children of their own, but none had been married."

6. *Ibid.* Also consider this comment from Dr. Kenneth S. Hines, a St. Joseph, Missouri clinical psychologist: "Hines said of the persons who commit the abuse crimes, 'You can find thousands of reasons for it, but most have a direct link to alcohol.'" ("Psychological Aspects of Abuse Are Far-Ranging," Child Abuse section, *St. Joseph* [MO] *Gazette*, September 21, 1985, p. 4.) This testimony has been confirmed by my conversations with people who work with victims of genuine abuse, and by the findings of the Attorney General's Task Force on Family Violence. As the Task Force Report states, "the relationship [between alcohol and abuse] is clearly there." (p. 101)

7.

During the 1960's, the advocates of abortion-on-demand argued that this policy change would reduce the number of unwanted pregnancies and so reduce child abuse. In fact, the exact opposite seems to have occurred. In an article for the *Canadian Journal of Psychiatry* [Nov.,

1979, pp. 610-620], Philip Ney, M.D., has shown that those Canadian provinces (British Columbia and Ontario) with the highest rates of legal abortion are also the provinces with the highest (and most rapidly rising) rates of child abuse. In contrast, provinces with low abortion rates (New Brunswick, Newfoundland, Prince Edward's Island) also enjoy low, even declining, levels of child abuse. Ney postulates that women's choice of abortion has led to diminished restraints on rage, to a devaluation of children, to an increase in guilt, to heightened tension between the sexes, and to ineffective bonding between the mothers and subsequent children. All of these factors, he notes, are closely related in the medical literature with abusive behavior toward children. (Allan Carlson, "The Child-Savers Ride Again," *Persuasion at Work* (a publication of the Rockford Institute), Vol. 8, #8, August, 1985, p. 8.

8. Germaine Greer, *Sex and Destiny* (New York: Harper and Row, 1984), p. 229.

9. "Deaths from 72 selected causes by age: United States, 1983," *Monthly Vital Statistics Report*, Vol 34, #6, Supplement (2), Sept 26, 1985, p. 23.

10. "Age-specific and age-adjusted death rates for 15 leading causes and selected components: United States 1979 and 1982-83," *Ibid.* p.20.

11. *Ibid.*

12. *Ibid.*

13. "Deaths from 72 selected causes by age," pp. 21-22.

14. As it happens, the government statistics *do* lump foster parents together with real parents when tabulating child abuse, and include just about any kind of alliance under the title of "family." (*Highlights 1984*, p. 45.)

15. "Sexual abuse is a taboo in our society." (Pamela D. Mayhall and Katherine Eastlack Norgard, *Child Abuse and Neglect: Sharing Responsibility* [New York: John Wiley and Sons, 1983], p. 11.) This social work text devotes its introductory chapters to breaking down the reader's religious and ethical beliefs and re-freezing him into a relativistic position. In the chapter on sexual abuse, a whole page is devoted to explaining why the "taboo" against sexual abuse is on its way to becoming passe (pp 178-179). Even so, this book noted that sexual abuse was most reliably associated with a "father" who was promiscuous or alcoholic (p. 39). And on page 101 it noted that "step/adoptive/foster parents . . . [are] associated with the greatest frequency of sexual maltreatment. . . . Nonrelatives and step/adoptive/foster parents are . . . often associated with sexual abuse. Almost half of the children were living with a single, unemployed female caretaker."

16. *Ibid.* Also Jan Paul, "Study Cites Failures on Child Abuse."

17. Detective Corporal George Haralson, a ten-year veteran with the Tulsa, Oklahoma Police Department's special investigations/child pornography division, a man who should know, says, "Adult pornographic materials are found in about 50 percent of the investigations regarding sexual abuse of children." (Debbie Fishback, "Officials Intensifying Battle Against Child Abuse," *Joplin* [MO] *Globe*, August 14, 1985.) In passing, I would like to commend the *Joplin Globe*, which has been one of the most careful, objective papers in the state of Missouri on the issue of child abuse.

18. *Highlights 1984*, p. 16. In other words, although the public has become accustomed to thinking of sexual abuse as referring to abuse occur-

ring within the home, the new statistics quietly incorporate *all* sexual abuse, including that perpetrated by non-family members.

19. Becky R. Gilmore, "Child sexual abuse is topic at meeting," *Nevada* (MO) *Daily Mail*, June 26, 1985.

20. "The [New Jersey] division [of family and youth services] did not begin to tabulate until last year how many of the reports included sexual abuse. In 1984, 9.6 percent were sexually related. Of those, nearly half were classified as 'mild fondling.'" Nancy Hass, "Other Victims in Child-Abuse Cases: Parents," *North Jersey News*, January 13, 1986.

21. "Statewide Child Abuse and Neglect Statistics for Calendar 1984," *Missouri House of Representatives Report*, p. 72.

22. On page C4 of the Wednesday, October 16, 1985, issue of the *Memphis Commercial Appeal* was an article, "Magazine Report Says U.S. Men Marry Later Than Their Dads Did" subtitled "Actions defy sex decline." The report was from New York (UPI). It described a survey by *Mademoiselle* magazine. The average unmarried American male has had sex with sixteen partners, among other things, according to the magazine article entitled, "Too Much Sex, Too Little Love . . . What Ails the U.S. Male." Here is a quote from the *Mademoiselle* report, "While only one out of five men professes to enjoy one-night stands, two-thirds expect to have sex by the third date and 80 percent by the fifth date." I thank Alida Gookin of Memphis for bringing this information to my attention.

23. I have a complete bibliography of studies on prevention programs. Not one of them involves a before and after study to determine how effective the program is in *combatting child abuse*. The only studies of effectiveness center around whether participants remember the information, not how it is used. This is not surprising, since an accurate study of this type is impossible to design, due to the dubious nature of voluntary reports about violence in the subject's family. However, though we lack *any* proof that prevention programs actually prevent child abuse, they are advertised as a sure remedy for social ills.

24. Becky R. Gilmore, "Incest is most common form of child sexual abuse" [a completely inaccurate title], *Nevada* (MO) *Daily Mail*, June 27, 1985.

25. Judith Reisman, "The Porno Industry: Giving Child Molesting Its Stamp of Approval," *The Rutherford Institute*, Jan/Feb 1986, pp 10-11.

26. Philip Noble, "Kids Should Have Sex—Pediatrician Says," *San Francisco Chronicle*, May 15, 1978, p. 21.

27. *Ibid.*

28. *Ibid.*

Chapter 4—The Immaculate Confession

1. One thousand child abuse deaths per year out of a child population of over seventy-two million. See Chapter 3.

2. Major physical injury was 3.3 percent of substantiated reports in 1984, that is, slightly over one percent of the 1.7 million total reports, or about 23,000 cases nationwide. That comes to approximately one out of every threee thousand children. See Chapter 3.

3. The 1984 sexual abuse rate was 15.88 per 10,000, or less than .2 percent. This includes "false positives," that is, cases reported as sexual abuse but that revealed no evidence of abuse, and cases perpetrated by non-family

members. It also includes activities far short of intercourse, such as "fondling." "National Estimate of Rates and Numbers of Children Reported as Sexually Molested," *Highlights 1984*, p. 17.

4. Consider this report by Allen R. McMahon, Attorney at Law:

For many years my practice of law was focused primarily on heated divorce actions. Back in the days before no fault divorce, each party in these actions would try to prove that the other party was at fault. The one determined to be the "innocent" party would get all the goodies plus custody of the children so it was very important to prove fault. In 1970 California instituted no fault divorce and in 1980, joint custody of children went into effect. This made it difficult for one parent to get sole custody of the children and completely exclude the other parent from visitation. It was not long after 1980 that things really got messy. It was at this time that I started to see false accusations of child abuse-/molestation/neglect. I have even heard of cases where attorneys have advised their clients that the only way to get custody would be if the other parent had done "something" to the child, therein planting this idea in their client's minds. The "usual" story goes something like this: The parents separate and either shortly thereafter, when one parent starts living with someone or marries, or when the noncustodial parent wants increased visitation or custody, the false accusations begin. The child is, in most cases, preverbal or barely verbal, five to six years old or younger.... ("'DIVORCE WARS' Don't Get Caught in the Cross Fire!" *The Voice*, a publication of the Los Angeles chapter of VOCAL, December 1, 1985.)

Thus spoke a lawyer. So also says Wayne I. Munkel, M.S.W., Medical Social Consultant for Cardinal Glennon Children's Hospital in St. Louis, in a letter to the House Committee on Children, Youth and Families that appeared in an official government report. Mr. Munkel, says in part,

I am estimating that in 1985 we will perform between 700 and 750 evaluations for sexual abuse at Cardinal Glennon Children's Hospital. We are experiencing a flood of referrals from both Missouri and Illinois.... As many as 10-15 percent of the evaluations involve the custody dispute between separated, divorcing, divorced spouses, and/or other co-habiting persons.... It is clear that parents and lawyers have determined that the only way to deny permanent visiting privileges of another spouse is to allege child abuse or sexual abuse. (*Missouri House of Representatives Report*, p. 66.)

5. "Violence to Kids Down in Past 10 Years: Study," an AP story out of Chicago, *Sedalia* (MO) *Democrat*, November 14, 1985.

6. *Highlights 1984*, p. 5

7. See Chapter 1.

8. Strauss, Gelles, and Steinmetz, pp. 20-22.

9. *Highlights 1984*, p. 5

10. *Ibid.*, p. 12.

11. *Ibid.*

12. "Position Statement of St. Joseph Health Center," St. Charles Missouri, September 30, 1985, *Missouri House of Representatives Report to the Speaker on Child Abuse Reporting Law*, December 1985, p. 114.

13. *Ibid.*

14. Pamela D. Mayhall and Katherine Eastlack Norgard, *Child Abuse and Neglect: Sharing Responsibility* (New York: John Wiley & Sons, 1983), p. vii., 102

15.

Gov. John D. Ashcroft had signed into effect a new law allowing children's testimony at the time the crime is reported to be used in court even if the child later alters that testimony. He said children sometimes changed their original testimony when pressure is put on them after the incident. The new law also provides for the use of videotaped statements under certain circumstances. (Thom Gross, "$250,000 Grant Will Permit Use Of Computer To Track Child Abuse," *St. Louis Post-Dispatch*, July 30, 1985.)

16. "A Five-Year-Old Takes the Stand," *Newsweek*, February 18, 1985, p. 73.

17.

A psychiatrist, appearing on behalf of the prosecution [in Brian Taugher's case] (at $1,000 a day) claimed that the child's behavior—not crying out, appearing altogether normal the morning following the alleged incident, waiting weeks before saying anything to her mother—was consistent with what he called the Child Sexual Abuse Accommodation Syndrome. But on cross-examination the psychologist acknowledged that his "syndrome" was nothing more than a description of how children behave; a youngster who hadn't been abused, he admitted, might have had exactly the same reaction. (David L. Kirp, "Hug Your Kid, Go to Jail," *American Spectator*, June 1985, p. 33.)

For a while there, the Los Angeles chapter of VOCAL was offering Dr. Lee Coleman's refutation of Dr. Rowland Summit's "Child Sexual Abuse Accommodation Syndrome" theory, provocatively entitled "False Allegations of Child Sexual Abuse: Have the Experts Been Caught With Their Pants Down?" A transcript of the 100-minute talk was $5, and the tape itself was $8. You might see if they still have a copy if you want to research this. The address is VOCAL, P.O. Box 4503, N. Hollywood, CA 91607. Dr. Coleman has also written a book called *Reign of Error*, which you can order through a VOCAL chapter or your bookstore.

18. "Sex Abuse Cases Likened to Witch Hunt," *Ogden* (UT) *Examiner*, July 22, 1985.

19. "Parents Battle Pain of Child-Abuse Allegations," *North Jersey News*, Jan. 13, 1986.

20. *Ibid.*

21. "The Youngest Witnesses," pp. 72-73.

22. *Ibid.*

23. David L. Kirp, "Hug Your Kid, Go to Jail," June 1985.

24. *Ibid.*

25. Paul Kilby, "Child-Abuse Accusations Called Latest 'Fad Crime,'" *Columbia Missourian*, July 29, 1985, p. 8A. In this same article, we find a program coordinator of Big Brothers and Big Sisters who, although admitting that "in child sexual abuse cases, it's the child's word against the adult's

word," continued that "studies indicate that children don't lie." Doctrine uber alles.

26. Frank Jones, "Horror Stories of Child Abuse: Fact or Fantasy?" November 21, 1985

27. VOCAL newsletter, July/Augst 1985, p. 4.

28. Reported in magazines and newspapers everywhere. The best summary of this case is found at the beginning of Allan C. Carlson's "The Child-Savers Ride Again," *Persuasion at Work*, August 1985.

Chapter 5—Negative Impact of the Child Abuse Hysteria

1. "Chilling Effect of Child Abuse Fears," *The Ozark* (MO) *Beacon*, August 28, 1985.

2. Deborah Peterson, "Study Details Problems of Child Abuse Among Blacks," *St. Louis Post-Dispatch*, October 28, 1985.

3. Pamela Schaeffer, "Child Abuse Laws Unfair to Minority Parents, Black Leaders Say," p. 8A. I would like to mention in passing that the city of St. Louis, with its higher proportion of black social workers, seems to have far fewer outrageous cases of family abuse than other counties in Missouri. Maybe we could compile a "social work perpetrator profile"—young, unmarried, female, fresh out of college with no experience or significant training in dealing with children, white middle or upper-class background—or older, white female with poor personal home life. Seems like these descriptions fit most of the really outrageous social workers.

4. *Ibid.*

5. Paul Kilby, "Child-Abuse Accusations Called Latest 'Fad Crime,'" *Columbia Missourian*, July 29, 1985.

6. "Child Kidnapping and Abuse Blown Out of Proportion," *Nevada* (MO) *Daily Mail*, July 8, 1985, p. 4. The editor of this paper has made possibly the most perceptive comments about child abuse hysteria of any journalist in Missouri.

Teachers are not the only workers affected by child abuse hysteria. The Philadelphia *Inquirer* quoted the associate executive director of a YMCA saying

he has already lost one of his summer day-camp counselors to the fear of being on the receiving end of a career-destroying allegation. And he had to have some "long discussions" with several others to keep them from quitting.

The above was cited in the VOCAL newsletter of July/August 1985. In the same newsletter, we find:

Many schools, day-care centers and day-camps in the Philadelphia area have been providing workshops and seminars for their employees aimed at preventing situations from which allegations of abuse may arise. Teachers are cautioned about "any kind of touching of children," to make sure there are other adults around when conducting a student activity in an isolated part of the building, and to refrain from transporting a student in a car "regardless of the situation!"

The schools' and camp counselors' fears are not unfounded. In a one-month period, I saw several clippings in my local paper about teachers and counselors who had been cleared of abuse, after being ravaged by months of slander and even threats.

Also in that same VOCAL newsletter (p. 5) we hear:

All but two insurance companies in Illinois who have formerly insured day care centers are now refusing to do so, which puts hundreds of day care centers in jeopardy. This is from fear of lawsuits from abuse charges.

7. Alida Gookin, "Tollett's Folly," *Jackson* (TN) *Journal*, November 21, 1984. The man who made this oppressive suggestion is Dan Tollett of the Tennesse School Boards Association. Mr. Tollett's idea is that public school children, who are now forced to sit through hours of child abuse awareness training and who come under the vigilant eyes of teachers steeped in child abuse dogma, are safe. However, children in private and home schools haven't yet become as paranoid as their public school counterparts. Thus, the idea of "agents from the Department of Human Services to privately interview such children four times a year to secure incriminating information about their parents."

8. Sandy Johnson, "Expert Says Two-Thirds of Abuse Reports Unfounded," Associated Press wire slug, December 17, 1985.

Chapter 6—"We Just Want to Help"

1. *What everyone should know ABOUT CHILD ABUSE* (Jefferson City: Missouri Division of Family Services, 1976), 1980 edition.

2. *Ibid.*, p. 7. "The abused child and family CAN'T HELP THEM-SELVES—They WANT TO BE HELPED, and *CAN* BE!" is one of the pamphlets's answers to the question "Why should I get involved?" This answer is given under the heading "for the FAMILY'S SAKE." All these capitals occur in the original, so you can see how emotionally hyped the entire presentation is.

3. *What Everyone Should Know*, pp. 8-9

4. *Ibid.*, p. 9.

5.

Delaware requires not only that doctors and other medical workers, social workers, school personnel and medical examiners report cases suspected of being child abuse and neglect, but also "any other person" with reason to believe it has occurred. And Michigan law makes any person who fails to make a report liable for civil damages.

Sally Bixby Duffy, "States' Efforts To Fight Child Abuse Discussed," *St. Louis Post Dispach*, March 31, 1985, p. 10D.

6. *What Everone Should Know*, p. 10.

7. Tammy's story was reported nationwide, but in secondary media. A short story appeared in *Jet* magazine, and Jack Anderson mentioned Tammy's case in his *Jack Anderson Confidential*, show 11, air date 11/27-28, 1982. As John McKay, a Kansas City lawyer, reported:

In July of 1979, Theodore Gully purchased Tammy Nelson, eight-year-old Tammy Nelson, for forty dollars for the purpose of having sex. He did in fact have sex with the eight-year-old child. He raped her. The rape was so severe this time that the child hemorrhaged, developed a massive infection. The mother, probably to cover her own steps, possibly out of guilt at what she'd done, did not take the child to get medical treatment for several days. When she did seek medical treatment, it was too late. The infection was at such an advanced stage that the child did die on August 10, 1979. Now this is ten months after the Division of Family Services had the exact, specific information that the mother was selling the child to Theodore Gully. In May of '79, the Division of Family Services received a second hotline phone call. Basically, the same allegations. . . . The case workers in both situations did not talk to a single neighbor, did not talk to the landlord, did not talk to the person who had made these hotline phone calls, did not make any attempt to contact Theodore Gully who was the perpetrator of the crime. (Transcript of the show, p. 7.)

8.   *Confessions of a Medical Heretic* (New York: Warner Books, 1979), pp. 167-169.
9. *What everyone should know ABOUT CHILD ABUSE*, p. 11.
10. *Ibid.*
11. VOCAL National Newsletter, September/October 1985, p. 5.

Chapter 7—"We Don't Want to Separate Families"

1. *Foster Family Care in Missouri: An Assessment*, p. 5. Prepared by the Missouri Coalition on Foster Care, Affiliated with the Missouri Association for Social Welfare, under a grant from the Missouri Division of Family Services and the U.S. Department of Health and Human Services. October 1981.
2. As Douglas J. Besharov points out,

At the present time, there are no legal standards governing the foster care decision. Juvenile court acts, for example, give judges unrestricted dispositional authority. Once initial court jurisdiction is established [e.g., once your child is taken into "temporary protective" custody] they set no limits—and hence provide no guidance—on which situations require foster care and which do not. Consequently, "decision-making is left to the ad hoc analysis of social workers and judges." (Douglas Besharov, *"Doing Something" About Child Abuse: The Need to Narrow the Grounds for State Intervention*, a reprint from the *Harvard Journal of Law and Public Policy*, Vol. 8, No. 3 [Washington: American Enterprise Institute for Public Policy Research, 1985], p. 584.)

3. Pp. 10-11.
4. *Foster Family Care in Missouri*, p. 101.
5. Dr. Robert ten Bensel of the University of Minnesota, School of Public Health, at the National Council of Juvenile and Family Court Judges, said, "I think Missouri has been the leader in planning for children. . . . It is the only state I've been in where the governor, the supreme court, the judges, the social services, the volunteers all have participated. This state is a mod-

el. . . ." (Carolyn Callison, "Education called key to end of child abuse," *St.Louis Globe-Democrat*, August 26, 1985, p. 5A.) Representative Kaye Steinmetz (D-Florissant) also made the statment that MO is a leader in the fight versus child abuse at a symposium on "Children in Crisis." Another speaker that day, Ernest A. Allen, charman of the board of the National Center for Missing and Exploited Children (a group that widely disseminated outrageous and false statistics on the extent of the missing children problem) disputed Ms. Steinmetz. He pointed out that some states require more people to report than Missouri. Mrs. Steinmetz countered that "the Missouri House was the first in the nation to have a Children, Youth and Families Committee" (of which she holds the chair). Mrs. Steinmetz was absolutely right: this committee has again and again thwarted the wishes of the general assembly and prevented bills giving families civil rights from becoming law. Mrs. Steinmetz, for example, personally killed a bill passed by the House that would have forbidden anonymous hotline reporting. Unhappily, this commit-tee ploy has "since been duplicated by other state legislatures." (Sally Bixby Defty, "States' Efforts To Fight Child Abuse Discussed," *St. Louis Post-Dispatch*, March 31, 1985.)

6. *Foster Family Care in Missouri*, p. 106.

7. Published also as a separate booklet. Charlotte Grimes, *Foster Care: Nobody's Child, St. Louis Post-Dispatch*, a collection of articles from Octo-ber 25-30, 1981.

8. *Foster Family Care in Missouri*, p. 111.

9. *Ibid.*, p. 110.

10. *Ibid.*, p. 116.

11. "While 77% of the children in the sample have siblings also in care, all siblings were placed together in only 28% of the cases." *Ibid.*, p. 101.

12. "Two out of every five children in care have experienced more than one placement, and for an unfortunate 20% of the sample, children have gone through four or more placements. Extrapolating to the total foster care population in Missouri, over a thousand children have been in four or more foster care placements; several hundred have been shuffled through seven or more placements." (*Ibid.*)

And extrapolating to the total foster care population of the U.S.A., we find 200,000 multiply-placed children, and 100,000 who have been bounced about at least four times.

13. Besharov, "*Doing Something,*" pp. 559-560.

14. *Highlights 1984*, p. 34. "The 17.7 percent receiving placement ser-vices [a euphemism for removal] is suggestive of a higher rate than was reported in 1982 and 1983." Since the total amount of reports is rising as well, this represents a dramatic increase in the number of children removed from their families each year.

15. Besharov, "*Doing Something,*" pp. 561.

16. Besharov, "*Doing Something,*" pp. 561-562.

17. Sandra Mathers, "Law Gives State Broad Powers in Child Abuse Investigations," *Orlando Sentinel*, December 10, 1982, p. A-17.

18. Richard Wexler, "Invasion of the Child Savers," *The Progressive*, one of the 1985 issues, as quoted in the VOCAL Sept/Oct 85 newsletter, p. 3. The article is based in part on a documentary Wexler produced for WXXI-TV, the public television station in Rochester, New York.

19. Telephone call in January 1986 from the president of K-PACT.

20. "Suit Filed Over Child-Custody Policies," *The Caswell Campaign*

Report, 320-29th Street West, Saskatoon, Sask. S7L 0M1, March 1985, p. 4.
    21. *Ibid.*
    22. VOCAL newsletter—September/October, 1985, p. 1.
    23. John R. Caswell, "Legislation Gives State Total Power Over Child," *The Caswell Campaign Report*, March 1985, p. 3.
    24. *Ibid.*
    25. Wexler, "Invasion of The Child Savers."

Chapter 8—"We Must Err on the Side of the Child"

    1. Kaye Steinmetz, "Protecting the Child," *Kansas City Star*, February 19, 1986.
    2. Reported by Laura Rogers, "Report to Legislative Committee on Abuse of Child-Abuse Hotline," *Report to the Speaker on Child Abuse Reporting Law by the Interim Committee on Children Youth and Families*, December 1985, p. 86.

> I [Laura Rogers] interviewed the director of a large residential care facility, a certified vendor of the D[ivision of] F[amily] S[ervices] in St. Louis, only a few weeks before this child died. Asking him how the children felt when they were taken away from their parents, he made this callous, indifferent remark. "They don't care. To them it's just another bed."

    3. "Emotional maltreatment is still the most likely to be opened for services (95.4 percent) followed by sexual maltreatment (88.7 percent) and deprivation of necessities (88.7 percent)." Major physical injury cases are only opened 84.9 percent. (*Highlights 1984*, p. 33.) Douglas Besharov also points out: "The reason for intervention in most cumulatively harmful situations is emotional harm to the child." (*"Doing Something" About Child Abuse*, p. 586.)
    4. *The People's Doctor*, Vol. 4, No. 10, pp. 3-4. Address: P.O. Box 982, Evanston, IL 60204.
    5. "Failing the Foster Children," an editorial, *St. Petersburg* (FL) *Times*, n.d., p. 14a. My source was a poor Xerox copy with the date, unfortunately, missing. An Associated Press article about these tragic events, entitled "13 HRS Workers Blundered in Baby's Death, Report Says," was printed in Florida papers on December 16, 1985.
    6. "Tangled tales of woe haunt MHR staff," *The Province*, August 25, 1985.
    7. Besharov, *"Doing Something" About Child Abuse*, pp. 577-578.
    8. *Missouri House of Representatives Report*, p. 85.
    9. Douglas J. Besharov's article "Child Welfare Malpractice," published in March 1984, points out the following areas of child protective worker liability:

- Liability for inadequately protecting a child (subheadings: Failure to accept a report for investigation; Failure to place a child in protective custody)

- Liability for violating parental rights (subheadings: Slanderous investigation [Dr. Besharov points out that social workers do have the right to interview everyone who knows you and mention that you are being investigated for child abuse—they only are legally liable for harassing, threatening, or browbeating parents or children]; Wrongful removal of children [this does not refer to taking children improperly, only to removing them without an easily-obtained court order, or, in allegedly emergency situations, without "good faith"—and at least half of the list of "good faith" reasons have nothing to do with imminent threat to life and limb]; Malicious prosecution; and Violation of confidentiality)

- Liability for inadequate foster care services (subheadings; Dangerous foster care placements; Failure to meet the child's needs for special care)

- Foster care "limbo" (subheadings: Failure to treat parents—lawsuits for this are usually dismissed; Failure to arrange the child's adoption)

To demonstrate a case of "wrongful removal" you will have to prove not only that you never assaulted, sexually abused, or neglected your children, but that you never made him eat "unpalatable substances" (do they mean liver?), made him stand in the corner, lived in a house with unbarred upstairs windows, refused to obtain or consent to any medical or psychiatric treatment for the child (the state gets to decide what treatment is or is not necessary), or appear to be "out of touch with reality" (this can easily apply to members of minority religions, since again the state gets to decide what constitutes faith and what is wacko). Even if you have never done any of the above, if the social worker fears you might flee with your children the removal will not be "wrongful."

10. Besharov, *"Doing Something" About Child Abuse*, p. 560.
11. *Ibid.*
12. *Ibid.*, pp. 560-561.
13. *Ibid.*, p. 586.
14. Jan Paul, "Abusive Families Must Focus On Goals, Expert Says," St. Louis *Post-Dispatch*, May 18, 1985, p. B1.
15. Cited in Wexler, "Invasion of the Child Savers."
16. Personal interview. The man, whose main work consists of trying to get the police involved in serious abuse cases in lieu of DFS and its "counseling" approach, asked to remain anonymous. He fears that his very successful work will be squelched by the Division if word gets around. If any journalist wants to contact this man, he or she should write to me care of the publisher.
17. Strauss, Gelles, and Steinmetz, *Behind Closed Doors*, p. 223.
18. Figures from the National Coalition of Jail Reform, quoted by Herbert G. Callison, "Getting Children Out Of Adult Jails," St. Louis *Post-Dispatch*, June 6, 1985, p. 3B.
19. In Columbia, Missouri, for example,

abused children taken into emergency protective custody often have to wait at the Boone County Sheriff's Department or the Columbia police station while social workers try to place them in temporary foster homes. (Bill Rogers, "Local Shelter Planned for Abused Children," *Columbia Daily Tribune*, October 19, 1985.)

20. Callison, "Getting Children Out Of Adult Jails."
21. June 5, 1985.
22. *Ibid.*

23. John R. Caswell, "Legislation Gives State Total Power Over Child," The Caswell Campaign Report, Vol. 1, No. 9, p. 3.

24. VOCAL newsletter, Sept/October 1985, p. 7. Elene's story, in extremely abridged form, also appeared in a *Woman's Day* article by Glenn P. Joyner entitled "False Accusation of Child Abuse—Could It Happen to You?" (May 6, 1986, p. 32).

25. "Treatment More Effective for Child Abuse Victims," *St. Louis Globe-Democrat*, Sept. 5, 1985, P. 4D.

Chapter 9—"In the Best Interests of the Child"

1. Solzhenitsyn, *The Gulag Archipelago*, Part One, p. 77.

2. Helen Huntley, "Custody Case Shuffles Girl Between Two States," *St. Petersburg Times*, Feb. 25, 1985, p. 4B.

3. John Camp, "In Molestation Case, Law Just Adds to Abuse," *St. Paul Pioneer Press*, January 11, 1984.

4. Memo dated February 10, 1986, from William R. Rapps, Director, re Alleged Impersonation of DOSS Employees, says in part,

Four confirmed incidents occurred on September 30, 1985, January 6, 1986, January 14, 1986, and January 20, 1986, in which one or more of the individuals described in the attached flyer attempted to impersonate employees of the Department of Social Services and falsely represented that they were conducting official business. Typically, the incidents involve entering or attempting to enter a household during daylight hours to investigate alleged child abuse hotline calls. These households are usually receiving benefits and have had some prior involvement with school, juvenile, or social services authorities. The individual or individuals may ask to search the house, examine female children for signs of abuse, and ask extensive questions. . . . Suspects may also show individuals a typed "report" describing the alleged abuse complaint and containing other information including names, dates of birth and other household information. . . . This "report" may also appear on printed DOSS or DFS letterhead.

The memo contained extensive descriptions of the suspects' appearances and manner of operation, plus composite drawings of the suspects.

5. On March 5, 1986, Department of Social Services Director Joseph O'Hara said, "The children were not molested." (Deborah Peterson, "Warning On Abuse Checks," *St. Louis Post-Dispatch*.) On March 11, the *St. Louis Globe-Democrat* reported O'Hara as saying at a press conference the day before, "there has been no outright child abuse by the imposters, although in four instances children were physically examined, two of them more thoroughly than would be necessary to check for bruises." (James F. Wolfe, "No motive found in fake child abuse probes.") Yet, reporting the same news conference, the *Post-Dispatch* reported: "In two of the cases, children were sexually molested by the imposters. The sexual molestation cases took place in a suburb of Kansas City in Jackson County, O'Hara said. In both cases, girls were subjected to a strip search and body cavities were searched, he said. . . . He said he would describe what happened to the children as sexual molestation instead of sexual abuse." (Terry Ganey, "Imposters Might Be Vigilantes," March 11, 1986, p. 1.)

I happen to know, since I was in close touch throughout the investigation with a woman who was spearheading citizen demands for full disclosure, that sexual molestation *did* occur. Yet both the Division and the media actually played this down. And once it was discovered that the imposters were "establishment" types from private agencies, the whole thing was dismissed with a "Ho, hum." At this moment, it is unclear if the people who did this will even go to trial.

6. Donna Whitfield, "Tyranny Masquerades as Charity: Who Are the Real Child Abusers?," *Fidelity* magazine, February, 1985, p. 26.

7. Barbara McLintock, "Family's Love Split by MHR," *The Province*, Aug. 25, 1985, p. 3.

8. *Ibid.*

9. "The 'Kiddie Car' on Patrol," *The Province*, Sept. 22, 1985, p. 5.

10. Gregg Middleton, "MHR's Kids Go Bad," *The Province*, Sept. 22, 1985, p. 4.

11. I have memos and school reports documenting that the girl is possessed by several different personalities. I also have documentation from the mother concerning the sequence of events, including the father's jailing for sexual offenses. Regardless of what the state may think of the mother, there can be no excuse for trying to reunite the children with this man.

12. Personal interview with VOCAL chapter head, April 17, 1986.

13. *Ibid.*

14. "Sex Abuse Cases Likened to Witch Hunt," *Ogden* (UT) *Standard Examiner*, July 22, 1985.

15. *Ibid.*

16. This theme, of promising custody to the accused if he will plead guilty, also has variations. Sometimes social workers will promise custody to the accused if he will help them invent a case against the parent with custody.

Jean Coyle, in her book *Bye Bye Baby*, tells the story of Linda McDonald of Houston and her little girl Charlene. When visiting a man to whom Linda had once been married for a short time, Charlene reported some "fondling" by this gentleman. Having been indoctrinated by child abuse hysteria, Linda immediately rushed Charlene to a police station. There a social worker appeared, drove them to the Department of Human Resources (DHR) Intake Office, and that was the last time Linda had custody of her daughter.

Among other features of this ugly case, in which DHR caseworkers apparently lied and fabricated a case against Charlene as a criminal transient (accusing her of passing bad checks, etc.—which even if true should have been handled in a court of law, and anyway has no bearing on whether a mother should lose her child), DHR tried to make a deal with the man Charlene had accused of fondling her.

> As soon as Satterwhite finished the hour's interview, three plain-clothes police officers from Mesquite walked in and arrested the accused. His wife.
>
> The next day, the couple later told us, Satterwhite called them and asked if they would sign notarized statements that Linda McDonald was mentally incompetent and should be in an institution. The accused man was told that *the child might be put into his custody if he would do this for Child Welfare.* Both he and his wife refused . . . (pp. 20-21).

17. Becky R. Gilmore, "Abusers and Victims Can Be Helped," *Nevada*

(MO) *Daily Mail*, June 28, 1985. Mr. Kirkwood, in the context of the interview, was talking about, first, a supervised meeting between the child and the perpetrator. But "putting them together" doesn't stop there. The ultimate goal of therapists is to "prove" the family healed by making the child go back to the perpetrator. As Henry Giarretto of Parents United, a California group using the therapy approach with incest cases, says, "The best approach for these families . . . is to prosecute the offender but to provide treatment and *allow for probation*." ("Family Violence Emerges From the Shadows," *U.S. News and World Report*, Jan. 23, 1984, p. 66. Emphasis mine.)

18. *Ibid.*

19. Ken Pryor, "Sexual abuse," *Columbia Missourian*, Aug. 8, 1985.

20. *Because We Care So Much!*, December 1985, pp. 5-6. Published by Tressler Lutheran Service Associates Inc., 25 W. Springettsbury Ave., York, PA 17403.

Chapter 10—Yours, Mine, and "Ours"

1. "Kidnapped Girl, 5, Found; Neighbors Held," *St. Louis Post-Dispatch*, May 13, 1985, p. 10A.

2. Jan Paul, "Combat Child Abuse, Group Told," *St. Louis Post-Dispatch*, May 16, 1985, p. 8A.

3. From Governor Ashcroft's Child Advocacy Day speech, Jefferson City, January 29, 1985. The governor said, in part,

I have become acutely aware of some of the barriers that must be overcome—and of the *need for cooperation* among those who share a common concern for *our children's* well-being. . . . Your presence here today proves that we have the most essential resource in place—a committed group of people dedicated to serving *our state's most precious resource, our children*. (Emphasis mine)

Governor Ashcroft's speech to the child abuse industry included, besides its plug for networking, his proposals for the General Assembly. He asked the legislature to "authorize a program of parent education" ($330,000), add a parent stress hotline, increase penalties for sexual exploitation, "authorize funds for training and assistance to child care workers," to "provide the funds to implement the 'Early Childhood Developmental Screeening Program'" ($3 million the first year), and "expand and strengthen our support for day care programs in Missouri" (a supplemental appropriation for one year of $1.4 million, plus an increase of over $1 million per year, plus another $556,000 "to expand day care as a treatment service for abused and neglected children.") Some of these proposals are sound, but most are just plums for the child abuse industry network. Governor Ashcroft wound up the speech this way: "Thank you for being here today and for your continuing committment to *Missouri's* children." The accompanying leaflet, "Brighter Lives for Missouri's Children," has this as its first line: "Children are Missouri's most valuable resource."

4. Said during a public speech. Cited by Concerned Women for America in their pamphlet *To Manipulate a Woman*.

5. "Hotline Viewpoint Faulted," *St. Louis Globe-Democrat*, 4/4/86, Mailbag. This letter repeatedly refers to the idea that children are the state's

"most precious resource," and even appeals to this dogma to support the idea that the state's resources need their families hotlined.

6. Jeanne M. Giovannoni and Rosina M. Becerra, *Defining Child Abuse* (New York: Free Press/Macmillan, 1979), pp. 36-37.

7. *Ibid.*

8. *Ibid.*, pp. 39-41.

9. *Ibid.*, p. 38.

10. Arnold A. Dallimore, *George Whitefield: The Life and Times of the Great Evangelist of the Eighteenth-Century Revival* (Westchester, IL: Crossway Books, 1981), Vol. 1, pp. 459-462. You'll be glad to know that, during one of Whitefield's absences, the older brother's lawyer came and took the children from the orphanage, restoring them to their own family. The magistrates thereafter so harassed and thwarted Whitefield that he declared he was almost tempted to wish he had never founded the orphanage. Let it be known that this entire episode was uncharacteristic of the ministry of this greathearted and generous Christian man.

11. Giovannoni and Becerra, pp. 51-52.

12. *Ibid.*, pp. 52-53.

13. *Ibid.*, p. 47.

14. Allan Carlson, "The Child-Savers Ride Again: Child Abuse and the Reign of Terror in Therapeutic America," *Persuasion At Work*, Vol. 8, No. 8, August 1985, p. 4.

15. *Ibid.*

16. *Ibid.*

17. *Ibid.*

18. Giovannoni and Becerra, p. 55.

19. Carlson, p. 5.

20. *Ibid.*

21. Giovannoni and Becerra, p. 61.

22. *Ibid.*, pp. 61-62.

23. *Ibid.*, p. 63.

24. *Ibid.*, p. 64.

25. *Ibid.*

26. *Ibid.* An inference.

27. VOCAL newsletter, vol. 1, no. 4, Nov/Dec 1985, p. 8.

The doctor that examined my daughter is employed exlusively by CPS in all child abuse cases and makes a lot of money, we found out in court. He is the self-appointed "expert" for our county and of course, an expert should be paid expert fees. Through CPS referrals alone, he sees 15 children a week and gets $195.00 per child. His office is 15 minutes driving time from the courthouse, so when he is needed to testify, they give him a call and he is on the witness stand in about an hour; of course he is paid the standard half day wage of $400.00 per court visit. So, assuming this man finds sexual or child abuse in any child, we can estimate that he probably appears in court for each child he sees. Figuring all this, the man would make an average of $38,675.00 per month, or $464,100.00 per year. One must wonder what motivates him, child saving or the all mighty dollar? (From a letter by Robin Richardson.)

28. Carlson, pp. 7-8.

29. "How United Way Money Was Allocated During 1985," *St. Louis Globe-Democrat*, September 5, 1985. This pie chart show 11.3 percent of United Way money spent on "Child Care/Child Abuse Prevention." Some of the other categories for allocations very likely contain child abuse-related activities, such as the 11 percent earmarked for "Family Problems," the 18.1 percent for "Youth/Family Programs," and the 4.5 percent for "Human Services Planning/Direct Services."

30. Don Mahnken, "Organizations rally to needs, aid children's home," *Springfield* (MO) *Leader-Press*, Jan. 8, 1986, p. 1

31. Carlson, p. 7.

32. "Judges More Involved In Child Abuse Cases," A.P. story, Springfield (MO) *Leader-Press*, Aug. 22, 1985.

Chapter 11—Bringing In The Thieves

1. The Joint Child Health Planning Task Force, *A Child Health Plan for Raising a New Generation*, submitted to (and endorsed by) James B. Hunt Jr., the Governor of North Carolina, published in "The International Year of the Child" 1979, p. i.

2. "*Neonatal screening* should be provided the newborn infant. . . . Further, assignment to an initial health care home should be verified." *Ibid.*, p. 23.

3. Part of the "follow-up and tracking service" includes

Acceptance by parents and/or young person of the need [for a health care home]. In some cases aggressive outreach and even governmental intervention may be appropriate to safeguard the child's well being." (*Ibid.*, p. 48.)

I.e., babysnatching is an option if the parents refuse to register their children with the health care "home."

4. Under the heading of "responsibilities belonging to the child and his family," p. 19.

5. P. 44.

6. Pp. 23, 73.

7. P. 46.

8. P. 4.

9. Pp. 13, 32.

10. P. 57. Although the report rather sanctimoniously states, "the advisor does not create conflicts with the natural or Health Care Homes but rather assists in resolving those already in existence," this advisor is also supposed to be "nonjudgmental and open," which means affirming the youth's rebelliousness as good and normal. The very presence of this state-ordained third-party adult who has power to meddle (without the parents' consent) in personal family matters, robs the parents of their authority.

11. P. 49.

12. P. 53.

13. P. 46.

14. P. 4.

15. P. 6.

16. P. 45. I have heard from several La Leche League members that women who believe in traditional discipline are no longer allowed to become La Leche League group leaders. Whether this is a formal or informal policy, it is unjust. To attack other women's families by joining with those who would label them "abusive" is the same as saying, "Take this woman's children away." La Leche League and ICEA were formed to help families stay together—this is just the opposite.

17. Pp. 43-59.

18. Laura Rogers, *Report of the Governor's Conference on Children and Youth*, 1982, self-published. 20,000 copies of this report were distributed to legislators, the media, and concerned citizens. That is the only reason why Missouri, in 1982, did not pass the proposed laws which would have made all children wards of the state at birth and given control of all children to "professionals" instead of to their parents.

19. Rogers, pp 1-2.

20. Missouri Parents and Children, *Impact Report on Federal Involvement in Child Development*, April 1982, p. 1. Quoted from Dr. White's speech at the Governor's Conference on the Young Years in 1982.

21. P. 2.

22. *Ibid.*

23. MoPaC *Impact Report*, p. 1.

24. Pp. 3-4.

25. Pp. 4-5.

26. P. 5.

27. P. 7.

28. P. 8.

29. Betty Howard (ed.), *Complete State Control of Every Family and Child in Florida through the Prevention Task Force Influencing the State Legislature* (Orlando: Pro-Family Forum, 1986), preface.

30. *Ibid.*

31. *Jefferson City* (MO) *Post-Tribune*, March 18, 1985, p. 11.

32. Alida Gookin, "Tollett's Folly," *Jackson* (TN) *Journal*, Nov. 21, 1984.

33.

A distinguished pediatrics professor at the University of Colorado (who published his lecture in a distinguished medical journal) recommended the creation of a corps of 60,000 "health visitors" who would go into the homes of ALL babies in this country until the child reached school age.

The professor, a leader of the National Center for the Prevention of Child Abuse and Neglect [sic] . . . is willing to effect his program through persuasion and education, but *if such methods fail, he believes in mandatory intervention through child-protection services.* (Emphasis mine)

Reported by Dr. Robert Mendelssohn, a nationally-respected pediatrician and author, in his newsletter *The People's Doctor* (P.O. Box 982, Evanston, IL 60204), Vol. 10, No. 4, p. 2.

34. "Child Abuse, Neglect Can Be Curtailed with Help from Citizens, Says DFS," *Franklin County* (MO) *Tribune*, July 31, 1985.
   35.

Eddie Bernice Johnson, HEW official, recommended at the Child Abuse Conference that a license to bear a child be issued only when a knowledge of parenting skills and techniques has been demonstrated and that parenting education be a prerequisite of our school system. (In Fort Worth, Texas, in the County Hospital in 1979 a program was started to *identify potentially abusive parents* and place them in Parenting Programs before they actually abused their children. A number of such programs are underway around the nation. (Betty Howard, *Complete State Control*, Appendix O.)
   [Missouri Supreme Court Judge Andrew J.] Higgins also suggested society might have to set standards to be met by persons wishing to have children. The state is, in fact, doing that to some degree, he said. "I believe that is what the legislature has been doing," Higgins said. (Sharon Doane, "Seminar on child abuse features noted panelists," St. Charles [MO] *Journal*, Oct. 27, 1985, pp. 1, 14A.)

36. Betty Howard, Appendix G, "Parenting Education."
   37. *Ibid.*
   38. *Ibid.*
   39. *Ibid.*
   40. Eric Brodin, "Destroying the Family: Swedish Style," *Washington Inquirer*, Oct. 11, 1985.
   41. "In Sweden the state now arrogates to itself the power to be the primary protector of the child. It can determine whether a single mild form of corporal punishment, verbal chastisement, or temporary restriction of the child's activities, constitutes an infringement of the law, by which the parent becomes subject to a jail sentence." (*Ibid.*)
   42. Betty Howard, Appendix G.
   43. "World Child Abuse Cited by U.N. Group," St. Louis *Post-Dispatch*, p. 11C.
   44. Nancy Pearcey, "Nairobi and the UN—changing the family by decree," *The Interim* (Canada), July/August 1985, p. 2ff. This excellent article is worth quoting at length. It will give you some idea of how a supposed crusade for "rights" is being manipulated into a call for coercion and the suppression of motherhood.

I was attending a meeting entitled "Prelude to Nairobi," held on June 2, 1985, in Toronto. It was billed as a way to support an upcoming United Nations conference and to learn more about it. The UN Conference (in Nairobi, Kenya, this July) is to celebrate the end of the Decade for Women. Its purpose is to hear governmental reports on their steps to implement a UN Convention on equality for women (the UN Convention on the Elimination of All Forms of Discrimination Against Women). . . .
   In many ways, the Convention calls for protecting women's right to work outside the home—but not their right to stay home with young children.

For example, it elevates the right to work to the status of an "inalienable right." That's paid work, the context makes clear, not housework or childcare. To enable mothers to exercise this "inalienable right," the Convention calls upon governments "to encourage the provision of the necessary supporting social services"—by that it means "the establishment and development of a network of child-care facilities." (Art. 12:2 (c)). . . .

In short, the Convention acknowledges the biological fact of pregnancy but not the biological fact of lactation—because that does take women from the workplace. It does not call for work patterns that enable women to work without compromising their parenting, such as better part-time work, work that can be performed at home, cottage industries, job sharing, flexible hours, work only during school hours, and so on. Clearly, the Convention supports only a limited range of "women's rights"—those that assume that women are primarily defined and fulfilled by work outside the home.

Surprisingly, *the UN Convention does not call for "equal opportunity" for women in work and public life—that is, the opportunity for women to participate as they wish. Instad, it calls for their "maximum participation."* . . . [emphasis mine]

Canada ratified the Convention in 1981. That means the government is legally bound to bring our laws into line with the principles of the Convention as long as we stay in the UN. Are Canadians aware of the path their government has embarked upon? . . .

What they are overlooking is that "rights" can become coercions. The "right" to subsidized day-care can put pressure on mothers to put their children into day-care. In Sweden, for example, a mother who wants to stay at home with her children is sometimes questioned by social workers as to her motives. In the rush for new rights, we are in danger of losing old ones. . . .

The UN Convention is objectionable not so much in what it says as in what it does not say. It does not call for the right of women to stay home, it does not call for work patterns which accomodate family needs. . . .

The result in practice is that when two rights conflict with one another, the unprotected rights will be over-ruled by those that are explicitly protected—the right to work over the right to care for one's own children. . . .

Is this all speculative and alarmist? Are we reading too much into the threat posed by the Convention to the family? Consider two instances where the Convention has had an effect already. International Planned Parenthood Federation, as mentioned earlier, has used the Convention to buttress abortion rights. Then again, a request for funding for REAL Women was turned down by Status of Women Canada, an agency that funds over 600 other women's groups, on the grounds that its view of "equality" did not accord with that of the Charter of Rights and the UN Convention on equality for women.

With a track record like that, we have little reason to be optimistic about the UN Convention. . . .

What's really interesting is the type of women Nancy Pearcey found at the "Prelude to Nairobi" meeting. In her words, the more than 200 women attending were expensively dressed, well-coifed, and looked for all the world like highly conventional ma-trons. . . .

At one point during the meeting, we sat at small tables of eight to ten women for small group discussions. Through our discussion it came out that most of the women at my table had stayed home while their children were young. Yet more than once they called for subsidized day-care so young mothers could participate fully in education and the workforce.

Nancy Pearcey wondered, and rightly so, "How could these women urge the government to take away from young mothers of today what they themselves had an opportunity to enjoy?" The answer:

The women at my table hinted at the social pressure they themselves felt at times. They felt "guilty" for not working, they said. . . .

45. Mary Pride, *The Way Home* (Westchester, IL: Crossway Books, 1985).

Chapter 12—If This Be Reason

1. "Successful Crimes," *Chronicles of Culture*, Vol. 10, No. 3, March 1986, p. 51. Mr. Fleming was talking about violent crime in general, but his comments are most appropriate for crimes against children as well.
   2.

. . . *Psychology Today* has, from the very beginning, taken its religious responsibilities seriously. Already in its second year (1969) they were observing that psychology must help man "face our own inner exper-iences without the guidance of traditional dogmas, ritual, or patriarchal authority—the foundation stones of Judeo-Christian religious exper-ience. Left without collectively sanctioned God-values and moral abso-lutes, we are compelled to erect our own morality, arrive at our own faith and belief, and discover the meaning of our existence." "Psycholo-gy Today, Psychology Tomorrow, Psychology Forever," *Chronicles of Culture*, Vol. 10, No. 3, March 1986, pp. 48-51. The article's author is not mentioned, but whoever you are, thank you for spending those arduous hours unearthing *PT*'s doctrinal formulae.

3. *Ibid.*, p. 51. The *PT* article in question is "The Building of Nations." It appeared in 1969.
4. *Ibid.* From a 1973 *PT* article.
5. *Ibid.* From a 1978 *PT* article. While we're at it, you also should know that in 1973 *Psychology Today* was proposing that parents be licensed to have children only when they demonstrated an adequate knowledge of psy-chological doctrine. As *PT* so sensitively put it, "We can no longer afford the luxury of allowing any two fools to add to our numbers whenever they please." In 1985, *PT* warned of an epidemic of mental illness affecting forty million Americans. This is firm proof that "mental illness" is being warmed up as the hit man for dissenters, since no way is one-fifth of the population

actually insane. As *Chronicles of Culture* acidly observed, "just how many registered Republicans *are* there?"

6.

... in the year 1950, in all of America, only 170 persons under the age of fifteen were arrested for what the FBI calls serious crimes (such as murders, forcible rape, robbery, and aggravated assault). ...

The rise in child crime, however, was staggering. Between 1950 and 1979, the rate of serious crime committed by children increased 11,000 percent! (John Whitehead, *The Stealing of America* [Westchester, IL: Crossway Books, 1983], p. 68.)

John Whitehead got his figures from Neil Postman, *The Disappearance of Childhood* (New York: Delacorte Press, 1982), p. 134. Do you realize that, in 1950, only .0004 percent of children aged fifteen and under were arrested for serious crimes? Think about our modern city schools filled with security guards, where students and teachers are regularly assaulted. What hath government programs for children and families wrought?

7. Gilmore, "Incest Most Common Form."

8. The divorce rate was almost nil at the turn of the century. Even since 1966 it has doubled. *Statistical Abstract of the United States* (Washington, D.C.: U.S. Bureau of the Census, 1983), p. 60.

9. Samuel Blumenfeld, in his fascinating book *NEA: Trojan Horse in American Education* (Boise, ID: The Paradigm Company, 1984), says on page 102, "The Department of Education estimates that there are 24 million functional illiterates in the United States, *virtually all of whom have had from eight to twelve years of compulsory public schooling.*" Functional illiteracy means the victim can't read the sweepstakes rules on a cereal box, library books, newspapers, or his IRS tax form. Blumenfeld continues, "Contrast this with the figures for illiteracy in 1910 issued by the U.S. Bureau of Education and quoted in the January 30, 1915 issue of James McKeen Cattell's own weekly publication, *School and Society*:

Statistics compiled by the Bureau of Education for use at the Panama-Pacific Exposition, show that of children from 10 to 14 years of age there were in 1910 only 22 out of every 1,000 who could neither read nor write. ... The following states report only 1 child in 1,000 between the ages of 10 and 14 as illiterate: Connecticut, District of Columbia, Massachusetts, Minnesota, Montana, New Hampshire, North Dakota, Oregon, Utah, and Washington."

10. Michael Bray is in jail in New York State with a five-year sentence for clinic bombing, while here in Missouri a judge recently granted a man who had raped an eight-year-old girl two years probation. As an October 1, 1984 *U.S. News & World Report* article says about those convicted of child sexual abuse, "Of those convicted, half end up on probation." ("Now, Nationwide Drive to Curb Child Abuse," p. 73.)

Pamela Klein, director of the Rape and Sexual Abuse Care Center at Southern Illinois University at Edwardsville, is on the right track. "Child abuse and incest are crimes and people should go to jail," she has said. "We believe counseling should be available inside the prison." As a newspaper article says, "Ms. Klein notes that people abuse children for different reasons, but that if they are compulsive abusers it can take at least five years of regular therapy to cure the people, mostly men, of their problem."

Here's she's somewhat of an optimist. "A study by the National Center on Child Abuse and Neglect concludes that more than half of parents who abuse their children mentally or physically are likely to do so again, even after treatment for abusive tendencies. The study by Deborah Dado . . . concluded that treatment programs made little progress. . . . Between 40 percent and 60 percent of the children included in the study were abused while their parents were in treatment." (AP article, "Violence to Kids Down in Past 10 Years: Study," *Sedalia* [MO] *Democrat*, Nov. 14, 1985.)

But to continue with Ms. Klein, who believes that therapy can cure the problem if therapy continues long enough—"What do you do over that five-year period if the offender is in the community? He's likely to be a repeater."

The article continues: "The average time actually served by child sex abuse offenders who are sent to Missouri and Illinois prisons is about 2 years; some offenders are put under court supervision or are referred to community mental health clinics in lieu of incarceration." (Abe Aamidor, "Child Sexual Abuse," *St. Louis Globe-Democrat*, Aug. 2, 1985, Living section.)

This can get even more sickening. One rapist (a twenty-one-year-old man convicted of sexually assaulting a seven-year-old girl in Kansas City, Missouri) has been "placed in a halfway house about a block from where the girl lives." The girl naturally is terrified, but the judge is unmoved. "While calling the case one of the saddest he has seen as a jurist, [Jackson County Circuit Judge Timothy] O'Leary said the man could not be subjected 'to the abuse of the prison population.'" ("Man Convicted of Sexual Assault Placed in Halfway House Near Victim's Home," *Jefferson City Post-Tribune*, May 16, 1985, p. 2.) Here you see what moving from Justice to Health has done: protecting the rapist is more important to this judge than protecting his tiny victim. As a perceptive letter to the editor of the *Tuscumbia* (MO) *Autogram-Sentinel* said, "How far can a parent's protection go when we have judges flashing green lights, uncaring and uninterested officials and laws that do not recognize this issue as the irreversible and damaging crime that it is?" (Debbie Leonard, "Child Molesters Should be Targets," Nov. 28, 1985.)

11. See, for example, Alexander Solzhenitsyn's account of the Kengir uprising in his epic *The Gulag Archipelago*. The entire multi-volume series is, among other things, one of the best looks at the psychology of bullies (in this case, the Russian authorities) ever written.

12. P. 235.

13. The newspaper report reads,

The Blue Springs man sentenced August 27 [1985] to four years in prison for twice sexually assaulting a teenage girl was sentenced Friday to seven more years for sexually assaulting another teenager. . . .

Wilson sexually assaulted a 14-year-old Blue Springs girl in his home at a party in January, *16 days after he was placed on probation for two counts of sexually assaulting another Blue Springs 14-year-old* in Independence in April 1984. . . .

In arguing for the maximum seven-year sentence, prosecutor Matt Whitworth told the judge, "The police department refers to him as the Charles Manson of Blue Springs. . . ."

Olathe, Kansas authorities want to try Wilson on a sexual assault charge in connection with an incident involving a 13-year-old girl. . . .

After he was sentenced, Wilson, loosely bound in chains, *strutted back to his seat and smirked* at the two Blue Springs detectives in the courtroom for the sentencing. (Stan Friedman, "Wilson Given Seven Years for Sexual Assault," Blue Springs *Examiner*, Sept. 7, 1985.)

14. The U.S. Attorney General's Task Force on Family Violence prepared a report in September, 1984, after months of hearings and research. It said, in part,

A recent research experiment is challenging these traditional beliefs that mediation is the appropriate law enforcement response. The results of the research demonstrated that arrest and overnight incarceration are the most effective interventions to reduce the likelihood of subsequent acts of family violence. A victim's chance of future assault was nearly two and a half times greater when officers did not make an arrest. (p. 24)

15. "Mediation is most often an equally inappropriate law enforcement response in family violence incidents. Mediation may assume that the parties involved are of equal culpability in the assault. . . . But an abusive relationship is generally demonstrably one sided. The abuser is usually physically superior and the victim is injured and fearful of further harm.

"Mediation not only fails to hold the offender accountable for his criminal actions but, worse yet, gives the abuser no incentive to change his behavior. Rather than stopping the violence and providing protection for the victim, mediation may inadvertently contribute to a dangerous escalation of violence." (*Ibid.*, p. 23)

16. Mary Ann McNulty, "Congressional Wives Push For Tough Laws Against Child Abusers," St. Joseph (MI) *Herald-Palladium*, Jan. 15, 1986.

17. Missouri just raised the training period from fifteen hours to forty hours. Strauss, Gelles and Steinmetz mention a Boston case in which a child died when returned home, the social worker ignoring protests by the foster parents that the children showed signs of abuse after parental visitation. The case worker also failed to follow up on the family after it was reunited. One girl had died from a beating and been thrown out in the trash.

Subsequent investigations into the case revealed that 65 percent of the state's protective service workers had less than forty hours' training in handling complex abuse and neglect cases. It also showed that two thirds of the workers currently handling such cases had less than one year's experience in protective services. Until the above case attracted public attention, the welfare department did not even require protective service workers to hold a college degree. (p. 229)

Does it make sense to let some kid fresh out of college loose on the streets to function as police, judge, and jury in child abuse investigations? Child protective workers do notoriously poor work, both failing to recognize dangerous situations and failing to respect family lifestyles. As Besharov says, "Studies in several states have shown that about twenty-five percent of all child fatalities attributed to abuse or neglect involve children already reported to a child protective agency." ("*Doing Something,*" p. 551.) These people are simply not capable of doing professional investigations.

18. Thom Gross, "Man Gets 2 Years' Probation in Rape of 8-Year-Old," *St. Louis Post-Dispatch*, Nov. 2, 1985. *The Joplin* (MO) *Globe* printed an excellent editorial on this outrage, here quoted in full.

If you ever wondered why so many people these days are distrustful of the criminal justice system, all you need to do is take a look at a non-sentence handed down by a St. Louis Circuit Court judge the other day in a case involving the rape of an 8-year-old girl.

The judge sentenced the man, who had pleaded guilty to the charge, to two years' probation.

The thinking of Judge Jack Koehr reportedly was that the 41-year-old admitted child rapist, whose criminal record showed three prior felony convictions through the early 1970s, had been something of an exemplary citizen for the last decade. The man had compiled a good work record and had stayed out of trouble with the law. Furthermore, immediately after the attack on the girl, he had sought help for alcohol abuse.

We agree that the fact an individual has held a steady job for more than a decade and has had no additional run-ins with the police during that time ought to carry some weight in the judge's decision. But only in a case of less severity.

What seems to have been lost in the judicial shuffle is that an 8-year-old child was victimized and that justice, not any outsized sense of revenge or retribution, demands punishment.

All sorts of rationalizations can be conjured up as arguments that the two-year probationary period is a severe enough penalty. The man cannot take a drink of alcohol for those two years, must remain in a special alcohol recovery program, has to seek psychiatric counseling and, of course, cannot break the law. One misstep and, wham, into the slammer he might go for whatever the law and the judge deem fit.

But being free to work, go home at night, take in a movie or eat out at a restaurant, even with the conditions imposed by the court, hardly constitutes serious punishment for so heinous a crime. Certainly it is not what most people might expect for anyone who rapes a child. That the individual is sorry for what he did indicates a conscience, but that is neither an acceptable excuse nor justification for leniency.

In this case, we believe, the judge erred. And in so doing, he has damaged the credibility of the judiciary and made a mockery of justice, especially for an 8-year-old victim.

"Matter of justice," Nov. 7, 1985.

19. Edelman, Charles, "Freedom From Religion," *American Atheists*, Feb. 1984. Cited in Jerry Berman, *The Criterion: Religious Discrimination in America* (Richfield, MN: Onesimus Publishing, 1984), pp. 14-15. Remember that *Psychology Today* is already trumping up a case against forty million Americans (those who strongly disagree with them), accusing them of harboring an epidemic of "mental illness." See footnote 5, above.

Chapter 13—Counterforce

1. Allan C. Carlson, p. 8.

2. Philip Ney, "Relationship Between Abortion and Cy," Nov. 1979, pp. 610-620. Cited by Allan C. Carlson, *op cit.*

3. Mary Pride, *The Way Home: Beyond Feminism, Back to Reality* (Westchester, IL: Crossway Books, 1985), pp. 24-31.

4. (Chicago: World Book, 1985), Volume 15, *Guide for Parents*, p. 86.

5. P. 96.

6. P. 90.

7. P. 118.

8. Lenore Weitzmann, *The Divorce Revolution: The Unexpected Social and Economic Consequences for Women and Children in America* (New York: Schocken Books, 1986). This book documents how once no-fault came in, divorced women and their children were financially victimized. Weitzmann shows that the women and children's standard of living dropped 73 percent immediately after the divorce, while the ex-husband's rose by 42 percent. This book is making waves among women everywhere, from Phyllis Schlafly to Betty Friedan.

9. *Childcraft*'s Parent's Guide, for example, suggest that parents introduce the subject of divorce in this way: "Your father (or mother) and I are not happy together, so we are going to try living in different houses to see if we will be happier that way. If we are, we will get a divorce." (p. 120) Nowhere in this section does the least bit of advice appear that parents should *not* get divorces, or that they should worry more about whether the child is happy than whether they are.

10. Besharov suggests a more careful definition would help screen out trivial and wasteful cases. His definition of child abuse differs from that of this book, but if this were at least a matter of public debate instead of private judicial decisions, anyone who objected to Dr. Besharov's definition could challenge it. His approach, in other words, is sound, and brings the whole question of "What is child abuse?" out of the realm of hysteria and into the jurisdiction of reason. Supporting a stricter definition than Besharov's are VOCAL and the Berean League Task Force, plus Pro-Family Forum, Eagle Forum, and state groups like Missouri Parents and Children. These groups are all calling for more rigorous definitions of child abuse.

11. Every pro-family group supports this.

12. This too.

13. In this I go farther than Besharov, who thinks children should be removed from "potentially harmful" environments, including houses with unbarred second-story windows, etc. Mounting opinion supports the removal of perpetrators, though—I couldn't find any writer who had seriously considered the issue of state abuse of families who opposed this. The U.S. Attorney General's Task Force is for it, as are all pro-family groups.

14. "The real problem with existing standards is that they place *too much responsibility* on decision-makers. Laws should explicitly recognize that social workers and judges cannot predict future maltreatment and the misguided attempts to do so can have serious side effects." *"Doing Something,"* pp. 579-580.

15. VOCAL eloquently begs for courts to "exclude any and all statements that suggest expertise in the area of psychology or psychiatry, since child protection workers and human services people do not have degrees in these areas. Reports should be devoid of personal bias or prejudice and state only

facts. These tapes should be available to the defendant's counsel." (VOCAL letter, n.d.) VOCAL also (due to sad experience) firmly opposes the theories of "experts" being introduced in court as fact, and the tendency to make judicial decisions rest on the personal impressions of some mental health professional.

In connection with this, let me mention that child protective agencies are already pushing a doctrine that only doctors employed by them can give accurate testimony about child abuse. As Florida subdepartment head Bob Horner says, commenting on the conduct of a caseworker who refused to contact the family doctor in the case of a child with hemophilia, "He was not a source of unbiased information. . . . He could say, yes, the child bruises, but he wouldn't know the situation we were investigating. That's why we hire child-abuse experts." (Sandra Mathers, "Child-Abuse Probe Has Parents Angry," *Orlando Sentinel*, March 23, 1983, p. A-8.)

Yet the agencies ignore the obvious bias of a doctor whose whole living consists of upholding social workers' actions in court. Do they honestly believe that a doctor who consistently found errors in social workers' conduct would last long at that job?

The behavior of the state medical "expert" on child sexual abuse in the infamous Johnson case (reported in *Woman's Day* of May 6, 1986) tells us something. Although in the course of the investigation five other doctors insisted that the little girl's hymen was fine, he alone tried to say it had been tampered with. Although nationally-known bacteriological experts denied that the slight vaginal discharge which had initially caused the parents to have their daughter examined contained any sexually-transmitted organisms, the state's doctor said it did. He even resorted to the extremely implausible story that the bacteria in question must have died on the way to the testing laboratory. As *Woman's Day* ironically observed, "Because Dr. Giese earns approximately $10,000 a month conducting such exams for the county and subsequently appearing in court, it was feared his findings might, unconsciously or otherwise, lean towards support of the CPS case." (Glenn Joyner, "False Accusation of Child Abuse.")

This is no isolated incident. Nor could we expect it to be. Even in cases where not nearly so much rides on a diagnosis, medical authorities advise patients to stay away from doctors who are always discovering the same disease. Surgeons get into a mindset of prescribing surgery for everything; chiropractors think all ills need their services; and child abuse doctors working for the state are under pressure to produce evidence for the state, not to clear parents.

16. The U.S. Attorney General's Task Force strongly recommends this.

17. Jacalyn Mindell, "Organizations unite in effort to reduce abuse of children," *Topeka Capitol-Journal*, April 3, 1986.

18. "Parents Battle Pain of Child-Abuse Allegations," *North Jersey News*, May 13, 1986.

19. Paul Johnson, *Modern Times: The World from the Twenties to the Eighties* (New York: Harper & Row, 1983). This massive work (817 pages including footnotes) is, for those who are patient enough to grapple with it, a damning indictment of all forms of totalitarianism. If the average social studies text resembles a brick building minus the mortar—history without a reason—Johnson's book is the missing mortar.

BIBLIOGRAPHY

BOOKS AND PAMPHLETS

Allen, Frank. *An Attorney Accused.* Pamphlet.

Bergman, Jerry. *The Criterion: Religious Discrimination in America.* Richfield, MN: Onesimus Publishing, 1984.

Blumenfeld, Samuel. *NEA: Trojan Horse in American Education.* Boise, ID: Paradigm, 1984.

Childcraft. Volume 15, *Guide for Parents.* Chicago: World Book, 1985.

Coyle, Jean. *Bye Bye Baby.* P.O. Box 264, Rowlett, TX 75088: Jean Coyle, 1984.

Dallimore, Arnold A. *George Whitefield: The Life and Times of the Great Evangelist of the Eighteenth-Century Revival.* 2 Vols. Westchester, IL: Crossway Books, 1981.

Roche, George. *America By the Throat.* Old Greenwich, CT: Devin-Adair, 1983.

Giovannoni, Jeanne M. and Becerra, Rosina M. *Defining Child Abuse.* New York: Free Press/Macmillan, 1979.

Greer, Germaine. *Sex and Destiny.* New York: Harper and Row, 1984.

Hacker, Andrew. *U/S A Statistical Portrait of the American People.* New York: Viking Press and Penguin Books, 1983.

Howard, Betty, ed. *Complete State Control of Every Family and Child in Florida through the Prevention Task Force Influencing the State Legislature.* Orlando: Pro-Family Forum, 1986.

Johnson, Paul. *Modern Times: The World from the Twenties to the Eighties.* New York: Harper & Row, 1983.

Kilpatrick, William Kirk. *Psychological Seduction.* Nashville: Thomas Nelson, 1983.

Mayhall, Pamela D. and Norgard, Katherine Eastlack. *Child Abuse and Neglect: Sharing Responsibility.* New York: John Wiley and Sons, 1983.

Mendelsohn, Dr. Robert. *Confessions of a Medical Heretic.* New York: Warner Books, 1979.

Morris, Barbara. *Change Agents in the Schools.* P.O. Box 756, California, 91786, The Barbara Morris Report, 1979.

Postman, Neil. *The Disappearance of Childhood.* New York: Delacorte Press, 1982.

Pride, Mary. *The Way Home: Beyond Feminism, Back to Reality.* Westchester, IL: Crossway Books, 1985.

Solzhenitsyn, Alexander. *The Gulag Archipelago, Part One.* Abridged by Edward E. Ericson, Jr. New York: Harper & Row, 1985.

Strauss, Murray A., Gelles, Richard J., and Steinmetz, Suzanne K. *Behind*

Closed Doors, Violence in the American Family. Garden City, NY: Anchor Press/Doubleday, 1980.

Weitzmann, Lenore. *The Divorce Revolution: The Unexpected Social and Economic Consequences for Women and Children in America.* New York: Schocken Books, 1986.

What Everyone Should Know About Child Abuse. Jefferson City: Missouri Division of Family Services, 1976, 1980 edition.

Whitehead, John. *The Second American Revolution.* Westchester, IL: Crossway Books, 1984.

————————————————— *The Stealing of America.* Westchester, IL: Crossway Books, 1983.

Winn, Marie. *Children Without Childhood.* New York: Pantheon Books, 1983.

Wood, Garth. *The Myth of Neurosis.* New York: Harper & Row, 1986.

NEWSPAPER ARTICLES AND EDITORIALS

Aamidor, Abe. "Child Sexual Abuse." *St. Louis Globe-Democrat.* Aug. 2, 1985, Living section.

"Aid Urged For Mentally Ill." *Memphis Commercial Appeal.* August 3, 1985.

"Animal Character Helping Kids Recognize Sexual Abuse." *St. Joseph* (MO) *News-Press.* September 18, 1985.

Bolch, Jennifer. "A Slap on the Hand Starts Lessons in Violence." *Dallas* (TX) *Times Herald.* Living section, March 20, 1979.

Brodin, Eric. "Destroying the Family: Swedish Style." *Washington Inquirer.* Oct. 11, 1985.

Callison, Carolyn. "Education Called Key to End of Child Abuse." *St. Louis Globe-Democrat.* August 26, 1985, p. 5A.

Callison, Herbert G. "Getting Children Out Of Adult Jails." *St. Louis Post-Dispatch.* June 6, 1985, p. 3B.

Camp Penuel. *The Mountain Echo* (MO). Special supplement, August 14, 1985.

Camp, John. "In Molestation Case, Law Just Adds to Abuse." *St. Paul* (Minnesota) *Pioneer Press.* January 11, 1984.

Chapman, Stephen. *Jefferson City Post-Tribune.* April 5, 1985.

"Child Abuse or Family Harassment?" *St. Louis Globe-Democrat.* Editorial, April 27-28, 1985.

"Child Abuse, Nelgect Can be Curtailed with Help from Citizens Says DFS." *Franklin County* (MO) *Tribune.* July 31, 1985.

"Child Kidnapping and Abuse Blown out of Proportion." *Nevada* (MO) *Daily Mail.* July 8, 1985, p. 4.

"Chilling Effect of Child Abuse Fears." *Ozark* (MO) *Beacon.* Supplement, August 28, 1985.

"Communication Needed to Combat Drug Abuse." *Salem* (MO) *News.* December 10, 1985.

"County Well Equipped to Handle Children With Problems." *Bloomfied* (MO) *Vindicator.* June 5, 1985.

Defty, Sally Bixby. "States' Efforts to Fight Child Abuse Discussed." *St. Louis Post-Dispatch.* March 31, 1985, p. 10D.

Doane, Sharon. "Seminar on Child Abuse Features Noted Panelists." *St. Charles* (MO) *Journal.* Oct. 27, 1985, pp. 1, 14A.

"Domestic Violence Group Needs Help." *Eldon* (MO) *Advertiser.* September 12, 1985.

"Failing the Foster Children." *St. Petersburg* (FL) *Times*. Editorial n.d., p. 14a.

Feder, Don. *Boston* (MA) *Herald*. Nov 11, 1985, p. 25.

Fishback, Debbie. "Officials Intensifying Battle Against Child Abuse." *Joplin* (MO) *Globe*. August 14, 1985.

Friedman, Stan. "Wilson Given Seven Years for Sexual Assault." *Blue Springs* (MO) *Examiner*. Sept. 7, 1985.

Ganey, Terry. "Imposters Might Be Vigilantes." *St. Louis Post-Dispatch*. March 11, 1986, p. 1.

Gilmore, Becky R. "Abusers and Victims Can Be Helped." *Nevada* (MO) *Daily Mail*. June 28, 1985.

———————————— "Child Sexual Abuse Is Topic at Meeting." *Nevada* (MO) *Daily Mail*. June 26, 1985.

———————————— "Incest Is Most Common Form of Child Sexual Abuse." *Nevada* (MO) *Daily Mail*. June 27, 1985.

Gookin, Alida. "Delusional Religious Beliefs." *Jackson* (TN) *Journal*. September 19, 1985, p. 3.

———————————— "Tollett's Folly." *Jackson* (TN) *Journal*. Nov. 21, 1984.

Grimes, Charlotte. *Foster Care: Nobody's Child. St. Louis Post-Dispatch*. Series, October 25-30, 1981.

Gross, Thom. "$250,000 Grant Will Permit Use Of Computer To Track Child Abuse." *St. Louis Post-Dispatch*. July 30, 1985.

———————————— "Man Gets 2 Years' Probation In Rape of 8-Year-Old." *St. Louis Post-Dispatch*. Nov. 2, 1985.

Hass, Nancy. "Other Victims in Child-Abuse Cases: Parents." *North Jersey News*. January 13, 1986.

"Hot Line Viewpoint Faulted." *St. Louis Globe-Democrat*. Mailbag, April 4, 1986.

Huntley, Helen. "Custody Case Shuffles Girl Between Two States." *St. Petersburg* (FL) *Times*. Feb 25, 1985, p. 4B.

Johnson, Sandy. "Expert Says Two-Thirds of Abuse Reports Unfounded." AP, December 17, 1985.

Jones, Frank. "Families Destroyed by Charges of Abuse." *Toronto* (Canada) *Star*. N.d., p. C1.

———————————— "Horror Stories of Child Abuse: Fact or Fantasy?" *Toronto Star*. November 21, 1985

"Judges More Involved In Child Abuse Cases." *Springfield* (MO) *Leader-Press*. AP, Aug 22, 1985.

"'Kiddie Car' On Patrol." *The Province*. Sept 22, 1985, p. 5.

"Kidnapped Girl, 5, Found, Neighbors Held." *St. Louis Post-Dispatch*. AP, May 13, 1985, p. 10A.

Kilby, Paul. "Child-Abuse Accusations Called Latest 'Fad Crime'." *Columbia Missourian*. July 29, 2985, p. 8A.

Lakes, Patricia. "Battle for Custody of Seized Children Becomes Nightmare." *Nelson* (British Columbia) *Daily News*. Nov. 7, 1985, p. 1.

Leonard, Debbie. "Child Molesters Should be Targets." *Tuscumbia* (MO) *Autogram-Sentinel*. Letter to the editor, Nov. 28, 1985.

Lerman, Saf. *St. Louis Post-Dispatch*. Parenting column, May 1, 1985, p. 6W.

"Magazine Report Says U.S. Men Marry Later Than Their Dads Did: Actions Defy Sex Decline." *Memphis Commercial Appeal*. New York (UPI), October 16, 1985, p. C4.

Mahnken, Don. "Organizations Rally to Needs, Aid Children's Home." *Springfield* (MO) *Leader-Press*. Jan 8, 1986, p. 1.

"Man Convicted of Sexual Assault Placed in Halfway House Near Victim's Home." *Jefferson City Post-Tribune*. May 16, 1985, p. 2.

Mathers, Sandra. "Child-Abuse Probe has Parents Angry." *Orlando Sentinel*. March 23, 1983, p. A-8.

————————————— "Law Gives State Broad Powers in Child Abuse Investigations." *Orlando Sentinel*. December 20, 1982, p A17.

"Matter of Justice." *Joplin* (Missouri) *Globe*. Nov. 7, 1985.

McLintock, Barbara. "Family's Love Split by MHR." *The Province*. Aug 25, 1985, p. 3.

McNulty, Mary Ann. "Congressional Wives Push For Tough Laws Against Child Abusers." *St. Joseph* (MI) *Herald-Palladium*. Jan. 15, 1986.

Middleton, Gregg. "MHR's Kids Go Bad." *The Province*. Sept 22, 1985, p. 4.

Mindell, Jacalyn. "Organizations Unite in Effort to Reduce Abuse of Children." *Topeka Capitol-Journal*. April 3, 1986.

Noble, Philip. "Kids Should Have Sex—Pediatrician Says." *San Francisco Chronicle*. May 15, 1978, p. 21.

"Open Mind." *St. Louis Globe-Democrat*. September 3, 1985.

"Parents Battle Pain of Child-Abuse Allegations." *North Jersey News*. January 13, 1986.

Paul, Jan. "Abusive Families Must Focus On Goals, Expert Says." *St. Louis Post-Dispatch*. May 18, 1985, p. B1.

————————————— "Combat Child Abuse, Group Told." *St. Louis Post-Dispatch*. May 16, 1985, p. 8A.

————————————— "Study Cites Failures on Child Abuse." *St. Louis Post-Dispatch*. October 30, 1985.

Peterson, Deborah. "Study Details Problems of Child Abuse Among Blacks." *St. Louis Post-Dispatch*. October 28, 1985.

Peterson, Deborah. "Warning On Abuse Checks." *St. Louis Post-Dispatch*.

Polk County Child Advocacy Program. "Child Abuse: The Facts." *Bolivar* (MO) *Herald-Free Press* and *Humansville* (MO) *Star-Leader*. Advertising Supplement, October 23, 1985.

Pryor, Ken. "Sexual Abuse." *Columbia Missourian*. Aug 8, 1985.

Pryweller, Jospeh. "Agency Helps Curb Child Abuse." *Columbia Missourian*. August 12, 1985.

"Psychological Aspects of Abuse Are Far-Ranging." *St. Joseph* (MO) *Gazette*. Child Abuse section, September 21, 1985, p. 4.

Rogers, Bill. "Local Shelter Planned for Abused Children." *Columbia Daily Tribune*. October 19, 1985.

"'Safety Net' to Promote Awareness of Child Abuse." *Southeast Missourian*. December 31, 1985.

Schaeffer, Pamela. "Child Abuse Laws Unfair to Minority Parents, Black Leaders Say." *St. Louis Post-Dispatch*. May 16, 1985, p. 8A.

Schweitzer, Lori. "The Difficult Art of Protecting Children." *Ventura* (CA) *Sunday Star Free Press*. p. 1.

"Sex Abuse Cases Likened to Witch Hunt." *Ogden* (UT) *Standard Examiner*. July 22, 1985.

Steinmetz, Kaye. "Protecting the Child." *Kansas City* (MO) *Star*. February 19, 1986.

"TEA Studies Child Abuse." *Lawrence County Record*. November 28, 1985.

"Tangled Tales of Woe Haunt MHR Staff." *The Province*. August 25, 1985.

"13 HRS Workers Blundered in Baby's Death, Report Says." Associated Press, December 16, 1985.

Tinsky, Jesse. "Girl's Size Spurs Suit by Parents." *Rocky Mountain News*, n.d.

"Treatment More Effective for Child Abuse Victims." *St. Louis Globe-Democrat*. Sept. 5, 1985, P. 4D.

"Violence to Kids Down in Past 10 Years: Study." *Sedalia* (MO) *Democrat*. Chicago AP, November 14, 1985.

Wolfe, James F. "No Motive Found in Fake Child Abuse Probes." *St. Louis Globe-Democrat*. March 11, 1986.

"Workers Acted Appropriately." *Nelson* (British Columbia) *Daily News*. Letter to the editor, Dec 3, 1985.

"World Child Abuse Cited by U.N. Group." *St. Louis Post-Dispatch*. AP article, May 19, 1985, p. 11C.

"Young Kindergarteners May Have Trouble." *Jefferson City* (MO) *Post-Tribune*. March 18, 1985, p. 11.

Zesch, Steve. "Court Again Orders Child Tested Because of Education at Home." *St. Louis Globe-Democrat*. March 16-17, 1985, p. 1.

PERIODICALS AND NEWSLETTERS

Anderson, Eileen. "Therapists and Power: The Unexamined Addiction." *National Association of Social Workers Newsletter*. May/June 1985.

Because We Care So Much!. Tressler Lutheran Service Associates Inc., 25 W. Springettsbury Ave., York, PA 17403, December 1985.

Besharov's, Douglas J. "Child Welfare Malpractice." March 1984.

Besharov, Dr. Douglas J. "An Overdose of Concern: Child Abuse and the Overreporting Problem." *Regulation: AEI Journal on Government and Society*. Nov/Dec 1985, p. 28.

Carlson, Allan C. "The Child-Savers Ride Again: Child Abuse and the Reign of Terror in Therapeutic America." *Persuasion At Work*, Vol. 8, No. 8. August 1985.

Caswell, John R. "Legislation Gives State Total Power Over Child." *The Caswell Campaign Report*, Vol. 1, No. 9. p. 3.

——————————— "Suit Filed Over Child-Custody Policies." *The Caswell Campaign Report*. 320-29th Street West, Saskatoon, Sask. S7L 0M1, March 1985.

Edelman, Charles. "Freedom From Religion." *American Atheists*. Feb. 1984.

"Family Violence Emerges From the Shadows." *U.S. News and World Report*. Jan. 23, 1984, p. 66.

"A Five-Year-Old Takes the Stand." *Newsweek*. February 18, 1985, p. 73.

Fleming, Thomas. "Successful Crimes." *Chronicles of Culture*, Vol. 10, No. 3. March 1986, p. 51.

Joyner, Glenn P. "False Accusation of Child Abuse—Could It Happen to You?" *Woman's Day*. May 6, 1986, p. 32.

Kirp, David L. "Hug Your Kid, Go to Jail." *American Spectator*. June 1985, p. 33.

McMahon, Allen R. "'Divorce Wars' Don't Get Caught in the Cross Fire!" *The Voice*. Los Angeles chapter of VOCAL, December 1, 1985.

Mendelsohn, Dr. Robert. *The People's Doctor*, Vol. 10, No. 4. P.O. Box 982, Evanston, IL 60204, p. 2.

Ney, Philip. "Relationship Between Abortion and Child Abuse." *Canadian Journal of Psychiatry*. Nov. 1979, pp. 610-620.

"Now, Nationwide Drive to Curb Child Abuse." *U.S. News & World Report.* October 1, 1984, p. 73.

Pearcey, Nancy. "Nairobi and the UN—Changing the Family by Decree." *The Interim* (Canada). July/August 1985, p. 2ff.

"Psychology Today, Psychology Tomorrow, Psychology Forever." *Chronicles of Culture*, Vol. 10, No. 3. March 1986, pp. 48-51.

Reisman, Judith. "The Porno Industry: Giving Child Molesting Its Stamp of Approval." *The Rutherford Institute.* Jan/Feb 1986, pp 10-11.

Steinem, Gloria. A public speech. Cited by Concerned Women for America. *To Manipulate a Woman.* Pamphlet.

"Violence in the American Family." *Journal of Social Issues*, 35. February, 1979, p. 15.

VOCAL Newsletter. July-Dec, 1985.

Wexler, Richard. "Invasion of the Child Savers." *The Progressive.* 1985.

Whitfield, Donna. "Tyranny Masquerades as Charity: Who Are the Real Child Abusers?" *Fidelity Magazine.* February, 1985, p. 26.

REPORTS, PAPERS, AND GOVERNMENT DOCUMENTS

American Association for Protecting Children, Inc. *Highlights of Official Child Neglect and Abuse Reporting 1984.* American Humane Association: Denver, 1985.

Ashcroft, John. "Child Advocacy Day Speech." Jefferson City, 1985.

Foster Family Care in Missouri: An Assessment. Missouri Coalition on Foster Care, October 1981.

Interim Committee on Children, Youth and Families. *Missouri House of Representatives, Report to the Speaker on: Child Abuse Reporting Law.* December, 1985.

Joint Child Health Planning Task Force. *A Child Health Plan for Raising a New Generation.* Submitted to James B. Hunt Jr., Governor of North Carolina, 1979.

McHugh, Mike. "They Can Take Your Children." Christian Liberty Academy, Illinois.

Missouri Statutes

Monthly Vital Statistics Report. Vol 34, #6, Supplement (2), Sept 26, 1985.

Rapps, William R. "Alleged Impersonation of DOSS Employees." Memo, February 10, 1986.

Rogers, Laura. *Impact Report on Federal Involvement in Child Development.* St. Charles, MO: Missouri Parents and Children, April 1982.

————————— *Report of the Governor's Conference on Children and Youth.* St. Charles, MO: Laura Rogers, 1982.

Schetky, Diane and Boverman, Harold. "Faulty Assesment of Child Sexual Abuse: Legal and Emotional Sequlae," paper presented at the annual meeting of the American Academy of Psychiatry and the Law, Albuquerque, N.M., October 10, 1985. (Typewritten.)

Statistical Abstract of the United States. Washington, D.C.: U.S. Bureau of the Census, 1983.

The U.S. Attorney General's Task Force on Family Violence, Final Report. September, 1984

RADIO PROGRAM

Jack Anderson Confidential, show 11, air date 11/27-28, 1982.